Social Work and the Community

Mart
Tel:

1 4 F

To be returne

Also by Paul Stepney

SOCIAL WORK MODELS, METHODS AND THEORIES (*edited with Deirdre Ford*) 2000

Also by Keith Popple

COMMUNITY DEVELOPMENT IN THEORY AND PRACTICE: An International Reader (*edited with Gary Craig and Mae Shaw*)

COMMUNITY WORK IN THE 1990s (*edited with Sidney Jacobs*)

RACISM IN EUROPE: A Challenge for Youth Policy and Youth Work (*edited with Jan Hazekamp*)

Social Work and the Community

A Critical Context for Practice

Paul Stepney and Keith Popple

First published 2008 by
PALGRAVE MACMILLAN
Houndmills, Basingstoke, Hampshire RG21 6XS and
175 Fifth Avenue, New York, N.Y. 10010
Companies and representatives throughout the world

PALGRAVE MACMILLAN is the global academic imprint of the Palgrave Macmillan division of St. Martin's Press, LLC and of Palgrave Macmillan Ltd. Macmillan® is a registered trademark in the United States, United Kingdom and other countries. Palgrave is a registered trademark in the European Union and other countries.

ISBN-13: 978–1–4039–9126–3
ISBN-10: 1–4039–9126–X

This book is printed on paper suitable for recycling and made from fully managed and sustained forest sources. Logging, pulping and manufacturing processes are expected to conform to the environmental regulations of the country of origin.

A catalogue record for this book is available from the British Library.

A catalog record for this book is available from the Library of Congress.

10   9   8   7   6   5   4   3   2
17   16   15   14   13   12   11   10   09

Printed in Great Britain by CPI Antony Rowe, Chippenham, Wiltshire

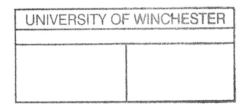

Contents

List of Figures and Tables

Figures

Tables

Acknowledgements

We are indebted to a number of people who have made this book possible. One is Neil Thompson who first suggested we might like to consider a scholarly critical text that explored the connection between social work and community, something both of us have had a particular interest in for most of our professional lives. Another is the late Jo Campling who as a Consultant Editor encouraged us to put these ideas in writing as a proposal to Palgrave some three years ago. We would also like to acknowledge the influence of our friend and colleague David Sawdon, who has become disabled by Motor-Neurone Disease, and whose ideas about community work and commitment to adult learning has encouraged many social work students and practitioners over the years.

Since commencing writing the book we have had the support of our families, friends and colleagues who have both encouraged us and challenged us through the gestation period. We are also indebted to the students we have taught in the UK, Finland, Hong Kong and Singapore who have unwittingly assisted us with feedback on our teaching inputs, which in turn has been informed by our researching and writing for the book. Further, we would like to thank all those at Palgrave who have patiently waited for the manuscript and together with anonymous reviewers who have provided us with helpful feedback. As with all contributions to the social work literature, however, we are responsible for any glaring errors, mistakes or plain misunderstandings.

The authors and the publisher would like to thank the following organisations and persons for granting permission to reproduce copyright material:

Peter Henriques, University of Wolverhampton, for granting permission to use the diagram on Ecological Models in Chapter 7; Professor Aila-Leena Matthies, University of Jyväskylä, Finland, for giving permission to reproduce the diagram on the European Research Network in Chapter 9; Russell House Publishing for granting permission to use the Community Social Work process diagram in Chapter 7; Statistical Office of European Communities, Luxembourg, for granting permission to reproduce two tables from the Eurostat Yearbook 2007 that are shown at the beginning of Chapter 9. Finally, all parliamentary material displayed in the book (for example, figure from Department of Health policy document in Chapter 9) is reproduced with the permission of the Controller of HMSO on behalf of Parliament.

Paul Stepney
University of Wolverhampton

Keith Popple
London South Bank University

Part I

The Social Construction of Community

The first part of the book, from Chapters 1 to 3, considers a number of wider developments and contextual themes in our understanding of community.

In Chapter 1 of the book we provide an introduction to the idea of community before outlining its significance for the remainder of the book. The key aims of the book are outlined and in particular we establish why our arguments are important in this early part of the twenty-first century. We consider the way in which the shifting and changing nature of community has impacted on the development of social work since the end of the Second World War. We look at the way community has become a central theme in a number of TV and radio 'soaps' as well as being a powerful aspiration in the political sphere.

In Chapter 2 we argue that to appreciate and understand the enduring interest and appeal of the concept of community we need to explore the different, and at times contradictory and contested, theories that highlight the term. We do this by examining the contribution of community studies to our appreciation of the diversity and changing nature of community from the industrial revolution to the present time. We then explore how the British government has increasingly intervened in what is seen as deprived or dysfunctional communities in order to regenerate neighbourhoods and increase economic activity. We note that a constant feature in British social and public policy since the mid-1940s has been the focus on improving life in communities and neighbourhoods. We end by considering a highly topical study from the Joseph Rowntree Foundation that examines the impact of economic migration of people from Eastern Europe on communities in the UK.

In Chapter 3 we are particularly concerned with globalisation and the policy of neo-liberalism that has had a significant impact upon levels of inequality and discrimination in local communities. We begin with an analysis of the impact of globalisation and neo-liberalism which stresses the value and the benefit of the economic free-market. We then move to examine how these have produced a range of inequalities, social problems and new patterns of exclusion that are presented through existing divisions of class, race and gender. Our concern then moves to the evolution of the UK's new communities, by which we mean economic migrants, refugees, asylum seekers and 'undocumented persons'. This is followed by consideration of what this means for rethinking community as a socially constructed concept. We conclude with the view that the notion of community, although associated with continuity and tradition in popular culture, has radically changed since the 1980s.

1

Introduction to the Idea of Community

Introduction

This book offers a critically progressive and we hope inspiring, contribution to contemporary social work theory and practice. It is primarily aimed at assisting a developing understanding of the relationship between social work and the concept of community. It is written and published at a significant time in the development of UK social work, and social work education, which in our view has much to gain from community-based approaches. The book seeks to effectively engage with the complex social problems inherent in a twenty-first century postmodern society that has closely adhered to the demands of globalisation and neo-liberal economics.

Social work practice is presently experiencing the challenge of the government's agenda for the modernisation of public sector services, the expansion of a mixed economy of welfare, and the changing organisation of social work and social care services for children and families and for vulnerable people. In the early part of the twenty-first century Lord Laming's report on the tragic circumstances surrounding the death in 2000 of Victoria Climbié (Department of Health and Home Office, 2003), followed by the publication of the Government Green Paper *Every Child Matters* (Department for Education and Skills, 2004) which determined the framework for Children's Services after the Laming Report, and the Children Act 2004 which implemented *Every Child Matters*, bringing together Education and Child and Family Social Work into a Children's Services structure, have all shaped services for children and young people. These children services are focused on improving protection, and balancing protection with prevention, in order to enhance the quality of care and improve children and young people's life chances.

The priorities for adult services are set to promote independence, improve consistency and provide user centred services. The National Framework for Older People (Department of Health, 2001, 2006b) has demanded that health and social services work together to improve the quality of services for older people in their own home, in residential care and in hospitals. This has been accompanied by the claim that the UK is facing a 'crisis in care' (Brindle, 2007) due to demographic changes, particularly the rise in the number of very old people in the population, greater geographical mobility, increasing divorce and more women in the labour market and therefore less available to care. At the same time there have been moves to introduce new thinking into the public and private pension systems (Department of Work and Pensions, 2006).

In the field of social work education, qualifying undergraduate and master degrees have replaced the Diploma in Social Work, and the General Social Care Council has been established to inspect and regulate social work programmes, to register social workers and to uphold sound professional standards. The Social Care Institute for Excellence has been established to commission and disseminate a developing knowledge base and to promote best practice in social care services. Social work post-qualifying (PQ) education has been given a boost with the Department of Health restating the view that all practitioners should undertake Continuous Professional Development (CPD) through one of the many approved PQ training courses.

At the same time government social policy has focused on social inclusion, community regeneration and sustainability, partnership working, multidisciplinary collaboration and the development of responsible citizenship. This was reinforced in 2006 with the introduction of the Respect Action Plan (Blair, 2006) to promote community cohesion and tackle anti-social behaviour. Considerable resources have been allocated to the prevention of family problems with initiatives such as Sure Start, which in the first phase emphasised the role of community in the reduction of disadvantage in the poorest areas (Glass, 2005, cited in Quinney, 2006, p. 92). Other developments that have been designed to address social exclusion at the neighbourhood level include the Social Exclusion Unit, which was abandoned in May 2006 in favour of the Social Exclusion Task Force, and the New Deal for Communities. However, as we will see these community-based social inclusion initiatives have had little impact in the fields of social work practice and social work education.

In response to this shifting scenario we have written *Social Work and the Community: A Critical Context for Practice* in which we explore the antecedents of community and social work, discuss and reflect upon the contemporary situation, and consider the future of social work in the UK and how it might gain from a re-examination of its role and purpose.

It is our contention that contemporary social work is facing a changing and problematic landscape. Modernisation has positioned social work as less involved in the enabling role in the community, and more associated with risk assessment and resource management. Some believe that the 'soul' has been stripped out of social work, or at best, the profession can be said to have lost its way (Butler and Drakeford, 2005a). Certainly the profession is increasingly being forced to operate within the government agenda of containment and management of the poor and excluded. Although the UK is considered to have one of the most powerful economies in the world and today's society is relatively wealthy and prosperous, there continues to be large sections of the community who are not sharing in this prosperity, and the gap between the most prosperous and the poorest continues to widen. Internationally, the gains that derive from the global market have brought losses for many groups and communities.

The government's own figures indicate 12 million people, which is just under a quarter of the UK population, now live in poverty. This is not a new phenomenon as during the period the Conservatives were in power (1979–1997) the proportion of people living in households below 50% of average income rose from 9% to 24% (Department of Work and Pensions, 2005). These figures are borne out by the findings from a Joseph Rowntree Foundation study that show that Britain is moving back towards levels of wealth and poverty last seen before 1968 (Dorling *et al.*, 2007). Although New Labour has attempted to reduce poverty with its policy of increasing Child Benefit, and the introduction and changes to the Working Families Tax Credit and the Children's Tax Credit, benefits for adults have become increasingly conditional upon meeting income and other work tests. New Labour philosophy has centred upon a policy of 'welfare to work' with a primary focus on paid work and entrance into the labour market as a means of combating poverty and reducing social exclusion. However, despite the government's attempts to 'give a hand-up and not a hand-out' there has been an increasing demand for personal social services as the UK faces an ageing population (the over 85-year-old segment of the population is considered to be the fastest growing of all age groups, and by 2051, 25% of the population will be over 65 (Department of Health, 2006b)). This has occurred at a time when there has been a decline in the value of real pensions and the introduction of a pension credit scheme which appears to benefit those reasonably well off by giving people who have saved for retirement additional financial reward; social and family fragmentation; the increasing cost of community care; and widening economic inequality. Alongside this there has been a failure of education polices to satisfactorily improve the outcomes for the lowest deciles of children and their opportunity to secure either a place in higher education or satisfactory, well-paid employment on leaving school (Walton, 2005).

Key Aims

It is against this shifting and disquieting background that we have written this book. One of our central tenets is to argue the need for both statutory and voluntary sector social work to reconnect with the communities that it is intended to serve. Without doubt we can claim that there are difficult and challenging times for social work and in embracing this we have set for ourselves seven key aims:

1. To offer a clear and coherent understanding and analysis of the importance of community in social work activity.

2. To provide a theoretical understanding for the location of community in contemporary practice and to analyse the significance of the term community as a central organising focus for social policy, both locally and globally.

3. To discuss the role of community in shaping the recent historical development of social work and social care.

4. To explore the way community might be used as a basis for developing anti-racist, anti-discriminatory and anti-oppressive practice including work with refugees and asylum-seekers.

5. To examine the potential for social workers to contribute to the creation of more environmentally sustainable communities.

6. To consider future prospect and scenarios for social work in the community, working collaboratively with other professionals across different organisational boundaries.

7. To construct possibilities for promoting progressive practice in social work and allied professions in an international context.

The Concept of Community

The concept of community has always occupied an important place in the development of British social work as well as in its contemporary theory and practice. Although as we will later see the term may be considered contested and contradictory, there is no doubt that in relation to social work, community has enjoyed a position of some significance. For example, Eileen Younghusband's report on the role of social workers in local authority health and welfare services identified community work as one of the three key constituents of social work. The other two approaches were acknowledged as case work and group work (Younghusband, 1959). Later the influential Seebohm Report (1968), which recommended the establishment of 'generic' local authority social work services in England and Wales, contained a complete chapter entitled 'community'. The Seebohm Report led to the reorganisation of social services with the recognition that community was an important element that needed involvement and consultation when delivering effective services. Nearly a decade and a half later the report of the Barclay Committee (1982) was to re-emphasise the case for an approach to social work based upon local, neighbourhood, decentralised strategies which advocated social workers practicing as close as could be possible to service users in what was known as 'patch' based work. In both the Seebohm and Barclay Reports community was seen as a source of mutual support and assistance. Six years later the reports by Wagner (1988) and Griffiths Report (1988) were to encourage more appropriate social care in the community. More recently there has been a recognition that the time to take seriously community in social work is now with us and that it might form the basis for promoting well-being, solidarity and respect (Jordan, 2007).

Defining the concept of community has never been straightforward. However, it is important to consider the concept in a little more detail as it provides us with key indicators as to why it has retained such a significant influence in social work.

At the core of the problem of defining community lies a paradox that the term is as much an aspiration as it is a reality. Nevertheless it is clear that the term community does have significant resonance for many people. Politicians of all parties have not been slow in realising this often using the term when wanting to best demonstrate their credentials to the often sceptical and critical voting public, or when calling for a consensus after difficult or contentious issues or events. For example, at the Labour Party Annual Conference in 1998 Prime Minister Tony Blair used community as the theme of his keynote speech talking of 'One Nation. One Community.'... 'The crude individualism of the 80s is the mood no longer. The spirit of the times is community.' Again, after the destruction of the World Trade Centre in New York on September 11, 2001 Blair used his Conference speech to restate the role of the community 'asserting itself' to bring people together in troubled times.

Community has been the central theme in a number of long running TV 'soaps' such as East Enders, Coronation Street and Emmerdale, and 'The Archers' on BBC Radio 4. In these fictitious neighbourhoods many of life's dramas and issues are played out to a keenly waiting public. 'Soaps' run a number of credible and simultaneous story lines, that provide viewers or listeners with both entertainment and education. So that issues such as teenage pregnancy, divorce, non-school attendance, the death of an elderly member of the 'community', alcohol and drug misuse, marital abuse and gay/lesbian relationships are used to reflect societies understanding of them as well as to consider strategies for coping with the resultant responses. The role of the neighbourhood or community is important in this context as it provides the everyday background (e.g. the pub, the small local convenience shop, the community centre, the local school) to the presenting issues and problems. The sociologist Hobson (2002) has argued that it would be a mistake to dismiss the 'soaps' as escapist and she reiterates the view above that to be successful the story lines have to connect with the audience's own experiences in their local communities.

Returning to the challenge of defining community it is helpful here to consider it in three different ways. The first is to recognise that when using the term community we can be looking backwards, maybe to a period in our own lives when even as the social scientists, social workers or the policy makers we are now, we might claim there existed a 'better' and more contented time. In echoes of Young and Willmott's classic study (1957) of Bethnal Green in London, perhaps it was a time when we knew our neighbours, we could walk or cycle safely to school, and when we could play out till dusk in a relatively risk-free neighbourhood. In one sense it feels like a paradise lost; a time of long summers and of people helping each other. The reality is that this version of community where the grass seemed greener, the light brighter and the taste of food was better, is an idealised nostalgic one. Rex and Moore (1967, p. 213) describe this as 'the myth of the golden past'. This is not to say that it did not *feel* safer to walk or cycle to school (there were many fewer cars), or it was possible to know your neighbours (there was less geographical mobility), and maybe the summers did *feel* longer, and maybe the vegetables did taste as vegetables should, but this version does not confront some of the harsh realities of community life. For example, the impact of unemployment on individuals and families; signs on boarding house windows stating 'No blacks, no Irish, no dogs'; racist attacks on minority groups; the impact of informal and formal sexist practices that left many women ghettoised in low-paid jobs; the physical and emotional abuse many children and young people experienced from their parents behind the closed doors of their homes; the intransigency of certain secondary head teachers who excluded pupils for growing hair longer than the prescribed limit, the impact of which was often to the detriment of a pupil's academic career and future life chances. We are sure all readers can add to this list concerning some of the negatives of community life in their childhood. So whilst looking backwards is important it is equally vital to recognise that the secure trusting feelings of a bye-gone community had elements that for many were not at all affirmative.

Practice Focus

Take a few minutes to recall a community from your childhood. What key features were important to you?

How does this differ from the community of today? What kind of relationship do you have with your present-day community?

The second way of considering the term community is by looking forward to a period in which communities are living in harmony, where there is a real sense of friendship and companionship, and where pluralism and a sense of solidarity and shared identity and interests are in the ascendancy. However, this is similarly an idealised view. It is not to state it cannot exist; however, it is an aspiration, something that drives us forward in the pursuit of something that might not be achievable but one which we are going to try to secure for ourselves and those close to us.

The looking back and looking forward approaches chime with the oft-used quote from Raymond Williams that:

> Community can be the warmly persuasive word to describe an existing set of relationships, or a warmly persuasive word to describe an alternative set of relationships. What is most important, perhaps, is that unlike all other terms of social organisation (state, nation society etc.) it never seems to be used unfavourably, and never to be given any positive opposing or distinguishing term.
>
> (Williams, 1976, p. 66)

Looking backwards with nostalgia or forward in an idealised manner reflects the enduring power of the idea of community. It provides us with a sense of security and belonging in an insecure and risk ridden world where rapid globalisation and the cult of the individual are powerful influences.

A more useful way of considering community is to consider it as it is *now*. The complexity of life in a post-industrial, postmodern society like the UK means we have to consider community in different ways than we did only 20 years ago. We will be looking at the diversity of community in more detail in Chapter 3, in the meantime it might help us to take the definition of community as emanating from the fact that people have something in common, usually in terms of geographical location or shared residence. It is equally possible to consider community in terms of shared elements other than location. For example, links or networks based on religion, ethnicity or occupation. These are often termed communities of interest. A third and important sense of community is based on people's 'spirit of community' that Willmott (1986) describes as a 'community of attachment'.

In Chapter 6 we consider two competing discourses associated with community. The first is moral communitarianism epitomised by New Labour's crusade in the disadvantaged estates of the inner city to create a new consensus around inclusion. The second is referred to as transforming community action by supporting marginalised groups in their collective struggle for communities characterised by social and cultural diversity.

In the postmodern era we can all belong to a range of different communities that may include, but not necessarily be bound or dominated by location or neighbourhood. We can belong to a multiplicity of communities that are based upon, for example, ethnicity, religion, nationalism, gender, sexuality, age, disability and lifestyles. New and different forms of communication and information technologies including the virtual community of the Internet have had significant consequences upon the notion of community. These new and emerging communities sit alongside and interact with other more established communities mentioned above. Whether these new virtual communities provide users with a sense of belonging or attachment in the way envisaged by Willmott remains unclear.

Community therefore remains a contested term. Whilst there are imprecise and value-laden definitions of the term, there have been as will see in Chapter 2, useful and detailed investigations aimed at better understanding the complexity of community. We need to be aware, however, there is some scepticism as to whether the community as a social construction exists in contemporary times. Our shifting understanding of the term, however, helps makes the case for us to explore the centrality of community in the evolution of social work.

Outline of the Book

We have divided the book into three sections. The first section, from Chapters 1 to 3, considers the wider developments in our understanding of community. In Chapter 2 we examine the contribution of community studies to our appreciation of the diversity and changing nature of community from the industrial revolution to the present time. We then explore how the British government has increasingly intervened in deprived communities in order to regenerate neighbourhoods and increase economic activity. We end by considering a study from the Joseph Rowntree Foundation that examines the impact of economic migration of East Europeans on communities in the UK. In Chapter 3 we are particularly concerned with globalisation and neo-liberalism which has impacted upon levels of inequality and discrimination in communities.

In the second section, from Chapters 4 to 6, we examine how the concept of community has become a central organising force in social policy, influencing both the nature and development of the welfare state. In Chapter 4 we explore the use of community in area-based policy using the Community Development Projects (CDP) as a case study. We argue that the CDP story is an important one in current debates in social work given the continuing appeal to community in contemporary policy and practice. Chapter 5 focuses on the development of community care and how such policy deploys particular notions of community and the family to achieve consent. The following chapter analyses how ideas associated with the new communitarianism have shaped New Labour's 'third way' modernisation project to reform the welfare state.

The third and final section of the book is focused on practice. To do this we have looked at different strands of practice. We start by looking at the current identity and status of community social work in Chapter 7. Practitioners are required to give greater emphasis to prevention and collaborative working, but to balance this with increasingly a proscribed protection regime. Drawing on a range of theory and research evidence we explore how this might be done. In Chapter 8 we focus on the location and role of community work and community action in contemporary UK society. Our view is that tension between these two practices and the state is an important one in a democratic society and one which demands high levels of skill and political understanding of its practitioners. In the final chapter we assess future possibilities for community-based social work in an international context. We argue in this chapter for a critical practice which offers an emancipatory way of working in the community and which can manage the contradictions that emerge.

Conclusion

Despite the difficult challenges that social work is presently facing, it is likely to survive. Social work is well placed to confront the dilemmas and problems of the coming decade and further, as it has a unique and important contribution to play in supporting and enhancing the lives of those living in desperate, uncomfortable, miserable and sometimes potentially dangerous situations. We believe social workers, who are working predominantly with marginalised people, are also well placed in their role as agents of progressive social change. Payne (2005b) has observed change and continuity is a constant theme in social work and we hope this book, which reports research findings, develops theoretical ideas and considers practice initiatives will make its own contribution to a social work that is critically progressive, reflective and ultimately transformative.

2

The Contribution of Community Studies and Increased State Intervention in Communities and Neighbourhoods

Introduction

To appreciate and understand the enduring interest and appeal of the concept of community, we need to explore the different, and at times contradictory and contested, theories that highlight the term. To operationalise this we have spent some time in this chapter considering a number of important community studies that reflect the diversity and changing nature and understanding of community from the impact of the industrial revolution up to the present time. Traditionally, community studies have been primarily concerned with the interrelationships of social institutions in a locality. Community studies have understood community as 'a space defined by multiple contiguous social networks' (Ray, 2006). Further, these community studies provide invaluable accounts of how people lived in particular neighbourhoods and the problems they encountered.

With this view informing our work, we will be considering studies that both emphasise theoretical expositions as well as those that have focused on the more detailed ethnographic studies that illustrate community life in a range of settings. We start with a discussion of the work of Frederick Tonnies whose work in 1887 began our understanding of the changing nature of community and provided us with an invaluable interpretation of community and association. The work of the influential Chicago School of Urban Sociology and the ideas they produced on racial discrimination in communities are then discussed. The work of one of the School's leading academics Wirth (1938) will be considered. In Wirth's view, the emerging urban society of the late nineteenth and early twentieth centuries were weakly integrated and characterised by tenuous relationships and superficial encounters. He argues that people's contact with each other is usually limited to a particular task or activity, consequently city life can be described as unstable and social order is likely to breakdown. This view can be examined in relationship to the role of social work in dealing with vulnerable people and unstable family relationships.

Fischer (1984), unlike Wirth, argues, that urban life can assist the formation of communities by means of a process of community gravitation, by which individuals gravitate towards like-minded or similar people to produce a critical mass and to establish 'thriving social worlds'. Similarly, Gans (1968) has argued that members of an urban population can live in stable communities and has argued that people's life chances to a great extent depends on their class situation and stage in life. Furthermore, the famous studies by Dennis *et al.* (1956) and by Young and Willmott (1957) reveal strong working-class communities existing in Featherstone in West Yorkshire, and Bethnal Green in London during the 1950s. Since Young and Willmott, other sociologists including Stacey (1969), Bell and Newby (1971) and Day and Murdoch (1993) have offered discussions on the value of community studies, and provided further conceptual analysis. We will consider the feminist critiques of community studies that have pointed to the sexist nature of the work. Further we will highlight community studies that have focused on ethnicity.

We then move our attention to explore how governments have increasingly intervened in community life in order to regenerate neighbourhoods and increase economic activity, before considering a 2007 Joseph Rowntree Foundation study that examines the impact of economic migration of East Europeans on communities in the UK.

This chapter provides the background for Chapter 3 in which we will consider the increasing diversity, inequality and discrimination that takes place in many communities. In this way these two chapters provide us with a clearer understanding of the relationship that presently brings notions of community and social work together.

The Slippery Notion of Community

As we discussed in Chapter 1, the idea of community is a continuing one that has exercised sociologists since the establishment of sociology as a recognised form of analysis and academic study. The work of Hillery

(1955) is useful here as the author discovered numerous and differing definitions of community in the sociological literature. However, some sociologists like Stacey (1969) have argued that efforts to clarify the meaning of community are self-defeating. Margaret Stacey's paper on the 'myth of community studies' was particularly influential as at the time she occupied a principal position in the emerging British sociological academy. Stacey's view that 'local social system' (1969, p. 139) could be a more appropriate term than the concept of community was to contribute to a relatively dormant period in the development of UK community studies. So much so that Abrams (1978, p. 11) claimed that

> the concept of community for its part is slowly being evicted from British sociology, not because there is general agreement on the empirical collapse of community, but rather because the term has come to be used so variously and different relationships, identified as those of community, have discovered in so many different contexts that the word itself has become devoid of precise meaning.

By the 1980s community life began to be studied again and explorations of both the notion of community and the study of discrete communities is now a central, if not a major strand in contemporary sociology. Traditionally, one of the main hurdles to many investigations has been that community can be considered in both subjective and objective forms. In their desire to establish sociology as an authentic social science discipline, sociologists have tended to err on the side of producing objective accounts that have not always satisfactorily captured the subjective elements of community as commonly expressed by local people in a sense of feeling or belonging. Whilst acknowledging the significance of objective accounts, we believe they contain inherent problems and for our exploration include some artificial and unhelpful aspects. What is needed is a more holistic and engaging investigation that recognises that most people, and here we include social scientists, social workers, practitioners in the community including community development workers, youth workers and policy makers, can simultaneously hold a conception of community that is both objective and subjective. In other words, we understand the concept of community to be based as much upon our social experience as on any informed theory. In this sense the idea of community is socially constructed.

Gemeinschaft and Gesellschaft

It would be difficult to satisfactorily examine the term community without first acknowledging the work of the German sociologist Frederick Tonnies (1855–1936) who considered the way in which people understood their communities and how they interacted with each other. In *Community and Association* (1955) (first published in 1887), Tonnies argues that the urbanisation of the Industrial Revolution in Germany had negatively impacted upon social life and led to the loss of community (or what he termed as *Gemeinschaft*). He portrayed *Gemeinschaft* as being made up of close-knit, traditional and personal relationships where people understood their social position in relation to each other. In Tonnies' view family and religion were powerful constituents in *Gemeinschaft*. According to Tonnies, *Gemeinschaft* was being replaced by *Gesellschaft* or association or society where relationships are based upon instrumental and transitory exchanges. In this scenario the individual rather than the community has greater importance. In *Gesellschaft* relationships are more likely to be specific to particular settings and purposes. The work of Tonnies is significant as his ideas of community represent the strand that contains romantic elements that we discussed in Chapter 1. He is lamenting a previous age when in his view people benefited from living in closer connection with each other, having ties based on locality and custom and which provided communities with cohesion and loyalty. He reflects with pessimism on the impact of industrialisation on a sense of community believing that community is about 'living' and has a particular naturalness whereas society is more 'rational' and mechanistic. In later years sociology was to grapple with the increasing complexity surrounding the idea of community.

Cities and Community

In the period from the late 1800s to 1930 the population of Chicago, USA doubled to 3 million people. This rapid development was almost entirely the result of immigration, first from European countries, and after 1918 from southern USA (Cressey, 1971). In an effort to understand these phenomena sociologists based at the Chicago School of Urban Sociology (CSUS) at the University of Chicago established a reputation for producing studies of discrete communities in the city that discovered important features of race relations and urban segregation. The CSUS studies of Chicago slum areas and ghettos offered the public an insight into both the dynamic of racial discrimination and the nature of different waves of immigration to areas of development. Researchers were able to identify a large number of individuals and families that had uprooted from established communities elsewhere, in many cases from another continent, and who were adapting to a different way of life, in a different place often in hostile and difficult circumstances. This constant changing scenario offered the CSUS an opportunity to examine these emerging communities and to test theories the researchers believed would assist them understand this new social phenomenon.

In later times the Chicago School was criticised for its various limitations in particular those relating to the 'uncritical and limited empiricism' of their studies (Mellor, 1977, p. 237). Nonetheless a major legacy of the CSUS is the important connection the sociologists made between ethnicity and areas of settlement, a theme examined in the British context by Patterson (1965) and Rex and Moore (1967) and which we discuss later in this chapter.

From the 1920s to the 1940s the CSUS was the base for a number of influential commentators on urban sociology who developed ideas that have particular resonance for our present understanding of cities and communities. Noteworthy is the influence of Wirth (1938) whose seminal work argued that urbanism could be considered a way of life. In passages that hark back to the earlier work of Tonnies he contrasts the closeness of village life to the impersonal nature of city life. He states that although people in cities live in close proximity to one another the contact between them is often fleeting and bounded by monetary or legal transactions. In his opinion, the increased mobility of city dwellers contributed to weak or fragile bonds between people with a major factor in many relationships being the competition for resources and status. Wirth claimed the general lack of co-operation between people led many to experience instability and absence of community spirit. Despite these observations Wirth recognises that people living in close proximity in cities can have the opposite effect with the creation of strong communities that display particular distinct characteristics. This is confirmed by the work of Dennis *et al.* (1956) in West Yorkshire and Young and Willmott (1957) in east London, and the study by Allatt and Yeandle (1992) focusing on Newcastle upon Tyne, in northeast England, which highlight the strength and resilience of working-class communities.

Before moving from the work of Louis Wirth (1897–1952) it is helpful for our investigation to consider the present-day implications of the ideas of this significant Chicago-based sociologist. The argument made by Wirth is that the impersonality of modern urbanism leads to instability and difficulties for urban dwellers. He believes it contributes to the breakdown of social order and unstable personal and community relationships. Wirth pointed to the higher level of mental breakdown and suicides in urban areas compared with rural areas – what the French sociologist Emile Durkheim (1858–1917) characterised as anomie. Contemporarily there is evidence that social exclusion, crime, family breakdown and issues of ethnicity is significantly greater and more intense in cities than in rural areas, even allowing for the issue of greater visibility.

In response to the inter-related urban problems of poor job prospects, high levels of crime, educational underachievement, poor health and problems of housing and the physical environment, the New Labour government launched in 1997 a strategy with the aim of regenerating specific urban areas and reducing disadvantage in communities in the greatest need. We will be briefly discussing these and other area-based regeneration projects later in this chapter, and in more detail in Chapters 3, 4 and 6.

Since the publication of Wirth's ideas, other urban sociologists have undertaken further work producing findings that counter his arguments. In particular, Gans (1968) argues that Wirth had overly concentrated on inner-city areas and had ignored the many more stable urban communities. Gans argues it is the poorest that suffer greatest in urban areas because they are in his view *trapped* and *deprived*. So unlike Tonnies and Wirth, Gans argues that thriving communities do exist in cities and that individual life chances and community breakdown has more to do with people's class position, income and stage in life than their location in either a rural or urban area. Giddens (1981) also criticises Wirth arguing that modern capitalism has transformed urban and rural life so that the defining feature now is not where people live but their income and their occupation and it is this which structures their life chances.

'Coal Is Our Life' – A View of the Working Class World in the 1950s

A community study that provides us with helpful insights into British working-class life up until the 1950s is the famous study of the small West Yorkshire coal-mining town of Featherstone (Dennis *et al.*, 1956). The authors explore a working-class world where most families depended upon mining for their livelihood with two-thirds of men in the town working in mining, with the majority of the other men employed in a local clothing factory and on the railway. At the time of the study there was a strict domestic division of labour with a separation of men's activities from those of women's. Few women were in paid employment, with most married women characterising themselves as 'housewives', and with the majority of the young and unmarried women in Featherstone being employed in domestic service, the retail trade, dressmaking, teaching or nursing. The majority of housing in Featherstone was built and owed by the local authority, with some property built by former mining companies but after nationalisation of the coal mines in January 1947 were owed by the National Coal Board. Therefore most families were tenants, not owner-occupiers.

This fascinating community study reveals to us a world where men's work had traditionally been insecure, and where their identity was related to a hard, difficult, and often dangerous, occupation. Men took pride in being 'real men who work hard for their living' (Dennis *et al.*, 1956, p. 33). This manual work gave the miners their working-class identity whilst the non-manual workers, that is the clerks and the managers, were not seen as 'us' but 'them'. The trade union movement and in particular the National Union of Mineworkers provided the miners with their sense of collective action and solidarity whilst the Miners' Welfare Institute and the town's six Working Men's Clubs (only one of which admitted women) and Featherstone's pubs were to provide the venues for the men's leisure activities of billiards, darts, cards, dominoes and various clubs and associations. Activities that were shared by both men and women included cinema going at the nearby town of Pontefract. Featherstone was noted for its strong sense of localism and competitiveness with other towns particularly through sport including rugby league, cricket and football. Important too was the colliery brass band that played at local events and took part in fiercely competitive brass band competitions.

The title *Coal is Our Life* for Dennis *et al.*'s book is apt as at the time of the study the mining industry dominated the relations between people in Featherstone. Few families did not have a direct or partial connection with the industry that influenced people's social, political and economic relations with each other, the state and the National Coal Board. The study gives us a sense of the continuity and community that people felt when most grew up in the same town, went to school with each other, worked with each other and spent leisure time together. The fact that the coal industry was the main employer meant that it was in the interests of everyone to ensure that the mine stayed open, worked efficiently and safely so that the next generation of boys and men could work there and families benefit from their wages. This gave the community its strength and enhanced people's commitment to each other. The strong local networks and close family ties inherent in the Featherstone community emphasised a clearly defined working-class life and like many working-class communities of this period gave people both their class identity and their gendered role and responsibilities.

Young and Willmott (1957): The 'Most Widely Read Work of Sociology in Britain'

Another key community study that was undertaken at a similar time as that in Featherstone is the examination of Bethnal Green by Young and Willmott (1957). Once described as 'the most widely read work of sociology in Britain' (Sanders, 1992, p. 15), *Family and Kinship in East London* should not be overlooked as the authors produced a classic community study that in more recent years has been criticised for its romantic images of traditional working-class life. Based at the Institute of Community Studies, Young and Willmott set out to investigate the impact of post-war changes on Bethnal Green in east London. The authors had expected to discover a breakdown in community life but instead found a neighbourhood, not dissimilar from Featherstone, in that it had retained its sense of community with strong extended kinship networks. The authors discovered that half of the local residents had been born in area. Although this was lower than in 1934 when 90% of the Bethnal Green residents were born in the east London, it still reflected and supported the strong sense of community. Again like Featherstone, women in Bethnal Green were identified as the key maintainers of wider kinship patterns with regularly visiting 'mum' seen as important in sustaining bonds of social solidarity.

One of the critics of this study, who argues that Young and Willmott presented a romantic view of community life in Bethnal Green emphasising the 'warmth, charm and humanity of working-class life', is the feminist commentator Elizabeth Wilson (1980, p. 64). Another is Cornwell who claims Young and Willmott painted a picture of the community they studied as being

> a place of huge families centred around Mum, of cobbled streets and terraced cottages, pen doors, children's street games, open-air markets, and always, and everlastingly, cups of tea and women gossiping together on the doorstep.
>
> (Cornwell, 1984, p. 24)

As Crow and Allan (1994) argue, the case against Young and Willmott is not that they denied the material hardship of those living in Bethnal Green, but rather they tended to selectively concentrate on aspects that in retrospect contained elements of sentimentality. One also needs to question whether the study could be described as 'scientific' as it relies heavily on ethnographic approaches that whilst offering interesting observations, cannot always be considered reliable. Undertaken less than 30 years after the Institute of Community Studies work, the studies by Holme (1985) and by Cornwell (1984) had discovered a rather different Bethnal Green community.

In the case of Holme she found that the sense of community was markedly less prominent with residents having become more home centred. She comments the corollary of the new home-centredness was

> the emptiness of the streets and corridors and staircases in the housing estates. Markets still flourished. Children sometimes played outside. Small groups of adults occasionally congregated. But no longer could it be said that people in

Bethnal Green were (in Young and Willmott's words) 'vigorously at home in the streets'.

(Holme, 1985, p. 45)

Meanwhile Cornwell has highlighted the importance of ethnicity in Bethnal Green and its role in determining inclusion and exclusion in the community. She discovered a degree of hostility from white residents towards the black and Asian residents in the area. Cornwell also observes the way in which private and public accounts of community are often at odds. Cornwell argues that Young and Willmott's explanation of community was based on public accounts, ignoring private accounts. She believes this 'partial and one-sided' view (1984, p. 24) gives precedence to the romantic and idealised account of the past.

Women and Community

Cornwell's study of Bethnal Green is valuable as she provides relatively recent insights into the role of women in community. In her authoritative study Cornwell reveals that men and women experienced and described notions of community differently. She found that men who lived in the area but worked outside of it identified the local pub as pivotal in their interpretation of community life. Women, however, who spent longer periods of their time in the neighbourhood, experienced and described a broader range of communal spaces including shops, school gates and local streets and friends' and relatives' homes.

In Chapter 3 we will consider in more detail the role of women in community organising but as a prelude it is useful here to briefly reflect on the nature of gendered relations and the impact on notions of community. We are aware that gendered relations have created levels of oppression that are reflected in, and reproduced by, institutions and social interactions. Patriarchal social relations have reinforced the role of women as the dominant child raiser and carer in both family and community life.

This expectation of women occupying the role of primary carers has had direct implications for the nature of community life for themselves, children and men. As Cornwell discovered, women are more likely to spend greater time in the community than men. They occupy more of the communal and private space and because of their role in bringing up children they will spend time with other women and children, often related to pre-school and school activities. Women frequently engage in unpaid activities that assist and enhance the welfare and education of others in communities. However, as Ashurst and Hall (1989) demonstrate, this can be at the expense of their own opportunities. In home life there is evidence that although men undertake more domestic tasks than previously assumed such as shopping and gardening, women continue to carry out the majority of housework and personal care much of which is unappreciated (Grenier and Wright, 2001). In community life, women frequently make a significant contribution in developing and resourcing provision such as play schemes and youth clubs that assist children, young people and themselves (Mayo, 1994).

Feminist critiques (Damer, 1989; Whitehead, 1976) have highlighted the sexist nature of some community studies that have portrayed women in a patronising manner. Further, Riley (1983) criticises the nature of some of the earlier community studies for failing to even consider gender inequalities whilst Elizabeth Wilson (1982) claims that community studies and the ideology of community has traditionally ignored the role of women, frequently confining them to the private sphere.

Ethnicity and Community

We noted above the significant dimension of 'race' and ethnicity in the study of community. The Chicago School with their detailed studies of the impact of large-scale migration on the city's urban areas were amongst the first to highlight how a person's 'race' and ethnicity can lead to exclusion and discrimination. The analysis provided by the Chicago School was to influence community studies undertaken in areas of migration and settlement in the UK. Before reviewing these studies it is helpful first to consider the background to immigration in Britain.

Major post-war migration to the UK began in June 1948 when the *SS Empire Windrush*, a former German pleasure steamer, docked at Tilbury, London after a journey from Jamaica. On board were almost 500 West Indians who had left the Caribbean island, predominately because they were facing a life of chronic unemployment and poverty, to seek a new life and employment in the UK. This mainly young male group were met with a 'Welcome Home' headline in the London *Evening Standard*: a reminder that some of them had been to Britain during the war to serve in the forces. The arrival of the *Empire Windrush* heralded a wave of immigration and settlement from the Caribbean as many sought employment in the UK which was enjoying the beginning of an economic boom based on the rebuilding of the country and its industries after the damage and destruction incurred during the Second World War. Immigrants found employment in the newly created National Health Service, and in the expanding service sector working for London Transport and the General Post Office as well as in a range of industries needing unskilled and manual workers. To meet the demand for workers the UK government encouraged the establishment of official employment agencies in the Caribbean to assist those seeking work and who wanted to move to Britain. The influx of immigrants from the Commonwealth was aided by the passing of the 1948 British Nationality Act that granted them favourable rights to enter the UK. However, the resentment and racism newly arrived immigrants experienced from some native-born Britons was considerable. Whilst their contribution to building a dynamic new Britain was thought valuable, their presence in local communities was not always welcomed. These translated into racist attacks by white residents on black people living in Notting Hill, west London and in the St Ann's community in Nottingham in 1958. Racist views were given a political voice through, amongst others, the Conservative MP and front-bench spokesman, Enoch Powell, whose 'River of Blood' speech at the Midland Hotel in Birmingham in 1962 predicted a massive inflow of 'non-white' immigrants and which is considered a key moment and turning point in British post-war race relations (Foot, 1969).

By the mid- and late 1950s some two or three thousand people were arriving from the Caribbean each month (Castles and Cossacks, 1973) and by the 1960s these figures were increased with immigration from the Indian sub-continent, in particular India and Pakistan. The attacks on immigrant communities coincided with a slow down in the growth of the British economy and the need for less dependence on the same numbers of unskilled and manual workers. In an attempt to address the problem, the Conservative government passed the Commonwealth Immigrants Act of 1962 that restricted the number of 'non-white' immigrants to the UK whilst protecting entry to whites particularly those from the 'old' Commonwealth including Australia and Canada, who could enter relatively easily. Inevitably, whites were more likely to possess specialist and in-demand skills.

Whilst in opposition Labour had opposed the immigration legislation of 1962, but when elected to government, and under pressure from its MPs that represented predominately white working-class communities, they introduced more stringent restrictions on the number of unskilled workers coming to the UK (Marwick, 2000). However, in an effort to improve community relations, the 1965 Race Relations Act established the Race Relations Board to deal with proven cases of discrimination based on colour or 'race'. It was at this time that two important studies were undertaken of communities in which newly arrived immigrants resided.

One study in Brixton in south London was by Shelia Patterson (1965) whose ideas were influenced by the Chicago School, in particular the contribution of Robert Park (1952, p. 79) who wrote that

> Once set up, a city is, it seems, a great sorting mechanism which . . . infallibly selects out of the population as a whole the individuals best suited to live in a particular region or a particular milieu.

This suggestion of communities being ordered into 'natural areas' and differentiated through complex processes of competition, immigration, settlement and succession has a resonance with biological ecology. In the natural environment, animals, insects, fish and birds engage in a constant battle to achieve some sense of balance and security in their environment in order to ensure a continuance of species. Park argued that this approach is not dissimilar to city communities where neighbourhoods emerge and evolve through the changes made by community members. Patterson's study of West Indians in Brixton draws on these ideas and refers like Park to 'ghettos' and 'zones' of settlement, which the author sees as negative features that can delay the assimilation of immigrants into communities. For example, ghettos, she argues

> perpetuate minority group values and traits, to limit social and cultural contacts between newcomers and local people, to reinforce local views on the alienness of the newcomers, and so to retard ultimate integration or assimilation.
>
> (1965, p. 195)

In contemporary times these views appear dated and naïve as they fail to satisfactorily acknowledge the racism directed at non-white people and the resultant need for minority communities to maintain and strengthen themselves through religious and cultural networks. At the time of writing, minority ethnic groups make up around 8% of the UK population (HMSO, 2004) with a greater presence of non-white people living in areas such as Greater London than ever before (ONS, 2002). Ethnic diversity in London and other major British cities is very different from when Patterson undertook her study almost 45 years ago.

Published 2 years after the work by Patterson, the study by Rex and Moore (1967), is similarly influenced by the Chicago School. However, Rex and Moore appear to use the Chicago School's ideas of different residential zones as a starting place for their own investigation. The authors consider the connection between 'race', community life and disadvantage in Sparkbrook, an inner area of Birmingham which contained a population of some 18,000 including English, Irish, West Indians and Pakistanis, and to a less extent Arabs, Cypriots, Indians and Poles. Rex and Moore's research, which is considered to be the classic community study of the period, discovered that Birmingham City Council housing policy, together with the private housing market, had aspects of both intended and unintended discrimination against different ethnic groups. To highlight this, Rex and Moore produced a classification of the varyingly desirability of housing. Identifying seven housing categories, they argued that the most favourable situation was reserved for those who were outright owners of their own property. The other classifications included those buying their own property through a mortgage, council tenants, council tenants in property awaiting demolition, private tenants of houses, owners of houses who rent out rooms in order to pay for mortgages or loans to purchase the property and finally the tenants of the rooms in these properties. They noted that it was in the suburban areas that property ownership was at its highest, whilst in inner area communities such as Sparkbrook there was likely to be a greater concentration of people from ethnic groups living in less desirable circumstances. Rex and Moore identified that Sparkbrook was a 'zone of transition' for many of its residents who appeared to have little control over their housing situation.

More recent studies on housing, 'race' and ethnicity confirm that people from minority groups continue to suffer discrimination and racism in the housing market. However, as Mason (2000) indicates, some minority ethnic groups, in particular those of Indian origin, have achieved well in the housing market and are as likely as whites to be in the home owner–occupier sector. Nevertheless, a high proportion of Bangladeshis and Pakistanis reside in property that is overcrowded and rented and which is located in inner-city areas.

Neighbourhood Decline and Renewal

In recent years the study of communities has developed to a more sophisticated and detailed level. In particular, the Economic and Social Research Council (ESRC) 10-year funding for the Centre for Analysis of Social Exclusion (CASE) based at the London School of Economics, and the studies produced by the Joseph Rowntree Foundation (JRF) have greatly added to our knowledge and understanding of the similarities and differences between different types of neighbourhoods. These studies have provided us with invaluable accounts of current policy initiatives, and evidence of the dynamic between international, national, regional and local circumstances, employment markets, and training and education opportunities, housing tenure, public and private sector provision and ethnicity. One of the key findings of both studies produced by CASE and the JRF has been the increase in intervention in communities and neighbourhoods by the local and central state. This is an important consideration in the development of communities in the UK and it is worth briefly reflecting on the nature and extent of this intervention from 1945 onwards. It was from 1945 that plans were drawn up and implemented to develop and rebuild the British cities that had suffered from chronic overcrowding before the Second World War, and which had experienced enemy bombing during the 1939–1945 conflict. We consider how the government has targeted the renewal of neighbourhoods and communities and in doing so has increased its intervention in areas where the poor reside.

Post-War Rebuilding of Communities

In the early post-war years the emphasis in Britain was on clearing and rebuilding bombed cities. For example, during the Second World War, Plymouth, a strategic naval port city in the south west of England, was badly destroyed by the German Luftwaffe. By Victory in Europe Day in May 1945 the city had suffered 602 air raid alerts, 59 actual bombing attacks, 1172 civilians killed and 4448 civilians injured, whilst figures for service personnel have never been published. The destruction of guild-halls, shopping centres, a theatre, hotels, cinemas, public houses and some 3754 houses with another 18,389 dwellings in need of major repairs led the city council to commence a major rebuilding programme (Gill, 1979, p. 197). The city's war-time mayor, Viscount Astor was at the forefront of moves to engage, as a consultant, the eminent town planner Professor (later Sir) Patrick Abercrombie, who was already working on a plan for Greater London. Working with Paton-Watson, Plymouth's city's engineer, Abercrombie drew up a rebuilding plan that had to deal

> not just with war damage but with all the pre-war defects of the city. A quarter of the population had still been overcrowded before the war, twice as many as Liverpool.
>
> (Gill, 1979, p. 198)

The outcome of this plan was that the central areas of the city were extensively rebuilt with commercial and retail property while new council estates were established in the outer areas. These new estates were mainly occupied by young families moving from inner-city areas, whilst between 1951 and 1981 inner areas experienced a large decline in the younger age group population and an increase in the proportion of elderly people (Maguire *et al.*, 1987, p. 26). The main problem that Plymouth continues to wrestle with today is that the outlying estates were built without sufficient social, commercial and retail outlets, leading to problems of social dislocation for its many communities (Bright, 2003).

Plymouth, with its lack of community facilities and services in its newly built estates, suffered from being one of the first British cities rebuilt after 1945. By the 1960s, central government was recognising that tackling poor communities was more than just building new houses and developing city centres. Instead it was accepted that improved services and living conditions needed to be developed alongside compensatory and support services.

The 1960s, 1970s and 1980s

From the late 1960s onwards a whole raft of government initiatives were introduced to provide more effective management of disadvantaged communities and to identify and tackle service-level deficiencies. The concept of community cohesion and well-being was recognised, perhaps for the first time as being important in regeneration and renewal. The initiatives in the 1960s included the Urban Programme, which launched in 1968, focused on funding social, educational and welfare projects in target-deprived areas. Initiated a year later, the Community Develop-ment Projects (CDP) addressed concerns that locality services needed better management and co-ordination. Although as we will see in later chapters this criteria was challenged by the CDP workers who saw the problem of poor communities to be due to the nature of capitalist society. Their analysis was borne out, as the 1970s was a period of fast growing unemployment and in turn severe neighbourhood decline (Lupton, 2003).

Against the background of rising unemployment in the 1970s and 1980s, both Labour and Conservative governments set out to tackle economic decline and change with a range of measures. The 1977 *Policy for the Inner Cities* (DoE, 1977) and the 1978 Inner Urban Areas Act heralded a move from social to economic regeneration in particular in the development of industrial estates. These Labour government initiatives were replaced when the Conservatives came to power in 1979 with schemes to support communities through private enterprise rather than public investment and in 1981, 11 Urban Development Corporations (UDCs) were estab-lished. These UDCs were funded from the public purse but were non-governmental organisations set up for a 10-year period to primarily create and stimulate private investment in localities. Similarly, Enterprise Zones were introduced to encourage private enterprises and to link with local authorities to speed planning and administrative processes. Five years later in 1986 Inner City Task Forces were established in 22 areas, again to boost economic opportunities in areas of high unemployment.

The 1990s

Although economic regeneration was the main thrust to supporting communities in the 1970s and 1980s, measures were introduced to improve neighbourhoods with agencies and schemes that were intended to improve people's living conditions. For example, over 500 council housing estates were upgraded through the Estate Action programme that ran from 1985 to 1994. With the Conservatives 'Right to Buy' scheme introduced in 1981, there was a need to ensure that as many council properties as possible were improved so they could be sold at discounted prices. Meanwhile, communities in London's Docklands were transformed with massive state funding that upgraded council property and encouraged the private sector to build houses, offices, retail outlets and entertainment complexes in an extensive waterfront area that was no longer serving as a working port. The development of the Docklands, however, was not without criticism from local people (Marris, 1987). Area-based initiatives continued to address communities in decline through 31 areas selected for City Challenge status. The scheme was launched in 1991 was a mix of economic revival and social welfare projects. By 1994 the Conservative government had instigated the Single Regeneration Budget (SRB), which comprised of finance 'top-sliced' from government departments and channelled through local multi-agency partnerships to deliver regeneration programmes.

New Labour and the Regeneration of Communities

Since their election to government in 1997 a corner stone of New Labour's programme has been to tackle social exclusion and highlight the role community regeneration can play in addressing poverty and enhancing its policy of 'welfare to work'. This was kick-started by the report from the Social Exclusion Unit (SEU, 2001), which built on an earlier report (SEU, 1998), which had documented the conditions in some of Britain's poorest areas, and led to the establishment of Policy Action Teams to develop strategic responses. The 2001 SEU report was to herald a move from short-term area-based projects, which had marked the previous decades, to more long-term strategic programmes that integrated the work of different departments but which delivered at a neighbourhood level. One of the key proposals was the New Deal for Communities which focused on 39 neighbourhoods of between 1000–4000 households that needed to tackle five areas of concern: unemployment and poor job prospects; improving health; tackling crime; raising educational achievement; and improving housing and the physical environment. The key to these interventions was the partnership of different agencies and bodies, and the involvement with local residents. This capacity building of local people was a departure from previous government-backed interventions and drew attention to the need for residents to be more involved in their own communities.

At the same time, New Labour launched 99 Education Action Zones, which were aimed at improving educational standards and tackling low school achievement. Simultaneously in 1998, 26 Health Action Zones were introduced to develop a new approach to public health that worked to link improving health and modernising services with other government concerns with regeneration, education, employment, housing and anti-poverty initiatives (see Chapter 4). These area-based, more strategic approaches were added to in 2000 with 15 Employment Zones aimed at addressing the needs of areas suffering from high long-term unemployment and in particular tried to assist older unemployed people back to work. Concern to eradicate child poverty led the government to introduce in 1998 Sure Start which was aimed at supporting families with direct provision for the under-4s, combined with advice to parents on health, nutrition nurturing and education. Nationally, there are now over 500 multi-agency Sure Start partnerships delivering programmes in communities.

Summary

A constant feature in British social and public policy since the end of the Second World War has been the focus on improving life in communities and neighbourhoods. We have observed that since 1945 governments have developed varying methods of tackling social and economic problems encountered by communities. Some of these have emphasised the social welfare and education aspects of redevelopment and renewal, whilst others have been concerned mainly with economic regeneration. New Labour, however, has attempted to integrate these two aims in a more coherent and strategic manner in order to achieve its commitment to social inclusion and to enable economic and social restructuring to take place. The government now has an Action Plan for the National Neighbourhood Renewal (SEU, 2001) that proudly claims that in a period of 10–20 years no one should be disadvantaged by where they reside. This is indeed a bold commitment to communities and we wait to see if this can be realised.

Recent Community Studies

We mentioned earlier the community studies produced by the Joseph Rowntree Foundation (JRF) have added to our understanding and knowledge of the diverse range of communities that reside in the UK. In particular, we would like to highlight and report on a recent JRF study that examines new immigrants from five Eastern European countries (Albania, Bulgaria [now part of the European Union], Russia, Serbia and Montenegro [which has since become an independent state] and Ukraine) living in the London Boroughs of Harrow and Hackney, and the City of Brighton and Hove (Markova and Black, 2007). One of the study's main focuses was to explore the interaction between the new European immigrants and the more established members of the local communities in which they settled. In particular, aspects of community cohesion are highlighted in our consideration, as there has been concern that any influx of migrants should not detrimentally effect how communities operate. Both new immigrants and long-term residents were interviewed in the three study areas.

Economic migration is not a new phenomenon in the UK, but with the enlargement of the European Union in 2004, and the inclusion of Bulgaria and Romania in 2007, Britain has experienced the impact of immigration of a different dimension to that felt in the period from the late 1940s to the 1980s when the majority of migrants came from the Commonwealth. Most of the new immigrants who were interviewed in this study had left their country of origin for economic reasons although Serbians and Albanians were more likely to report political instability as their prime reason. Two Russians of Roma origin stated they left their country because of racial discrimination. All groups said that factors such as family, friends or marriage were important in their choice of the UK as a destination. The Bulgarians, Russians and Ukrainians also mentioned the ease of securing an entry visa as a factor.

Over 50% of the respondents had been in the UK for more than 5 years, with the majority being well educated. Forty per cent of them had a university degree or above, a further 54% had completed secondary education or college, and some 6% had no qualifications. Interestingly, more than two-thirds of the immigrants described their level of English on arrival as either 'none' or 'basic', whilst 70% of Albanians said they had no English at all when they arrived. However, by the time the fieldwork was carried out self-reported English proficiency had improved significantly amongst all groups, with Albanians describing their English as 'fluent' or 'adequate'.

In regards to housing tenure over half the immigrants were living in private rented accommodation, with slightly more owner-occupiers in Brighton, whereas in Hackney social housing was a major form of tenure. The majority of the new immigrants were in managerial, professional or associate professional positions in business, health and social work, wholesale, retail trade and repair work. However, over half of those interviewed had entered the UK labour market through jobs in the hotel and restaurant sector, construction or 'other' services (mainly domestic cleaning). Most were assisted in finding their first job through fellow nationals although their first employer was usually a white British employer. The majority reported a white British person presently employed them.

The interesting observation for us is that only 35% of the new immigrants felt a sense of belonging 'very strongly' or 'fairly strongly' to their neighbourhood. This compared with 72% of the long-term residents interviewed. The authors of the study believe this reflects a real lack of identification amongst the new immigrants with the neighbourhoods in which they resided. However, 63% of the new immigrants reported they felt they belonged to the UK and the majority of immigrants said they had a greater sense of belonging to their borough or city of residence than to the local neighbourhood. Those who did indicate a sense of belonging with their neighbourhoods were those with children or those who did not plan to return to their home country soon, those living in council property and those with less education.

Among long-term residents, women (74%) were more likely to express feelings of belonging to the community than men (67%), but only 30% of new immigrant women, and 40% of new immigrant men felt a sense of community.

There were signs, however, that both long-term residents and new immigrants (87% in each group) valued the diversity in the three study areas, with both groups reporting that their neighbourhoods were places where people got on well. Although over half of both groups reported talking to a neighbour at least once a week, immigrants were less likely to talk to their neighbours. Those with children present were more likely to talk to their neighbours. All residents reported fairly high levels of social interaction with people from other ethnic groups, with 72% of immigrants and 85% of long-term residents interviewed confirming they had friends from different ethnic groups.

What does this study inform us about community cohesion? There is little doubt that the study does evidence that the relations between the new immigrants and the long-term residents in the three areas showed some signs of a 'cohesive community', particularly through diversity and social interaction. In respect of the new immigrants, however, they did not indicate the same sense of belonging to the neighbourhood as other residents and they were not involved to the same degree in certain forms of community participation. The study shows a clear link between housing tenure and community cohesion with owner-occupiers and council tenants more likely to participate in community activities and feel part of their neighbourhood than those in private rented accommodation. Community participation was lower among the new immigrants than the long-term residents with the later group more likely to be involved in volunteering, in social clubs and in tackling local issues. New immigrants were more involved in sports clubs than long-term residents. Levels of community participation increased the longer immigrants lived in the UK. The main concern that the study highlights is that where there is a problem of cohesion, it is reported at the local level. Immigrants feel part of the UK but not always part of their local community and therefore do not participate in local affairs. One of the reasons for this is that the three areas studied were described by the researchers as having aspects of being places of 'transit' with a high degree of movement in and out of the areas. One of the long-term residents thought this was eroding community spirit.

Interestingly, the perceived tension between new migrants and members of indigenous groups around competition for jobs, community facilities and space did not emerge in this study. This is not to suggest that such tensions do not exist, but the boundaries that separate social groups and the signs of segregation are now quite difficult to read and interpret.

Summary and Conclusion

In the previous chapter, we noted that theories of community are contested and that there is a need for some greater understanding of the changing nature of community. This chapter has assisted this process by considering community through some of the work of key thinkers in this area, together with the lessons that can be drawn from classic community studies. We have seen that these studies have attracted criticism and debate, which further underlines the problematic nature of the concept. However, the studies capture the diverse experience of local people often at a time of social dislocation and change. Community therefore becomes a site for the reproduction of social relationships and inequalities derived from divisions of class, race and gender.

We have highlighted how the state has increasingly intervened in community life, usually to assist community cohesion, to encourage economic regeneration and to regulate and monitor poor neighbourhoods. New Labour's approach to community has been to adopt the concept to promote its polices to regenerate some of the UK's poorest areas.

The influx of new migrants from Eastern Europe has been considered and the 2007 JRF report offers us some helpful understandings of community cohesion in areas where long-term residents and migrants live.

Finally, it is clear from this chapter that in an era of globalisation and increasing individualism we need to rethink our understanding of community if we are to successfully use this information to assist those using and demanding personal social services. This debate will be explored further in the following chapter.

3

Rethinking Community – Globalisation, Neo-Liberalism and Inequality

Introduction

The aim of this chapter is to provide a critical examination of community as a site for ideological conflict and oppression. We are concerned here with the impact of inequality and discrimination and examine these in terms of class, 'race'/ethnicity and gender. We also consider the establishment of new communities in Britain with the influx of economic migrants, asylum-seekers, refugees and 'undocumented persons'.

We discovered in the previous two chapters that the notion of community has been a central organising feature in the reproduction of social and economic relations. The main focus of this chapter is the changing character of locality, and the varying nature of the impact of difference, diversity, inequality and discrimination in contemporary communities. To do this we are examining the significant impact that globalisation and the neo-liberal economic agenda has had on the UK. This background will assist us address the key questions which enable us to rethink community and reflect upon what we might learn from this shifting social phenomenon for the theory and practice of social work.

Globalisation

Since the end of the Second World War five momentous changes have taken place in the balance of international forces:

- The retreat from colonisation and empire in Asia, the Middle East, Africa and the Caribbean, by the European 'old' major world powers, Britain, France, Spain, the Netherlands and Portugal.

- The ascendancy of independent countries particularly in Africa, and south east Asia, which, rid of former colonisation, and in tandem with the rise of independence movements, are now an important influence in determining world affairs particularly at the United Nations.

- The creation and then collapse of the Soviet bloc and Soviet fashioned socialism; the fall of the Berlin Wall and the formation of a unified Germany; the rise of a host of smaller eastern European countries that have encouraged the influx of foreign capital and know-how, the unleashing of the capitalist mode of production of goods and services, and the introduction of Western-style political and welfare systems; and the enlargement of the European Union to accommodate many of these eastern European countries.

- The further increase in the power and influence of the United States of America so that it's now *the* dominant world power and in turn shapes the activities of the global market.

- The elevation of China as a major international power, and through its role as a major exporter of manufactured goods, is presently the fourth largest economy in the world.

In more recent years we have become aware of a further and powerful influence, globalisation. Globalisation is not a new concept and has arguably been evolving ever since Christopher Columbus crossed the Atlantic in 1492 in search of riches in East Asia and instead reached the Bahamas. Since then the economic, religious, social, political and cultural influence of the dominant 'known world' has spread to encompass large swathes of the globe. From the 1980s onwards, however, economic expansion has increased at a remarkable speed with the emergence of a transnational, global or world economy, where markets and enterprises operate globally in what has been described as a 'borderless world' (Ohmae, 1990). Markets that at one time were internal to a country or a region have now extended their reach around the world. This process has created important new linkages and dependences among national economies. Enormous transnational corporations, for example, Wal-Mart, General Motors, Exxon Mobil, Ford Motors, General Electric, Chevron Texaco, Conaco Philips, Citigroup, Royal Dutch Shell and Toyota; influential international political and economic institutions such as the World Bank, the International Monetary Fund, the World Trade Organisation and the United Nations; and huge regional trading systems such as the European Union and the North American Free Trade Association have emerged as the key structures of this century's global new economic order.

There is little doubt that information and communications technology and largely unregulated capitalism are the powerful drivers in the development of globalisation. We can witness the tremendous energy being given to the pursuit of finding new markets for constantly changing goods and services, the bottom and important line of which is capital accumulation and increased corporate profitability.

At the same time globalisation has brought us 24/7 news from around the world. Through viewing television we can observe the impact of war, famine and invasions, as well as negative weather forces like drought, tornadoes and hurricanes. We can listen to the words of politicians, observe the rise and fall of celebrities, and experience the impact of music, film and media from almost all areas of the world.

This interconnectedness and interdependence means that it is now possible to journey to some of the most inaccessible areas of the world and see cultural images associated with advanced industrial countries. For example, it is possible to travel to isolated villages in Africa, India and South America and see images of Coca Cola, and survey children and young people wearing replica shirts of leading international football clubs and major countries and be able to watch their favourite teams on satellite connected TV sets either in their homes, or in public places like village squares and small cafes.

As noted above a key driver of globalisation is quickly changing high technology, which it has been thought could have a homogenising effect on society. Whilst it is claimed that the impact of this phenomenon breaks down traditional cultures and introduces lifestyles that are efficient to the globalisation project, some such as Beyer (1990) argue that this does not necessarily mean a global westernised modernity. However, the argument often made is that if developing countries are to become modernised or 'developed' they need to become westernised. This drive to westernise the world is thought to lie behind many of the conflicts in the world at the present, particularly those in the Middle East where Moslems experience their religion and traditional ways of life as being threatened by the transmission of western values.

The nature of new advanced technological means that it is possible for the financial world to switch and move capital around the world at the push of a button. One commentator has stated that 'markets are no longer geographical locations, but data on a screen transmitted from anywhere in the world' (Writson, 1988/1989, p. 72). The swift changes in the market can be seen, for example, since the deregulation of the London Stock Exchange in 1986 where the FTSE 100 index has risen by almost 300%. However, a third of the top 100 companies listed then had disappeared by 2006. This was due to companies being merged, or swallowed up by others. In other cases, companies were no longer listed in the top 100 as others overtook them as market leaders (*The Guardian*, 2006). It is considered unlikely that we will return to a situation where individual nations can exercise meaningful power over the workings of this new world order, or can effectively influence the corporations that are driving globalisation. Strange (1995, p. 298) argues that these corporations have 'to a large extent emasculated state control over national economies and societies'. However, according to Driver and Martell, governments do have a key role in assisting the globalisation project.

> In the global economy... capital is mobile and demand is affected by factors beyond national boundaries. Governments cannot... control capital but can intervene to improve the capacities of labour. They have limited control over demand but can be active on the supply side, through education and training. This can provide for a skilled and flexible labour force to attract investment and ensure competitiveness.
>
> (Driver and Martell, 1998, p. 42)

Increasing numbers of the world's population now travel more than they did previously. The lower real cost of international travel, and the growth in travel possibilities means that we are not just enjoying short and long holidays (such as weekends in Europe and long haul holidays to places with stunningly beautiful beaches) but many citizens are more frequently visiting family and friends who now live and work abroad, as well as travelling to far-off places on work-related business. This has blurred the boundaries between nation states as travellers from the rich world increasingly penetrate poorer and isolated parts of the world. An example of the impact of this increased travel is the substantial volume in the number of flights coming in and out of the UK. In 2005, British airports handled 229 million passengers, a growth of 7% a year in the previous 3 years, and on this trend are likely to cater for 500 million passengers by 2021 (*The Times*, 2006). London Heathrow Airport that has led the way in passenger expansion which has seen the construction of Terminal 5 and the demand to build a third runway.

Finally, we cannot leave unstated a dominant and significant feature of globalisation; that nation states are not equal and there exists a hierarchy of power in which the more military powerful tend to dominate weaker countries. Whilst military power is only occasionally used, by forming key influential alliances, these powerful countries can act as a coercive and prevailing influence on others. The world's most powerful country is the USA, which through its enterprise economy, together with the political pressure exerted by the government in Washington, whether Republican or Democrat, has since 1945 been engaged in establishing global hegemony through ideological and economic leadership.

Neo-Liberalism

The ideology and the workings of neo-liberalism, which stresses the value, and benefit of the economic free-market has been a central driving force in the development of globalisation since the late 1970s. The core premise of neo-liberalism is that the market is pre-eminent at producing and distributing goods and services, is best at rewarding managers and workers and is more efficient than state or bureaucratic planning. It is thought, for example, that the collapse of the Soviet bloc was due in part to the inability of its closed centrally planned communist economies to compete in a global economy that had become increasingly integrated and expanded.

Consequently, neo-liberalist ideology has been traditionally hostile towards public expenditure, public borrowing, taxation and the collective provision of public services, which it believes to be a parasite on the wealth-generating private economy. The neo-liberal thesis is that high levels of taxation to fund public programmes lessens incentives to work and means that the production of goods and services is less than it could be, thereby reducing economic growth. Any social welfare provision therefore must not damage the system of rewards and must be justified by the benefits it brings to the economy. A key reason for this is the neo-liberal view that economic and social inequality is fundamentally necessary to reward 'success' and to provide the incentives for the creation of wealth.

It is therefore argued that private provision is more efficient and is generally more superior to public provision. The neo-liberal position argues that competition, which is a cornerstone in the furthering of private markets, creates greater efficiency by removing inadequate and inefficient providers and suppliers (Adams, 1993).

A further element in the expansion of neo-liberalism is the harnessing of rapid technological change with the application of computers and other electronic refinements to both the production process and the marketing of goods and services. We have witnessed the increased use of adaptable machinery and the switch in some industries to advanced automation and robotisation with the result of changing the nature of the involvement of labour in the process to maximise profit. In turn this has created new opportunities for small businesses to carve out viable and specialised market niches that provide individuals with further and different employment prospects.

The introduction of Post-Fordist production methods has replaced large factories and work places producing mass-produced goods. Instead there is evidence of increased flexible working practices, including home-working, part-time work, seasonal work and smaller group working. This has led to the weakening of labour bargaining, and is claimed to reduce work place autonomy and increase financial and work insecurity (Hutton, 1996).

Social democracy, which is based on the principle of plural social institutions and a parliamentary system of different and competing political parties, has put in place systems that protect the public from the untrammelled impact of the free market. Social democratic countries like the UK have given people protected rights in key areas affecting their lives such as in employment with a statutory minimum wage and maternity and paternity rights. However, the neo-liberalist ideology has emphasised that these rights have to be balanced with individual responsibilities, and the duty of people to protect themselves. For example, by encouraging individuals to consider taking out personal health insurance, to invest in personal pension plans and not to rely on the state for personal care when elderly, but to utilise the private care sector for their residential and nursing needs when too ill or too infirm to look after themselves.

The neo-liberal approach has led to nation states being more concerned with international competitiveness than social welfare, social justice or social rights. Governments are mindful of their countries' position in the international economic pecking order and are encouraging their citizens to ensure they take every opportunity to remain competitive in the employment market. In the UK social welfare has become a vehicle for advancing this goal through, for example, support for those with young children to participate in the labour force by offering them inexpensive child-care facilities; along with wage subsidisation, a key element of the government's 'welfare to work' policies.

The following quote from Scholte (2000, p. 14)) emphasises the pressure on governments to move to a mixed economy of welfare and where the market should offer services that traditionally the state used to provide.

No state has escaped the downward pressure of neo-liberal globalisation on government guarantees of material welfare.

Finally, neo-liberalism depends on nation states being strong in relation to public order, social morality and defence. The outcome has been that at the same time as the private market has been liberalised, the public sector has had increasing controls and regulations placed upon it. The Conservative governments from 1979 to 1997, and since then New Labour, under Tony Blair and Gordon Brown, have reduced the autonomy of public institutions and established and strengthened centralised compliance and scrutiny. The purpose here has been to ensure the standardisation of practice, to raise the quality of service, and to maintain order in increasingly problematic communities. The expectation, however, is that the private market needs less regulation in order it can seek out profit.

Another feature of New Labour's policies, given the prospect of variable compliance from front-line workers, has been the introduction of rankings or grading for schools, hospitals, universities, social work services and other key public services including all local authorities. For example, it is now possible to access a range of league tables for universities based on research grades, ranking according to teaching, on the number of first class degrees a university awards each year, on the amount spent on books and journals in the university library, the number of students taken from educationally disadvantaged backgrounds to widen participation and so on.

Globalisation, Neo-Liberalism, Inequality and Social Problems

A key feature and consequence of globalisation and neo-liberalism is inequality. Although there is recent evidence in the UK that the bottom 10% of the population now have an improved real income than before New Labour came to power in 1997, the richest 10% in the UK have during the same period seen their income increase much more in real terms. The improvement for those at the bottom has come about through increases in tax relief and benefits for those with children and those receiving state pensions (Hills and Stewart, 2005). This needs to be placed alongside evidence from Paxton and Dixon (2004) that from 1990 to 2000 the percentage wealth held by the wealthiest 10% increased from 47% to 54%. These trends are confirmed by a Joseph Rowntree Foundation report (Dorling *et al.*, 2007), which examines how poverty and wealth are distributed in the UK. In a study that looked back 40 years the authors discovered that already-wealthy areas had tended to become disproportionately wealthier, and there was evidence of increasing polarisation, where rich and poor now live further apart. The study also shows that both poor and wealthy households have become more geographically segregated from the rest of society.

There is also a widening gap between rich and poor countries. According to the United Nations Development Programme (2005)

- The richest 20% of the world's population receives 75% of world income.

- The poorest 20% receive 1.5% of world income.

- The richest 50 individuals in the world have a combined income greater than that of the poorest 416 million.

- 2.5 billion of the world's population live on less than US $2 per day.

It is increasingly recognised that widening inequality presents its self as social exclusion and exacerbates problems such as crime and unemployment. By social exclusion we mean individuals or groups who as a result of multiple deprivation are not able to fully participate in the economic, social and political activities enjoyed by the majority of people. Social exclusion can present itself through crime with some criminologists such as Jock Young (1998, 1999) suggesting that certain criminal activity is due to individuals experiencing being on the margins of 'respectable society' and not enjoying its benefits, in particular in terms of meaningful, well-paid work. Similarly, globalisation and neo-liberal economics have had the effect of excluding people economically as work is transferred to regions and countries where labour unions are weak and employment costs are low. This has produced job insecurity and unemployment that has high-lighted the widening gap between people (Grint, 2005).

Inequality in the UK is presented in three main ways, through class, race and gender. We want now to consider these in more detail before drawing together the different overlapping strands presented here and examine them in the context of their impact on contemporary community life.

Class

Class is a key but contested theme in present-day society, and has been with us for many centuries. The novelist Jane Austen (1775–1817), for example (1996 [1813]), writing in *Pride and Prejudice* offers us a perceptive and at times humorous observation of class in eighteenth century England that was more sensitive to class differences than now.

It was the German social, political and economic theorist Karl Marx (1818–1883) who was the first to analyse and develop sociologically the notion of class. One of the key points Marx made was that classes are both mutually dependent and antagonistic. With the financial support of a wealthy Manchester-based mill owner, Friedrich Engels (1820–1895) and himself a commentator of the plight of workers (Engels (1999) 1845 (first published)), Marx studied the relationship between the owners of capital (the bourgeoisie) and those who sold their labour (the proletariat). In his classic work *Das Kapital*, Marx develops the notions of surplus value, class conflict and the exploitation of the working class. Marx and Engels devoted a good deal of their working lives to developing the theory that became known as Marxism. Marxism suggests that capitalism contains the seeds of its own destruction and predicts the 'overthrow of capitalism' by socialism and the ultimate 'withering away' of the state with the emergence of a class-less society of communism. A reading of Marxist theories are valuable in understanding some of the powerful forces in capitalist societies and still have significant value in helping us identifying the nature of the contradictory class positions between the bourgeoisie and the proletariat. In particular, the antagonistic relationship between the two major classes and the struggle to extract profit from labour (Harman, 1997; Wheen, 2000).

Whilst Marx's prediction that socialism and then communism would overcome capitalism has proved inconclusive, it would be incorrect to conclude that class no longer exists. The majority of social scientists argue that class remains *the* main grouping of social stratification in societies such as the UK and arguably *the* most important analytical sociological concept. Max Weber (1864–1920), also a German sociologist, but living later than Marx, has influenced our thinking about how social classes are hierarchically arranged. Unlike Marx, Weber argues that class positions are related to positions in the labour market and produces status differences. Marx on the other hand saw class as related to positions in the process of production.

It has proved controversial and difficult, however, to agree a consensual definition of what class means and what it covers in contemporary society. As a result, and particularly in 'official statistics', class and status are often collapsed into one concept. It is argued that in this way it can be applied in a more meaningful manner. The British Social Attitudes Survey (BSAS) and the General Household Survey (GHS) are examples of 'official statistics' that provide us with rich sources of information on how people live. The statistics cover areas such as consumption, education, health, employment as well as providing valuable information to enable us to make comparisons between countries. These statistics also provide us with valuable data that can be interpreted on the lines of gender, geographical location, income and race and ethnicity.

Class is an important lens in which to understand how inequality and discrimination operates at the level of community. The work of the French sociologist Pierre Bourdieu (1930–2002) is of assistance here as he argues that social class can be closely linked with lifestyles. Bourdieu presents the analysis that individuals increasingly distinguish themselves from each other based on cultural capital (such as education, appreciation of the arts, fashion, consumption patterns and lifestyle) rather than according to purely only economic factors. Bourdieu also argues that social capital is an important feature in people's lives. He sees these as the networks that people create and maintain and which provide them with support and identity (Bourdieu, 1992).

Bourdieu's theory on the impact of class and culture has been used in the UK by the sociologist Beverly Skeggs who studied the lives of 83 women over a period of 12 years in northwest England. Skeggs (1997) found that Bourdieu's theories were valuable when examining social and cultural capital, and economic factors of the women's lives. Skeggs argues her study demonstrates that the lack of social capital in the women's lives reflects a wider deficiency of positive identities for working-class women in the UK. Whereas for working-class men there are positive identities that are transmitted through the relationship with work and the status attached to certain kinds of employment, for working-class women there are no such positive identities. According to Skeggs, for many women being labelled working class is a negative term. For example, the women Skeggs studied were sensitive to the stereotyping of working-class women as 'tarty' and were acutely aware they were discriminated against because of their class position. Instead, the women wanted to present themselves as competent and able women, and saw getting married and having children as a way of securing social respectability and responsibility. These women experienced being working class as marginal, and at times a hindrance to their lives, and what was important for them was their gender.

There is no doubt that whilst class divisions remains a core contributor in economic and social inequalities in the UK it is difficult to precisely describe and analyse class. However, this should not prevent us from recognising that class location is inextricably linked with advantage and disadvantage, and a person's class location reflects and generates inequality and exclusion in communities. As Goodman *et al.* (1997) argue, earnings inequality, a key factor in determining class location, is the largest single factor in overall inequality in the UK with a widening gap between those on the lowest and the highest incomes. Whilst there are always exam-ples of people who have experienced significant upward social mobility, earnings, poverty and class are closely linked and together with a person's place of residence will have a major influence on their life chances.

Gender

Moving to gender it is now widely recognised that women are disadvan-taged when living in a patriarchal society that favours men and oppresses women through its social, political and economic institutions. This disad-vantage is reflected particularly in employment and income inequality. In most western countries, women make up almost half of the official labour force.

> However, nearly half are employed part-time. Also, despite legislation designed to ensure wage equality they continue to earn roughly three-quarters of male wages for the same work. Moreover, they tend to be segregated within certain female-designated employment enclaves such as the caring professions (in health, social work and education) or in low-paid industries and services including catering, garment manufacturing and clerical work.
>
> (Cohen and Kennedy, 2000, p. 105)

Homans' (1987) study in the mid-1980s investigated gender employment inequality, demonstrating how NHS managers were discriminating against women applicants to scientific posts. Women applicants were seen by managers as more likely to be away from work to have children, and to care and look after their children during their school years. More recent evidence of discrimination indicates that the NHS is the largest employer in the UK with more than 1.3 million staff of which 70% are women, and among non-medical staff this figure rises to 82%. The research carried by Dr Jan Bogg and her team from the University of Liverpool has shown that health professionals believe the NHS suffers from an institutional gender bias that favours the progression of men over women despite women being the major users of the NHS (Women's National Council, 2000). The outcome of this, and other informal discrimination, is that women continue to be over-represented in the more insecure and poorly paid job sectors, and despite some gains women remain under-represented in the higher paying sectors (Rake, 2000). According to Apter (1994), many women struggle with often-contradictory feelings in wanting a family and caring for children whilst aspiring to a career and economic independence.

Since the 1970s women's availability for paid employment has increased in many ways, including the increasing mechanisation of housework that has reduced the time needed to carry it out. However, one of the principle reasons for the availability of women in the labour market has been the increased pressure on household budgets due to the relative rise in the cost of purchasing homes and the desire to acquire a widening range of consumer goods and services. Similarly, increased divorce rates have also led to many women needing to work in order to support themselves.

Whilst there has been pressure for women to take paid employment, there have been contradictory pressures for them to remain at home and spend more time engaged in unpaid work in the home and community. The promotion of community care in the UK, and in particular the conclusions of the Griffiths Report (1988), and the implications of the NHS and Community Care Act 1990, have been premised upon women undertaking often time consuming and demanding roles that are termed as informal care (see Chapter 5). However, it has been shown that women (and men) engaged in providing informal care found it eroded their social networks, with many experiencing difficulties in maintaining close relationships (Atkin and Twigg, 1994). What is clear is that women are usually those who attempt to juggle the dual roles of undertaking paid employment whilst caring for others at home and community (Plantenga and Hansen, 1999). Women also undertake the majority of intimate personal care (Twigg, 1998). There are an estimated 5.5 million people in the UK undertaking informal care and who are in paid employment or are in full-time education in addition to looking after another member of their family.

In addition, due to people living longer and new medical treatments, it is estimated that every year an additional 2 million people become carers. That's 6,000 people each day.

(Cameron, 2006, p. 1)

Women's subordinate position in society has been challenged by feminism, which offers a critique of patriarchy as well as providing an ideology which has been embodied by the women's movement, and which is committed to women's emancipation. Within feminism it is possible to identify a number of theoretical positions including liberal feminism, radical feminism, socialist feminism and black feminism. There are, however, a number of other approaches in feminist thought and many writers cannot be easily assigned to any one position. In fact, strands of feminism have come in the late twentieth and early twenty-first centuries to challenge notions of traditional understandings of what it is to be a woman or man. Instead, they have argued these are not fixed identities and there may not be 'objectively' correct ways of viewing the world.

Meanwhile, many feminist writers have centred their analysis on the role of the family and women's position within it. They have pointed to the dominant ideology that presents the family as a 'natural' and relatively unproblematic unit and that 'women's place is in the home'.

Far from being a 'natural' arrangement or individual choice based on mutual love and respect in which the emotional, sexual and domestic needs of adult partners are met and their children cared for, it is a social institution in which women's labour is exploited, male sexual power may be violently expressed and oppressive gender identities and modes of behaviour are learned.

(Bryson, 2003, p. 176)

Feminists argue that this perpetuates the expectation that women's main focus is in the domestic arena and by implication should be prepared to undertake unpaid caring. This has implications for women in the community as they are seen as the key players in the life of a neighbourhood, and are often engaged in community and collective action. Both Bornat *et al.* (1993) and Dominelli (2006) observe that it is women who are in the front line of negotiations over nurseries, schools, housing health and other welfare agencies. Therefore, it is not surprising to learn that women have been central in community-based actions to organise, defend or protest about such services.

What is also important for us as we consider community is the way institutionalised gender disadvantage operates to restrict the life opportunities of women. For example, women with young children maybe unable to take up certain employment because of a lack of or inadequate childcare facilities. This further confirms women's role as primarily carers and

dependent on state benefits, part-time work, or places them as economically dependent on men.

'Race'/Ethnicity

We are aware that 'race' is a cultural, political and economic concept,
not a biologically derived one as previously argued by anthropologists. In
the social sciences, ethnicity is a more appropriate term used to refer to
groups or societies that share a common sense of identity; usually based
on a shared nationality, culture, history, religion, language and customs.
Ethnicity and racism are important for us to consider in our exploration
of social work and communities.

In the UK the term *minority ethnic* rather than *ethnic minority* is often used
to indicate that there is an *ethnic majority*, usually meant as British White.
Sometimes the term *visible minority* has been deployed to distinguish those
groups that experience more overt forms of racism and discrimination due
to their skin colour. These are useful ways of considering ethnicity as it
signals that ethnic identification has a part to play in community life.
People can identify and align with others who share the same ethnicity
as themselves as well as being able to interact with those outside of their
ethnic group. Ethnicity then is a relational process and marks the often-
blurred boundaries of identification between different ethnic groups.

One of the reasons why 'race' is used less in the social sciences now
than before is the politically charged nature of the term. In particular, the
word 'race' has links with ideologies that have used the term to emphasise racial purity, racial difference and racial hierarchies. Racism, which
feeds from the notion of different racial groups, is the belief that one's
own 'race' or ethnic group is superior to others. Such beliefs can be used
to justify discrimination, including violence towards those perceived as
inferior.

Organisations can be accused of being racist, as the Metropolitan Police
Force was in the Stephen Lawrence Inquiry. This Inquiry was set up
to examine the brutal killing of a black teenager, Stephen Lawrence, in
London in 1993. The Public Inquiry, which reported in 1999, concluded
that 'institutional racism' existed in the Metropolitan Police Force. Going
against earlier claims by the Metropolitan Police Commissioner, Paul
Condon who declared no racism existed in the London Force; Lord
Macpherson's report defined 'institutional racism' as 'the collective failure
of an organisation to provide an appropriate and professional service to
people because of their colour, culture or ethnic origin' (Macpherson,
1999). The Macpherson Report had wider significance for all public services
and was a catalyst for increased government action to tackle racism more
effectively in the public sector. It was also a wake-up call to government

to demonstrate greater urgency in responding to the perceived growth in racism and the challenges and dilemmas that are an integral aspect of a changing multicultural society.

Racially motivated crimes are a particular concern for minority ethic communities. The Office of National Statistics (2002) has estimated that racially motivated incidents represented 12% of all crime against minority ethnic people (compared with 2% for white people), with 42% of victims of racially motivated crime saying they were 'very much affected' by the incident. This compares with 19% of victims of others forms of crime. Although minority ethic people are more likely to be attacked in communities they are also more likely to be stopped and searched compared with white people. The Metropolitan Police Authority (2004) reveals that in London black people were eight times and Asians five times more likely to be stopped and searched than white people.

Whilst racism continues to exist institutionally, or formally, there is evidence that racism operates informally in neighbourhoods with people from minority ethnic groups feeling their different expressions of cultural, religious and language are under threat. Politically, this has been demonstrated in the activities of the British National Party (BNP) that has made electoral gains in specific communities. The BNP was also thought to play a part in 'shaping the tensions' that led to unrest on the streets of Burnley and Oldham in 2001 (Solomos, 2003, p. 169). Although the BNP remains a relatively small party with limited appeal, New Labour appears to be acutely aware of the impact that immigration and race has on urban communities. It has demonstrated concern for the backlash from the host community in their social exclusion agenda which aims to address multiple deprived communities in an effort to stem the activities of extreme right parties and to develop a policy context for the development of race equality through its many urban policies and regeneration programmes (see Chapter 4). This approach combines both tackling racism, and addressing the needs of minority ethnic communities (Home Office, 2002).

Evidence shows that people from minority ethnic groups are over-represented in prisons, young offenders intuitions, mental health institutions and amongst children in care. Robinson (1995) presents some of the reasons for the over-representation of black people in mental health services claiming that it is the manner in which black people are perceived and are assessed for mental health that is at fault, with many being examined against white middle-class norms. To deal with this Robinson argues that social workers and psychotherapists should be 'provided with frequent opportunities to examine their feelings about blackness and to evaluate the relevance to black people of psychotherapeutic theories, research and techniques' (p. 160). Robinson argues that social workers have focused on the inadequacies and weaknesses in black families and not on their strengths and competencies. The author argues that social workers need to accept that black families cannot be assessed on the basis of cultural preconceptions, but rather they need to be assessed in the context of a racist society. According to Robinson, the best way for social workers to work with black families is to 'recognise the strength in black family systems rooted in value orientations different from their own' (p. 86).

The theme of working culturally, sensitively and appropriately with minority ethnic groups is taken up by Thompson (2001) who states that social workers need to account the ethnicity of the service user in order that assessment is not based on 'dominant white norms' (2001, p. 73). He argues that it is imperative on social workers to understand the service users' cultural background in order that the assessment is 'based on understanding and analysis rather than ignorance and assumptions' (2001, p. 73). Payne (2005a) makes a similar point when he argues that social workers should enquire as to the culturally specific requirements that service users may have. This he states 'will be regarded as respectful' rather than making 'assumptions from broad generalisations in text books' (2005, p. 280).

Unfortunately there is a dearth of research on social work with minority ethnic groups. The outcome is that social workers have frequently failed to make adequate and fair assessments and judgments. Instead they have based their decisions upon their own stereotypes. There is a need to address this with work that considers the individual and family needs together with an understanding of the communities and neighbourhoods in which people from minority ethnic groups reside. This will give social workers greater opportunities to develop meaningful and effective anti-discriminatory practice.

Minority ethnic communities have used collective action, both to confront racism and discrimination, and to forge alliances to protect and support cultural, religious and national groups. This action has encompassed a wide range of issues within minority ethnic communities including mother tongue teaching, cultural and religious provisions, special schools, and ethnic music, dance and arts. However, whilst emphasising these specific and entirely appropriate cultural aspects and needs, it should not be forgotten that social and economic decline has impacted particularly hard on certain minority ethnic groups. This together with overt and covert racism, has led to increasing political awareness and participation on a local level. Often feeling denied representation and influence in conventional political groupings, certain minority ethnic groups are becoming politically active in different forms of community action, both at the neighbourhood level and one identified by nation, religion, age or political persuasion.

New Communities

So far this chapter has demonstrated how globalisation and neo-liberalism are affecting UK society. We have also considered three discrete but interconnected areas of discrimination and inequality, class, gender and 'race'/ethnicity. To this we need to consider the evolution of the UK's new communities, by which we mean economic migrants, refugees, asylum-seekers and 'undocumented parsons'. The development of these communities in Britain is an example of how globalisation perpetuates and extends inequality. For example, Carrington and Detragiache (1999) demonstrate that approximately 30% of the better educated in Africa, the Caribbean and Central America are leaving these areas to work in knowledge-based economies elsewhere.

As we noted in Chapter 2, the majority of minority ethnic communities, primarily people from the Caribbean islands and India, Pakistan and Bangladesh, came to the UK during the period from the late 1940s to the 1980s. The vast majority had a connection with the UK through being citizens of Commonwealth countries and travelled to Britain as economic migrants in the hope of establishing a more prosperous life for themselves and their families. Multiculturalism was the favoured approach by public authorities in this period in their attempt to encourage the development of cohesive communities that could contain these different ethnic and religious groups. The multiculturalism model was deployed particularly in schools and local authority departments to assist the management and integration of first, second and third generation migrants. Consultation with community leaders and support for certain minority ethic associations and activities was similarly aimed at building cohesive communities which both celebrated difference and diversity and attempted to achieve some form of social equality.

However, since the 1990s immigrants have come from a much wider range of countries, especially non-Commonwealth and non-European Union states. These new migrant groups are highly diverse, with their own gender and age formations, and different languages and religions. Vertovec (2007) titles this 'super-diversity' and states that:

> Some are mostly women, such as Slovakians and Filipinos. Others are mostly men, such as Algerians and Albanians. Some are mostly single people, others have families. Some are particularly made up of young people in their 20s, others have a fuller range of ages. Immigrants today range from the highest-flying skilled professionals to those with little education and training. Many hope to remain in Britain and become new citizens, while others plan to stay for only a relatively short period.
>
> (Vertovec, 2007, p. 94)

According to Vertovec, Britain now has up to 80 different migration categories and immigrant legal statuses including asylum-seekers, refugees and 'undocumented persons'. It is these last three groups that attract the ire of the popular press who consistently highlight the 'burden' they make to the welfare system. These accounts, which make up the dominant discourse in this area, fail to communicate to the public the trauma and often extreme difficulties these new migrants have left behind, and continue to live with in the UK, and the considerable human assets they have in their own communities and can bring to the wider society (Rousseau and Drapeau, 2003).

What Does This All Mean for Rethinking Community?

There is little doubt that globalisation and adherence to neo-liberal economics has had a considerable impact upon communities in terms of uncertainty, greater fragmentation and less solidarity. Here concerns about inequality and divisions are displaced by an emphasis on inclusion and social responsibility. Whether it relates to what we view on our televisions, or the type of employment people now occupy, to the shape and scope of the public sector, it is impossible to escape the impact of these two major features in our daily life. Paradoxically as globalisation and neo-liberalism gains momentum, and people's mobility and access to information increases, there is evidence that an increasing number of people are challenging what appears to be the consummate power and impact of multinational corporations, global finance, the entertainment industry and the expanding breadth and accelerating pace of consumption (Cohen and Rai, 2000). People are making connections between their lack of power over the governments, companies and organisations that determine much of their daily life and their drive to take greater individual and personal responsibility for determining their own paths in life. The outcome has been a growth in organisations that connect people with each other both locally and globally. The World Wide Web and global networks of communication have enabled millions of people to develop links that have in numerous different arenas culminated in social movements. People are widening their emotional loyalties and ties beyond their immediate families and community to newly emerging forms of expressions that appear to have unbounded interconnections and interactions. These social movements and connections have meant a change in how people consider political activity. Membership of the traditional political parties has decreased at the same time as people have become engaged in identity politics, the 'counter culture' and decentralised non-hierarchal grass-root activity. All these are producing new and different forms of community.

There are class, gender and 'race'/ethnicity dimensions for these emerging communities. A key constituent of the emerging forms of community is an opposition to discrimination and inequality. For example, in identity politics, or 'emancipatory politics' as described by Giddens (1991), an important element is the struggle against oppressive structures that have constrained people's lives. In the USA in the 1960s the Civil Rights Movement emerged as a powerful social movement to argue for the same rights for black people as given to white people. In the UK the trade union movement emerged in the nineteenth century to represent their members through collective action against the power of employers and managers. Contemporary trade union agendas are based on justice in the workplace and in wider society. The women's movement which is a major example of identity politics or 'emancipatory politics' has an extensive agenda for women including equal opportunities in education, employment and pay, improved facilities for child care and self-determination on issues such as contraception and abortion.

As we have noted, in general, structured inequalities and discrimination operate along the core lines of class, gender and 'race'/ethnicity. This is not to dismiss other forms of inequality and discrimination in relation to age, disability, religion, sexuality, nationality and civil status. For example, the disability rights movement has been especially influential in promoting the rights of disabled people (Oliver and Campbell, 1996). As we noted previously that whilst class is considered by the majority of sociologists to be the main grouping of social stratification in industrialised societies, they have problems in convincingly defining the term.

As the speed and intensity of globalisation has increased and deepened, and the impact of the neo-liberal economic agenda is felt internationally, there has been a significant counter movement that has attempted to re-create and reconnect with notions of community. This has led to the emergence of global social movements (GSMs) that according Cohen and Rai (2000) represent a 'post-national phase' with political action becoming more unconventional, open, direct, participatory and focused. These movements have linked local and global struggles that are addressing and connecting key areas in particular human rights, women's movements, peace movements, labour movements and environmental movements. Some movements have extensive international networks, whilst others are small scale. There is, however, no transnational framework or forum to bring these movements together, which according to Cohen and Rai seriously weaken the possibilities for protest and opposition leading to political change.

> We need to think of the possible emergence of an alternative global society. The GSMs are part of this alternative vision and practice of globalization, one in marked conflict to the global offerings of the TNC (trans-national corporations), the World Trade Organization and the World Bank.
>
> (Cohen and Rai, 2000, p. 16)

And to cite Craig, Mayo and Taylor (2000, p. 327)

> This growing connection between economic globalisation on the one hand and declining social standards and environmental degradation on the other, is the seed from which growing political opposition is emerging.

What is clear is that the anti-globalisation movement has made connections between the environmental crisis, the role of unregulated capitalism and the disproportionate effect on the poor.

At the same time Britain, like many others countries, has experienced the establishment of new communities whose diversity and differences we are only now beginning to grapple with. These communities need social work support in ways that are sensitive and appropriate. The work by Butler (2005) highlights the need for skilled practitioners to recognise that these new communities are defined by their exclusion from basic human rights including the security of food, family life and freedom from violence (Butler and Drakeford, 2001; Williams, 1996).

As we noted in Chapter 1, the state has been quick to recognise the value of emphasising the concept of community and in a plethora of policies and practices has used the term to describe and designate its activities at the local level. We have, for example, community policing, community justice, community schools, community wardens, community health visitors and even community prisons. In 2006, the Prime Minister, Tony Blair, who was influenced by the work of the American sociologist Etzioni (1993) created the position of Secretary of State for Communities and Local Government, together with a ministerial team with a strategic role to build inclusive and cohesive communities. These developments are a recognition that the impact of globalisation and the adherence to the neo-liberal agenda has created significant problems and in particular social exclusion at the community level. Again concerns about justice and rights in the community have been reworked in recent policy initiatives with a discourse of inclusion and choice. Whether New Labour's attempt to address poverty in neighbourhoods will have the desired effect remains to be seen, and this question is taken up in Chapter 4 and that concerning the rise of communitarianism in Chapter 6.

It has been argued, however, that the British states interest in community is driven by the need for containment, management and surveillance of difficult and disruptive areas and their residents. The state's role to enhance the well-being of its people is based on the premise that the market should be protected and extended. Troublesome communities need to be policed and if necessary individuals punished and made an example of. So community, which could be seen as offering a much needed identity and refuge from relentless economic growth, is also a site of friction and unhappiness.

Summary and Conclusion

There is little doubt that the notion of community has radically changed in the last 20 years or more. It has moved from a notion built on geography and in particular upon neighbourhood, or alternatively based on inclusion into a set of social formations with identifiable social, religious, ethnic or cultural parameters, to one that reflects a high degree of contradiction, producing a number of partial, conflictual and unequal effects for different groups.

New Labour has been instrumental in attempting to find new approaches of addressing these issues, in particular through the Third Way and the reform of the welfare state. New Labour's modernisation policy constructs idealised representations of community that emphasise opportunity, responsibility and 'choice'. These have become key aspects of the inclusion agenda. Examples of this can be found in the continuation of area-based initiatives for problematic communities, often in the inner city, and the development of community care. These themes will be explored further in the three chapters in Part II.

Part II

Community as an Area of Social Policy

The second part of the book examines how the concept of community has become a central organising force in social policy influencing both the nature and development of the welfare state. We will focus on the way in which particular communities, defined as dysfunctional or problematic, become the target for policy intervention by the state in socially and politically significant ways. This section will take up a number of themes introduced in Part I and situate them within their wider policy context. For example, New Labour's modernisation policy has constructed idealised representations of community where social divisions and arguments about redistribution may be displaced by an emphasis on choice, opportunity and inclusion. In such a policy paradigm, wider concerns about inequality and injustice subside, and the citizen is reminded about their social obligations and responsibilities rather than rights.

In Chapter 4 we will explore the use of community in area-based policy using the Community Development Projects (CDP) as a case study. Although these projects were set up in the 1970s and have been much written about (see Craig and Mayo, 1995; Loney, 1983; Mayo, 1975), they remain a potent symbol of what happens when the state conducts poverty experiments at the local level. It will be argued that the CDP story is particularly relevant to current debates in social work given the continuing appeal to community in contemporary policy and practice. Area-based experiments also provide important lessons for both practitioners and service users as policy has increasingly sought to promote inclusion in the management of problem communities.

Chapter 5 focuses on the development of community care and how such a policy deploys particular notions of community and the family to achieve consent. Although community care has received widespread support, partly as a reaction against institutionalisation and segregation (Payne, 1995), it relies heavily on the domestic labour of women in their role as informal carers. The chapter will consider how arguments about rights and the entitlement of different groups have influenced the making of community care policy. A number of contemporary issues are examined, including the impact of financial constraints on local authority spending, partnership working between health and social care and an expanding role for the voluntary sector.

Finally, Chapter 6 analyses how ideas associated with the new communitarianism (Giddens, 2000) have shaped New Labour's 'third way' modernisation project to reform the welfare state. Communitarian themes now underpin the inclusion agenda in many areas of policy and the drive to transform the welfare state from an institution that 'provides passive support to one that provides active support to help people become independent' (Blair, 2000, p. i). In offering a critique of New Labour's 'third way' approach to policy reform, the chapter will briefly consider an alternative discourse based upon transformative action that seeks to move the debate beyond the notion of community to consider the struggle for more inclusive communities (Hughes and Mooney, 1998). The impact of policy on practice will be illustrated in relation to developing a more preventive approach in child care and more general concerns about the reshaping of social work.

4

Community as an Organising Focus for Social Policy

Introduction

During the post-war period the concept of community has increasingly become a central organising focus for policy analysis and debate. This can be seen in responses to the rediscovery of poverty in Britain's inner cities in the 1960s (Abel-Smith and Townsend, 1965) through to New Labour's New Deals for communities in the new millennium. The idea of community has featured prominently in a raft of contemporary policy proposals designed to modernise and reform the welfare state, particularly in adult community care, children's services and mental health. Also in the forging of a new partnership role with the voluntary sector – see Chapter 5. The notion of an active community has been advanced to signify a new relationship between the state and the citizen, premised upon a belief in the need for the state to demand more from those who receive its services. Such an embracing and ever more demanding policy prescription has, as will be explored in Part III, influenced the nature of contemporary social work practice, captured by the slogan 'tough love' (Jordan, 2001).

As already noted in Part I, the idea of community is not fixed or static but a highly contested concept 'frequently invoked in a variety of ways by different interest groups' (Pain *et al.*, 2001, p. 254). It is therefore replete with constructed meanings that reflect deep-seated divisions and conflicts based upon class, race, gender, age, disability and sexual orientation (Stepney and Evans, 2000). The variable experience of different groups is revealed, for example, in working-class communities that have conflicting gender interests as women experience their community both as a source of friendship and support but also as oppressive and restrictive (Williams, 1997). This means that ideas about community feed into the policy-making process through discourses of inclusion, partnership and so on, and these can be unpacked to reveal the interests and underlying values they uphold.

To assist consideration of these issues, the chapter is organised into three interlocking sub-sections:

1. The first section examines the way ideas about community have informed responses to poverty through the growth of area-based policies.

2. The second revisits the CDP story. CDP represents one of the state's most interesting and controversial poverty experiments during the post-war period, and one that continues to resonate in contemporary policy debate.

3. The third and final section offers a critique of area-based policy, identifies the lessons that can be learned and assesses the implications for practice.

The Rise of Area-Based Policy

The growth of area-based initiatives (ABIs) as responses to persistent poverty and widening inequalities is perhaps one of the defining features of UK social policy in the post-war period. Their significance is that they reveal a fundamental contradiction in policy – namely, the preoccupation with local and spatial solutions to inherently structural problems (Hamnett, 1979). There are now a substantial number of separate ABIs in England concerned with issues ranging from community safety to health improvement, and the majority of these are co-ordinated by the Office of the Deputy Prime Minister (www.rcu.gov.uk/abi).

The popularity of ABIs as a policy formula with successive governments is that they essentially offered a 'third way' approach before the 'third way' became articulated in official New Labour policy. In other words, the 'third way' aims to find a new middle path between 'some of the dualisms that have dominated previous policy practice, such as that between structure and agency, and this is particularly true of the area-based approach' (Alcock, 2004, p. 88). Further, ABIs may offer a symbolic way of balancing the freedom of the market with a commitment to social justice (Stepney, 2000), whilst tackling poverty through practical policies to combat exclusion at the local level (Hills *et al.*, 2002). ABIs appear to offer a winning combination, ostensibly with more political advantages than risks, and this helps to explain their attractiveness to policy makers. The continuing use of ABIs as a central plank of New Labour policy has enabled policy makers to move the debate from a concern with urban poverty and inequality to a concentration on tackling exclusion.

The early literature and conception of ABIs came from the USA. However, this literature reveals a problem of 'quantitative abundance and qualitative impoverishment' (Rose and Ashcroft, 1979, p. 2), and that legacy has influenced recent policy evaluation. As in many other policy areas, the UK government has conducted a love affair with ABIs that drew upon a substantial US experience of spatial approaches to poverty.

In the past, the American 'war on poverty' programmes in the 1960s, such as, Community Action Programme (CAP) and Operation Head Start (the original model for Sure Start in Britain) were researched in two distinct ways. Those from a policy perspective sought to evaluate whether material resources had been redistributed in favour of the poor (Marris and Rein, 1967). They concluded that the war on poverty was essentially 'a series of demonstration projects with high visibility, low costs and modest redistribution' (Rose and Ashcroft, 1979, p. 6). The second tradition from the same period derived from political science and questioned whether the projects had tackled the exclusion of the poor. The conclusions drawn suggested that whilst poverty had not been eliminated the programmes did provide a basis for a political awakening of groups previously excluded from mainstream political processes (Bachrach and Baratz, 1970). These two principle lessons in regulating the poor through inclusion and modest redistribution (Piven and Cloward, 1972) were subsequently taken up in Britain as positive indicators to justify the area-based approach.

If the 1950s was characterised by hopes of social reconstruction after the harsh realities of war, epitomised by the message from prime minister Harold Macmillan that the people had 'never had it so good', then the 1960s was a decade marked by fears of social unease and impending doom. The source of this sea change was a fundamental reassessment of the nation's health and prosperity following the rediscovery of poverty in Britain's inner cities in the 1960s (Abel-Smith and Townsend, 1965) and television dramas highlighting the social problem of homelessness in 'Cathy Come Home'. By the end of the decade, the state embarked on a series of 'poverty experiments' to devote resources to tackling what was defined as urban deprivation. This reflected two potentially conflicting developments,

> first the increasing pressure for state intervention in social as well as economic concerns; but second, the increasing public awareness of the contradictions and limitations of existing political and administrative institutions in responding to local needs.
>
> (Mayo, 1975, p. 14)

Clearly the hope was that by setting up a series of urban poverty programmes targeted on particular communities, the problem of deprivation could be contained and tackled in a more cost-effective way. Such an approach was also aimed at improving the efficiency and credibility of local government at a time when this was being questioned. A number of community programmes were set up and the National Community Development Project (CDP) was one of the most interesting of the state's poverty experiments. CDP continues to resonate in contemporary debates about social policy and social work practice in the community.

The CDP Story: An Effective Response to Poverty or Gilding the Ghetto?

The CDP story began in 1968 at the Home Office when James Callaghan was Home Secretary. The American 'war on poverty' experience was in the process of being digested following an inter-governmental conference and, in 1969, a working party was set up to consider whether a similar kind of project would be suitable for tackling poverty in Britain's declining urban areas. The working group comprised of:

- senior civil servants from the Home Office;

- a junior minister in the Labour government;

- academics such as Professor AH Halsey from Oxford University who had been instrumental in setting up and evaluating the Educational Priority Area (EPA) programme aimed at tackling educational under-achievement through 'positive discrimination' in inner-city schools; and

- professional social work representatives.

The working party was placed under the stewardship of Derek Morrell, a senior civil servant from the Children's Department at the Home Office, who subsequently became the founding father and, according to internal minutes, the architect of CDP. Derek Morrell saw the need to counteract the forces of fragmentation and disintegration in society at the local level, and had previously been involved in establishing the Schools Council. At a meeting in Coventry to discuss establishing the first community development project, Morrell had set out the central task of CDP:

> The most difficult step will be...the crucial task of raising the people of Hillfields from a fatalistic dependence on 'the council' to self sufficiency and independence.
>
> (Internal Home Office Minutes, 14.07.69, cited in CDP, 1977)

Inherent in CDP was the notion of 'Gilding the Ghetto' that came from the minutes of the inter-governmental conference. Miss Cooper, Chief

Inspector at the Home Office said that there was an element of looking for a new method of social control. 'Gilding the Ghetto' or buying time was thus from the outset part of the official planning of CDP. This later became the title of an influential project report published in 1977 by the CDP inter-project workers group.

The dominant set of ideas at that time which informed the search for new solutions to the problems of Britain's urban areas might be described as the 'culture of poverty' thesis. Here deprivation was seen to be both cyclical, transmitted from one generation of poor parents to the next, as well as culturally determined and sustained in the community. Such ideas had been deployed to explain the persistence of poverty alongside afflu-ence amongst Black and Hispanic groups in USA and the people of the barrios in Mexico and Latin America (Lewis, 1968). The political signifi-cance of cultural deficit theories is that they attempt to explain a central paradox in democratic market economies, epitomised by USA and Britain, concerning the reason deprivation exists alongside conspicuous wealth and affluence (Harrington, 1962). Here, poverty is explained as a conse-quence of the lifestyle of marginal groups and the culture prevalent in declining neighbourhoods of the city. The implication is that such groups have failed to take advantage of the opportunities on offer and have been left behind as a result.

The official view emanating from the Home Office about Britain's inner-city crisis extended the culture of poverty thesis by acknowledging that other factors might be contributing to the problem. In particular, the need for reform of local government services to make them more responsive to poor and disadvantaged groups. The dominant view was that the poor had 'slipped through the net' of the welfare state as a result of personal char-acteristics, cultural inadequacy, poorly co-ordinated services or a combi-nation of these factors (Mayo, 1980).

The culture of poverty thesis was linked to community inadequacy rather than individual pathology. Hence, 'the social pathology of the poor person had been replaced by the social pathology of the poor area' (Rose and Ashcroft, 1979, p. 13). This view of policy makers was consistent with an optimistic vision espoused by liberal academics in American univer-sities during the 1960s who had been advancing an 'end of ideology' thesis. This suggested that the good society (closely tied up with 'the goods society' and viewing the poor as part of its expendable waste products – see Pearson (1975)) had not only arrived but indicated that only minor reform would be required in future to smooth out societies remaining rough edges (Lipset, 1960). From this perspective urban poverty was presented as an unfortunate blot on an otherwise fair and functional social landscape. Further, the blot could be removed by a judicious programme of self-help allied to technical and administrative reform, rather than requiring any fundamental social change. These ideas would be central to any solution the Home Office working party proposed.

What emerged in 1969 was a plan to set up a number of community-based projects 'aimed at finding new ways of meeting the needs of people living in areas of high social deprivation' (Home Office Press Release, 1969, p. 1, cited in CDP, 1977). Twelve community development projects were established in collaboration with local authorities in the following local areas or 'pockets of poverty': Batley, Yorkshire; Benwell, Newcastle; Canning Town and Southwark in London, Cleator Moor, Cumbria; Hillfields in Coventry; Glyncorrwg, Glamorgan in South Wales; Vauxhall in Liverpool; North Shields, Tyneside; Glodwick, Oldham; Paisley in Scotland; and Saltley in Birmingham. The areas were selected on the basis of a multiple deprivation index, concentration of immigrant families and in localities where local authorities were responsive to the need to provide better co-ordinated services in partnership with local people.

The CDP approach was based upon an action-research or experimental social policy model, with community development workers employed by the host local authority and researchers engaged from various universities. Three-quarters of the funding came from the Home Office whilst the remaining sum was the responsibility of the local authorities.

The CDP brief for project staff was informed by three assumptions:

1. the culture of the 'deprived' was the primary cause of urban deprivation;

2. a programme of self-help offered the most effective solution; and

3. community-based research into the problems would assist in promoting reform of government policy both locally and nationally.

(amended from CDP, 1977, p. 4)

There is evidence to suggest that initially the various CDP Project workers attempted to keep to the Home Office brief (Craig and Mayo, 1995; Loney, 1983). In very general terms, they investigated and established local needs, organised meetings, set up community groups around identified issues and initiated specific projects in collaboration with local people (Mayo, 1975). A number of reports were written about the problems local people faced living in poor housing in declining inner-city neighbourhoods characterised by high unemployment, inadequate community facilities and suffering problems of acute environmental stress and decay. Such problems were, of course, not confined to the project areas and similar troubles associated with poor housing and social disadvantage could be found in other cities at that time. Many examples of poor quality housing can be cited as planners sought solutions to the urban crisis through high rise development, such as, the Red Road flats in Glasgow, the Ronan Point tower bloc that subsequently collapsed in the east end of London and the sprawling Hulme development in Manchester (see Pain *et al.*, 2001, p. 209).

The CDP reports were generally well produced and of high quality. They were critical of government policy and contained some pointed recommendations for action well supported by evidence from the appropriate research team. For example, in Oldham the problems ethnic minority families faced in getting access to affordable and suitable local housing were reported and presented to the local council (Shenton and Barr, 1974). However, an early indication both of the problems that lie ahead and the inadequacy of the Home Office brief was revealed when the various reports were submitted by CDP teams to local and central government. The project teams waited for a response, and waited, but nothing happened (CDP, 1977). Although, it is difficult to generalise given the diversity of the relationships that existed between project staff and local authorities at the time, it would seem that in many cases the reports were received with a mixture of bemusement, indignation and even hostility (Benington, 1975). The response from the Home Office was one of embarrassing silence, whilst behind the scenes concerns were being expressed about the critical nature and style of CDP reports, and of projects appearing to be getting out of control (Donnison, 1982).

The other part of the brief, designed to promote community self-help, also began to be questioned. An inter-project working group was set up to examine the problems and cost to the community of industrial change (CDP, 1976). The group identified the structural nature of the problems facing many traditional industries located in the old urban areas viz. coal, iron and steel, shipbuilding, textiles, railways, the motor industry and so on. These industries had witnessed low levels of investment, rising costs, low productivity, competition from cheap imports and by the 1970s were shedding labour as a precursor to transferring production out of the UK to developing countries where labour costs were low and communities more malleable. The high levels of unemployment, industrial decay, environmental degradation and poor infrastructure services were all a direct consequence of this disinvestment from Britain's urban areas and an early indication of the social costs of economic globalisation. De-industrialisation also led to out-migration of the more able and mobile socio-economic groups from the inner city leaving behind many poor people caught up in a spiral of decline. As the subsequent CDP reports made clear, the social costs of industrial change were largely borne by the urban working class and ethnic minorities (CDP, 1976), the very local people that CDP was designed to assist. It also became abundantly clear that self-help could do little more than ameliorate these structural socio-economic problems.

Since the 1950s the most run down parts of the inner-urban areas, where housing was cheapest, had attracted immigrants from the New Commonwealth to come and settle. The prospect of a better life had brought many immigrants to Britain. There were distinct waves of immigration that corresponded with the needs of the UK labour market. With the decline in manufacturing, immigrant labour was required to fill jobs in the emerging service sector as well as public services like the NHS (Castles and Cossacks, 1973). This began to create in Britain the kind of ethnic segregation that had been observed in many American cities. There were inevitable tensions between members of ethnic minority groups and the indigenous working class competing for jobs and scarce local resources. It was not long before racism began to scar the social landscape of the inner city.

The problem of racism as a response to sporadically planned migration in Britain in the 1950s and 1960s connects with a very contemporary phenomenon that has uncomfortable echoes of these earlier tensions. The problems of community cohesion, exclusion and multiculturalism have become particularly sensitive issues as a result of the arrival in Britain of new migrants, including refugees and asylum-seekers from central and Eastern Europe. Unplanned migration throughout Europe due to global conflicts, disasters and a range of political and economic forces has placed additional pressures on local community resources and the welfare state. The dynamics of globalisation has unsettled existing divisions of race, class and gender, and the state's ability to manage socially differentiated populations. According to Clarke (2001) 'globalisation has produced new trajectories and forms of migration into and within Europe' (p. 36). This raises a series of troubling questions about citizenship, social benefits, access to 'free' health care and leads to conflict around issues of race, culture and identity (Clarke, 2001).

Migration has also provoked a reaction from politicians, especially those on the right, as well as middle England that appears to support a fortress Europe policy. It is important for social workers to stand firm against such trends, work to heal divisions and develop a critical analysis of the issues. The lessons from our own history should be a reminder that the profession has a duty to challenge oppression and support new migrants to fight persecution in the community, no matter what form this takes. CDP provided a model of good practice in this respect and should not be consigned to the archives as part of our collective historical forgetfulness. Many of our inner-city policies were forged during this earlier period.

The problems of racism and policing the urban areas emerged during the late 1950s and early 1960s against a political backdrop shaped by the dire predictions of social unrest articulated by public figures, most notably Enoch Powell MP (Hall *et al.*, 1978). Racism had already erupted in what the media dubbed 'race riots' on the streets of Notting Hill in London in

1958, and later in other British cities during the 1960s. This prompted government action and led to the first Commonwealth Immigration Act in 1963, explicitly designed to control the number of immigrants entering the country by introducing a voucher system to recruit more skilled labour. In 1967 the first Race Relations Act was put on the statute book to tackle racism in public places and, although the legislation had many loopholes, it did make discrimination an offence. Hence by the time CDP was being launched the question of race was seen as central to the problem of urban deprivation and consequently this influenced both the choice of local areas and the initial focus of project staff. Thus, working with minority groups became an important and essential dimension of CDP's work at the local level.

The degree to which individual projects could redefine the Home Office brief is a relevant question here. This had implications for the way problems could be tackled – given the disjuncture between the initial theoretical assumptions and the structural analysis developed by the local action-research teams. Much depended upon the configuration of local political interests, the quality of the work being done, the level of support and whether the project workers were politically skilful at exploiting opportunities at the local level. Paradoxically, the continuities in public administration with no party once in government warmly committed to extending community participation beyond consultation 'created a political space within which the projects were able to innovate' (Rose and Ashcroft, 1979, p. 14).

The ability or perhaps more accurately the capacity to innovate was important in enabling project workers to mobilise and support community action. It follows that there were many examples of politically astute and committed community action that flowed from this in the various project areas. However, there were clearly limits on how far the initial brief could be reinterpreted in favour of a structural analysis without causing consternation in government circles and an inevitable hostile reaction. Further, the political nature of some of the reports, such as, *Whatever Happened to Council Housing? Slums on the Drawing Board, The Costs of Industrial Change, Profits Against Houses*, persuaded the Home Office that something had to be done to curtail project activities as the first step to closing down CDP altogether.

The parameters of control began to be revealed especially in relation to those projects where disputes between CDP workers and the local authority had escalated to the point of open conflict. In Batley, Saltley and Cleator Moor following well-publicised arguments with local politicians the projects were all closed down prematurely (CDP, 1977). By 1975 following a management review that had been resisted by project staff, the Home Office was actively seeking ways of speeding up the closure of the remaining projects (Loney, 1983). From a central government perspective, CDP had created unmanageable conflicts at the local level, and had, through the publication of critical reports disseminated to a receptive national audience become a major political embarrassment (Mayo, 1980). With 75% of the CDP budget coming from central government a withdrawal of this funding provided the neatest solution to the crisis. Local authorities were informed that their project could continue, but 100% of the funding would have to be found locally as no further central government money would be available. Not surprisingly this quickly heralded the end of CDP, as local authorities were unwilling to find the substantial additional funds involved. One by one the projects closed down, with the last project in Oldham closing in March 1978.

Two Contemporary Examples of Area-Based Policy – Sure Start and Health Action Zones

The demise of CDP did not lead to the abandonment of area-based policy. On the contrary ABIs have continued as an important tool of policy makers seeking to tackle exclusion especially among children. However, contemporary ABIs have a sharper focus and more extensive controls closely tied to meeting government targets (Alcock, 2004).

The Sure Start programme is a central government initiative designed to improve child health through developing services for under 5s in local areas and providing support to families for promoting inclusion. A key theme underlying this approach is capacity building. Capacity is seen as giving access to resources and skills in the community and finding ways of using these more effectively (Attree, 2004). It may be evaluated with reference to hard outcome measures, such as, new skills, qualifications and the reduction in the number of families without a member of the household in work, as well as softer measures associated with community participation and well-being (Pierson, 2002).

The Sure Start initiative is currently being evaluated at a national level drawing on data from each local project (Tunstill *et al.*, 2005). Early indications suggest that progress has been made in developing preventive services for children and involving parents in such activities. Those who participate are reported to show improved confidence and self-esteem, enhanced social skills and better awareness of health and educational matters affecting their children (Attree, 2004). However, the inherent limitations of the programme have also been revealed. For example, many families in severe need remain outside the project areas in neighbouring communities and, as a result, do not benefit from Sure Start initiatives and resources. Conversely, some families within the designated project boundaries are not 'deprived'. Further, the most 'hard to reach families' may remain untouched by the project's initiatives that benefit those who actively participate (Attree, 2004, p. 160). The impact of Sure Start in reducing wider inequalities remains unclear and few projects are likely to reach government inclusion targets for employment (Tunstill *et al.*, 2005). Similar findings can be found for other ABIs such as Health Action Zones.

Health Action Zones (HAZ) may be seen as another 'third way' approach this time geared towards health improvement. They contain elements of an Old Labour commitment to tackling health inequalities first identified in the Black Report (Higgins, 1998), whilst embracing the market and competitive bidding so much a feature of New Right health policy under Mrs Thatcher (Clarence and Painter, 1998). HAZ were established in 26 areas and implemented in two phases during 1998, covering both urban as well as rural areas. Although the urban areas closely matched those identified by Black as having the ten highest standardised death rates, other communities were selected as demonstration projects of what might be achieved at the local level – in the words of New Labour's Health Secretary of the day 'all demonstrated a will to modernise . . . to help themselves' (Frank Dobson, 1998, cited in Powell and Moon, 2001, p. 49).

The HAZ experiment was intended to have a 7-year lifespan and backed with £4 million to cover start up costs. They reflected a desire to achieve greater equity through partnership working and adopting a whole systems and evidence-based approach to health improvement (HAZnet, 2000). The notion of partnership, combined with community empowerment directed at areas which could demonstrate a capacity to improve health in a cost-effective way, characterises the HAZ initiative. The emphasis has been on working in places with the potential for improvement, rather than place poverty *per se* or people poverty (Powell and Moon, 2001). In the event, many of the HAZs have not fulfilled the promise of tackling health inequalities and have been discontinued. HAZ activities have either been absorbed by the local primary care trust or taken up by local voluntary sector projects (Davies, 2001).

Area-Based Policy – Towards a Critique

ABIs can be sharply criticised on at least four grounds. First, for confusing people poverty and place poverty, and failing to acknowledge that most poor people do not live in poor areas (Powell *et al.*, 2001). Secondly, as the CDP experience indicates, the problems of poor areas are not fundamentally due to the character of the people who live there or the culture of the local community. These factors may give us rich descriptive narratives and some fascinating insights into life at the sharp end of society, including the survival strategies that people adopt to enable them to live at the edge of the welfare state (Jordan and Stepney, 1999). Thirdly, any serious analysis of urban poverty must start with locating the problem of exclusion within the wider social and economic system and the global market that reproduces inequalities in access to resources and power alongside conspicuous wealth.

There has been an interesting theoretical debate about ABIs that derives from the work of the French Marxist school of Manuel Castells (Castells, 1977). At the heart of this debate is 'the urban question' and whether the problems of the inner city are less of an urban problem but more related to the crisis of advanced capitalism (Craig *et al.*, 1982; Saunders, 1979). From this analysis under conditions of globalisation, capital will migrate from the old industrial and urban areas in search of more profitable locations across the globe. But the city and by implication the community does have significance not least as the site of social reproduction (relationships, socialisation and training) as well as collective consumption (services including welfare that are collectively provided by the state). According to Castells, the community offered opportunities for the growth of new social movements based around consumption issues to do with schools, health, transport and so on, which he predicted could potentially become new arenas of the class struggle (Castells, 1978). In Britain unlike France and Italy, such struggles have rarely linked directly to social class or been seen by those involved in this way. However, the growth of the service-user movement does illustrate the significance of groups tackling oppression by organising on the basis of gender, disability, mental health status and so on. And such groups as the disabled people's movement and 'survivors speak out' against oppression in the psychiatric system demonstrate that collective action retains the capacity to link community-based struggles with wider issues concerned with structural change (Cooke and Shaw, 1996; Ledwith, 2005).

A fourth criticism of ABIs is that the confidence of policy makers in devising solutions to problems of place poverty based on better co-ordinated services and more 'joined-up' government may be over-optimistic and misplaced (Pollitt, 2003). The emphasis on local partnership working, such a prominent feature of ABIs, whilst important for information sharing and the development of collaboration, has taken on the mantra of becoming something of a panacea that does not necessarily lead to better practice (Alcock, 2004). One of the positive features of ABIs is the aim to promote the active involvement of the local community. This is likely to increase the credibility of the project in the eyes of local people, support the inclusion agenda and assist in building up social capital. However, there is a long history of community involvement becoming tokenistic and increasing the legitimacy of the project sponsors but falling well short of empowering local people (Craig and Mayo, 1995). There is also the problem of co-opting local people into self-help activities as an end in itself (Berner and Phillips, 2005). The story of CDP as we have seen illustrates the problems of attempting to promote self-help and community involvement without empowerment. Further, the literature on community participation tends to neglect the social and economic costs of participation, which may fall disproportionately on poorer people (Rose and Hanmer, 1975) and women (Williams, 1997).

What Lessons Can be Learnt from Area-Based Poverty Experiments and What are the Implications for Social Work?

The demise of CDP far from signalling the end of ABIs, as has already been noted, provided important lessons for government, professional workers and local people concerning the potential benefits as well as risks of using community development supported by action-research as a strategy for tackling urban poverty. For government the political risks associated with funding staff to engage in community action, backed up by independent research, were perceived to be too great. It was seen as a recipe for political agitation against the established order. Community development work would not be sponsored by the state in this way again. Instead the notion of self-help and voluntary effort to promote greater responsibility and independence remained in many subsequent community projects, but set within the context of centrally determined inclusion targets and extensive local controls. The voluntary sector and local community groups became the beneficiaries of new partnership initiatives and moved from outside to inside the policy making citadel, but subject to close accountability and regulation (Taylor, 2001). Both Sure Start and HAZs reveal these mechanisms very clearly. Aligned to this was the need to ensure that community-based projects were geared more closely towards the needs of the labour market with again the American workfare model providing the example.

There are many points of continuity as well as change in policy that can be identified. In very general terms it would appear that the lexicon of policy makers has moved from a concentration on people poverty and the problems of dysfunctional communities to a concern with place poverty defined by indices of social exclusion. Promoting inclusion and participation through self-help legitimised by the rhetoric of empowerment has become something of a panacea for ABIs. However, since 1997

New Labour has promoted a new 'third way' approach where the capacity to modernise is seen as being equally important as the ability to reduce inequalities.

Specific aspects of New Labour's area-based policy include:

- modernisation and reform of local agencies to deliver more joined-up services;

- use of partnership arrangements with a range of stakeholders in statutory and voluntary sectors to facilitate modernisation;

- targeting of resources to those in greatest need or most at risk especially children to achieve greater prevention; and

- clearer lines of accountability with performance targets for staff and league tables for agencies to promote the choice agenda in local communities.

For professional social work staff in local authorities, opportunities to engage in community development would appear to have become more limited, although this approach has continued in the voluntary sector but again subject to more subtle and pervasive forms of control – this will be taken up in Part III. This also meant that opportunities for social workers to engage in preventive work in the community will need to be carefully argued and justified, a problem reinforced by care management and the growing emphasis on protection and risk management in child care and work with vulnerable adults. Prevention can and should be combined with a protection role based upon good research evidence (Department of Health, 1995; Holman, 1998) and this is being finally recognised post Climbié (Laming, 2003) with the development of the *Every Child Matters* framework in the new (2004) Children Act (Department for Education and Skills, 2004).

The implications for social work are highly significant in that a knowledge of the local community, its networks and resources, can provide important information to enhance the possibilities for preventive practice (Stepney, 2006a). Research has consistently identified a range of factors associated with the assessment of children in need, including availability of social support, relationships with peers, school attainment, economic circumstances and the accessibility of local resources (Department for Education and Skills, 2004). And these cannot be assessed and appropriate decisions made to balance protection with prevention without good quality information and reliable local knowledge (Stepney, 2006a).

With no research teams at their disposal, as in CDP, social workers will need to build evaluation into their work and become more research minded. Developing partnerships with both community members and other professionals can support such endeavours provided they are mutually rewarding and geared towards meeting community needs. However, the risks of promoting a more critical and empowering practice and thereby incurring the displeasure of powerful interests should not be underestimated (Ledwith, 2005). The appeal to community remains strong and compelling but its translation into practice continues to prove problematic. The idealised representation of community in the minds of policy makers may be at variance with reality or indeed what local people may wish. Nonetheless, there are numerous models of good practice in this area, and the work of Bob Holman in Easterhouse, Glasgow (Holman, 1998), the continuation of Sure Start (Attree, 2004) and work of voluntary sector agencies like Barnardos, Age Concern and local survivor organisations in mental health and the disabled peoples movement illustrate what can be achieved.

For local people the heady days of organising for change and establishing locally managed projects has given way to more carefully managed programmes of self-help. Many of these are geared towards inclusion, through labour market activation as in the New Deals, and run by special advisers rather than by community workers with closed agendas and devoid of radical objectives. Another policy pill apparently on repeat prescription from government is participation and partnership. Participation may be prescribed either around selective issues or connected to the new care trusts and linked to multi-agency working, where the views of service users and community members may be sought. The new trusts are of course the organisational framework to achieve joint working between health and social care staff, along with certain sections of the community, especially those with time and resources to spare. However, evidence suggests that significant sections of the community may be missed out leaving the majority feeling disengaged and disconnected with local services (Dowling *et al.*, 2004).

Summary and Conclusion

In this chapter we have noted how the concept of community has become a central organising force for policy formulation and debate. The popularity of ABIs has been explained in terms of their high visibility, modest redistribution and capacity to promote inclusion at the local level. The story of CDP provides a telling example of an initiative where the aim of inclusion through self-help was rejected by local project staff in favour of a more structural analysis of urban poverty. This resulted in political conflict and the premature closure of the projects. With the election of a New Labour government in 1997 a raft of new ABIs have been set up, reflecting a new 'third way' approach to the problem of poverty now referred to in policy discourse as the need to meet targets to combat exclusion. However, a brief analysis of two contemporary projects, Sure Start and HAZ, reveals that results have been at best extremely modest and the impact in reducing inequality unclear.

ABIs have increased both in number and scope and whilst job activation through the New Deal for Communities has become one of the officially sanctioned roads to inclusion, there are projects addressing such diverse issues as neighbourhood renewal, community safety and environmental protection (Alcock, 2004). All reflect a third way approach to policy making in the community – a subject that will be taken up in Chapter 6. Alongside the growth in ABIs has been the development of community care policy and this will be the focus of the next chapter.

5

Community Care: Promoting an Empowering Service or Using the Market to Contain Costs?

To the politician, community care is a useful piece of rhetoric; to the sociologist it is a stick to beat institutional care with; to the civil servant it is a cheap alternative; to the visionary it is a dream of the new society in which people really do care; to social services departments it is a nightmare of heightened public expectation and inadequate resources.

(Jones *et al.*, 1978, p. 114)

Introduction

The term community care has become a highly contested and ambiguous concept. It tends to be interpreted in a variety of ways, as the above quote illustrates, leaving provider agencies with the dilemma of matching rhetoric with reality at a time of finite resources. Its use in policy debates can be traced back to the 1930s when it was used to refer to non-institutional provision (Denney, 1998). More recently community care has been defined as 'the various efforts to help ensure that people who are in need of care remain in the community' (Thompson and Thompson, 2005, p. 1). This is likely to consist of a package of care including practical, personal, social and emotional support to help maintain or restore people to a safe and satisfactory level of independence (Centre for Policy on Ageing, 1990).

Almost everyone appears to be in favour of community care, although this seems more of a reaction against institutionalisation than a commitment to developing genuinely participatory and empowering services (Payne, 1995). The de-institutionalisation consensus has spanned both

71

liberal and conservative opinion (Scull, 1984), and whether on the grounds of human rights or saving money both agreed that institutional care should be radically scaled down. The shape of the new policy was revealed in the late 1980s when the Griffiths Report (1988) recommended an enhanced role for the voluntary and independent sectors as part of a new mixed economy of care. This was followed by the Conservative government's decision to grant social services a leading role in managing community care services, as outlined in the 1989 White Paper *Caring for People* (DoH, 1989). The decision was greeted perhaps surprisingly with almost universal approval. This was unprecedented because, then as now, social services departments were publicly criticised for their failings in child protection and care of vulnerable adults, as well as an alleged inability to develop preventative services to tackle wider inequalities. Consequently, the view that emerged from practice has been one of guarded optimism, cautioned by the fear that in community care social services and its partner agencies were being handed a poisoned chalice.

As a policy, community care deploys particular notions of community based upon traditional familial ideology where social relations are imagined, idealised and reflect traditional gender roles. From the beginning, in political debate the policy has been imbued with fine words and ambitious promises. However, the experience of service users, carers and staff suggests that the reforms contained some positive but potentially conflicting intentions. On the one hand, they were intended to provide a needs-led service and empower users, whilst on the other, they were designed to achieve better value for money and the containment of costs (Payne, 1995). It is clear that successive governments were determined to reduce public spending on the central funding of residential and nursing home places, which had risen dramatically from £10 million in 1979 to £2.5 billion in 1993 (Wistow, 1995). Hence, the desire to contain costs was accorded a higher priority than the wish to empower service users and, as a result, improvements to services would have to be funded through efficiency savings.

With the election of New Labour in 1997 there has been a shift from a contract to a partnership culture in community care and a new compact with the voluntary sector (Balloch and Taylor, 2001). Partnership working featured prominently in the modernising social services White Paper (DoH, 1998a) where a whole chapter was devoted to it. Dismantling the so called 'Berlin wall' between health and social services to create a 'seamless service of care' was presented as one of the top priorities. However, the importance of the voluntary sector and community organisations was acknowledged but it seems very much as an afterthought, as they only featured in the final few lines of the chapter (Balloch and Taylor, 2001, p. 5). The need for partnership with the voluntary sector, as well as the independent sector and service users has subsequently been reinforced in the NHS Plan (DoH, 2000), although more recently this has been somewhat overshadowed by the arrival of the choice agenda (DoH, 2006a). It would seem that policy makers have recognised the difficulties agencies face in providing high quality care services from limited resources, but are now espousing the benefits of multidisciplinary collaboration and choice as solutions to those problems.

The Historical Legacy – But Whose History?

A short historical detour may be instructive to establish the reasons why people appear to be so keen on community care and why the fragile consensus underpinning the policy has held for so long. The consensus may mask many deep-seated divisions and conflicts that have a long history – a history punctuated by contradictions, not least between political rhetoric and reality (Walker, 1997). First, as noted above, support for care in the community is in part a reaction against the longer tradition of segregation, a legacy of nineteenth century social policy that consigned people with disabilities and mental health problems to the asylum (Scull, 1984; Stedman-Jones, 1984). Second, it is helpful to recognise that a range of provision has always existed, from institutional care to what was termed outdoor relief, both have origins in the Victorian poor laws. What has gradually changed is:

(a) the balance between the various elements;

(b) the basis or eligibility criteria for admission to care;

(c) the nature and extent of the responsibilities of the state;

(d) the changing role of the state from monopoly provider to planning, monitoring and regulation over a mix of provision involving public, private, voluntary and informal sources of care.

Third, as noted in Part I, the warmly persuasive concept of community is informed by at least two opposing discourses (Abrams, 1980; Williams, 1983):

● A belief in community as mutual aid, charity and voluntarism – a legacy of Victorian philanthropy that promotes individual responsibility in the poor and dangerous classes (Pearson, 1975). It is the incorrigible, deviant and feeble minded who, within this discourse it is argued, should be consigned to a modern institution or subject to surveillance and control in the community. This view based on the notion of self-help, informs much of the Conservative and some of New Labour's approach to community care.

- The second discourse centres upon the belief that community has the potential for promoting social solidarity and collective responses to adversity. This draws on a tradition associated with social change grounded in the experience of the labour movement and oppressed groups everywhere. Since the 1980s it has found expression in the struggles of black people, women, older citizens, disabled people, mental health survivors of the psychiatric system, gay and lesbian people, and has informed the struggle for more inclusive communities (Bryan *et al.* 1985; Dalley, 1988; Gilroy, 1987; Hughes and Mooney, 1998).

In the mid-1990s Tony Blair attempted to combine both traditions in his 'third way' modernisation of the welfare state utilising the notion of moral communitarianism – see Chapter 6. Prior to this, politicians were inclined to leave many of the tensions that derive from these two contested discourses about community unresolved.

Community Care in the 1980s

During the 1980s Margaret Thatcher attempted to revitalise the traditional family and promote individual responsibility whilst rolling back the frontiers of the state. The Thatcher government were ideologically committed to a patriarchal model which stressed this first discourse in community care at the expense of the second. It was to be based on the informal care provided largely but not exclusively by women (Finch and Groves, 1980), and signified an important shift from 'care in the community' towards 'care by the community' with the community taking more responsibility for its more vulnerable members (Ungerson, 1987).

This form of community care based on welfare pluralism made sound economic sense to a market-minded government given predicted demographic trends, especially relating to older persons:

- increasing cost of hospital and residential provision;

- rising cost of social security budget and other forms of social support;

- changes in the labour market especially involving greater participation by women;

- rising rates of divorce and greater geographical mobility; and

- a crisis in care with less women willing and able to do the caring.

Overall the government came to the uncomfortable conclusion that they were sitting on a 'resources time bomb' that required concerted action. They rather overlooked other demographic evidence that suggested that the growth in residential care for older people had in fact not risen more than the increase in the proportion of the very old (those over 75) in the population (Firth, 1987). The problem for Margaret Thatcher was that too much of the financial support was coming from central government, thus breaking another pledge of reducing public spending, and in the process creating a perverse incentive in favour of residential care that had inhibited the development of domiciliary community care services. According to Walker (1997), government policy in the 1980s had three constituents, which taken together would inexorably lead to the residualisation of public services.

First, there was a fragmentation of social provision indicating a change from a public to a pluralist welfare model. The monopoly role of the state was ended creating conditions for the development of a mixed economy of care. Second, there has been increasing marketisation of services with the introduction of a quasi-market in both the NHS and social care (Hoyes and Means, 1997). Further, the discipline of the market was introduced and expected to shape the organisation of all public services (Pollitt and Harrison, 1992). The purchaser/provider split has been one of the predictable outcomes of this process. In a buoyant care market the private residential homes sector and much later domiciliary care agencies and the voluntary sector have expanded significantly, funded by higher levels of user-financed resources, means tested local authority support and a new mix of state funding (Means and Smith, 1998; Scott and Russell, 2001).

Third, according to Walker (1997) there has been a twin track policy of decentralisation of administration, combined with increased responsibility at the local level, alongside centralisation of control particularly over expenditure. In theory, decentralisation could lead to greater user involvement and an enhanced role for the voluntary sector. Moreover, this has been one of the more positive outcomes of the policy as user groups and community organisations have entered into partnership arrangements with state social services.

Assessing the Research Evidence, Including Seminal Research by Davies and Challis (1986)

As already noted, there was a good deal of scepticism prevalent in the years leading up to the implementation of policy encapsulated in the 1990 NHS and Community Care Act. However, there were also genuine hopes and expectations. In the UK the work of Davies and Challis (1986), particularly the evaluation of community care projects in Kent, influenced policy makers at the Department of Health as well as social work practitioners. Part of the optimism amongst practitioners was based on the potential for developing high quality preventative services. Alongside this there was a genuine fear that this kind of research might be seen as being almost too helpful and cost effective, by demonstrating how to provide preventative services at lower unit cost. In turn such research evidence might be used by central government to justify reduced funding for local authorities.

Davies and Challis (1986) established a research project with a quasi-experimental design in collaboration with Kent Social Services. The project involved selecting 100 frail older people from the active caseloads of social workers in the county and this became the experimental group. The older persons were all living in the community with varying degrees of support, but had reached the stage in their lives where residential care was being considered as a distinct possibility.

A team of experienced social workers was selected for the project to work with the experimental group and given reduced caseloads and a decentralised budget. The social workers were able to purchase services and construct individual packages of care most appropriate to the needs of the older person to enable them to continue living independently in the community. However, the care packages were subject to certain conditions. The cost of the purchased care was set at a ceiling which was two-thirds the cost of residential care, thus ensuring that there was an inbuilt cost saving. In the experimental group, a mixture of care was provided ranging from informal care by relatives, semi-formal support from voluntary sector providers like Age Concern, and mainstream services provided in-house by the local social services department (the private domiciliary care sector in Kent was undeveloped at that time). Outcomes from the experimental group incorporating the experiences of the older people were then compared over a 12-month period with those from a matched control group. The latter received traditional services and other forms of support from social services teams across the county in the usual way.

The results for those older people in the experimental group were extremely impressive. At the end of the 12-month period, admissions into residential care had been halved, mortality rates substantially reduced and significant improvements reported on a range of quality of life measures. Further, this was achieved at a lower cost when compared with the previous system of service delivery and on average two-thirds the cost of residential care. It all seemed too good to be true, and on closer inspection some concerns were raised, particularly on the question of reliability. It was suggested that the most complex cases were filtered out, such that the complex reality of a social worker's caseload was not fully represented in the study. Also the workers selected were an elite corps of the most experienced staff and were thus not representative of the range of abilities typically found in a social services team. Although this scheme was an unbridled success with frail older people, the question was asked whether it could be replicated elsewhere with a random group of service users and similar results achieved with other user groups.

Other studies have to some extent answered these criticisms and concerns. For example, Cambridge *et al.* (1994) in a study of 200 clients with learning disabilities found that care management had provided a helpful and co-ordinated service in response to assessed need. They concluded that 'most people with learning disabilities are demonstrably better off living in the community than in hospital' (p. 105). Means and Smith (1998) similarly point to various positive achievements in a climate of uncertainty and resource constraints experienced by local authorities. Pockets of 'innovative practice' have emerged in planning better agency partnerships and moves in some authorities towards more integrated housing and social services provision. However, they are less optimistic about achieving consensus at the boundary between health and social care and the role of GPs in the new primary care trusts. Significantly, they call for greater investment in rehabilitation and prevention that characterises care in other European welfare states, especially Scandinavia (Means and Smith, 1998). Finally, Challis *et al.* (2002) report encouraging results in the management of frail older people involved in the Gateshead community care scheme.

Overall, the research carried out during this important period influenced as well as reflected the emerging shape of policy development, and this will be examined more closely in the next section.

Community Care in the 1990s

Following the publication of the influential Griffiths Report (1988), the stated aim of community care policy was to create 'high quality, needs led, co-ordinated services which maximised choice' (Denney, 1998, p. 202). The mechanism for delivering such services was to be the market within a mixed economy of care, thus revealing the enduring legacy of Thatcherism. The full social cost of community care was never really spelt out and policy appears to have been shaped by a determination to make greater use of the market, the voluntary sector and informal care by the family rather than the state. It was thus a modified version of an old tune designed to find cheaper community alternatives to institutional provision (Blakemore, 1998, p. 171). At the local level, social services would change from being sole providers to purchasing care from a number of state, voluntary and independent or private sector providers. Later John Major's government introduced a rule prior to implementation in April 1993 that 85% of new funds from the Special Transitory Grant to local authorities for community care (STG) should be spent in the non-state sector.

The official aims of community care policy were encapsulated in the 1990 NHS Community Care Act and can be summarised as follows:

- providing services to enable people to live in their own homes whenever possible;

- making support for carers a high priority;

- providing proper assessment of needs and good care management with individual care plans, the basis for service provision;

- promoting the development of a flourishing independent sector;

- making providers of services more accountable; and

- securing better value for money by introducing a funding structure based upon an internal market (adapted from Department of Health, 1989, cited in Denney, 1998, p. 202).

Two principal objectives from the White Paper (Department of Health, 1989) were to shift the balance of provision away from residential homes towards domiciliary care and in doing so encourage a greater diversity of provision in the independent and voluntary sectors. By 1996 not every local authority had met this target, although the role of the independent and voluntary sectors had increased substantially (Lewis and Glennerster, 1996). According to Means and Smith (1998), between 1992 and 1997 the volume of public-funded (not provided) domiciliary care increased by 57%, whilst public funded residential care rose by less than 5%. Moreover, this growth was in no small part due to the dramatic increase in the number of private sector providers. The latter's share of the market increased from 2% in 1992 to 44% in 1997 (Means and Smith, 1998). Regarding the voluntary sector, the state sought to alter the balance of funding from annual grants to contracts and service agreements (Kendall and Knapp, 2001). By the mid-1990s, fees, including 'sweetheart deals' with preferred voluntary agencies, accounted for 75% of social services spending in the voluntary sector (Scott and Russell, 2001). The reasons were basically to provide an incentive for voluntary organisations to work more closely (and harmoniously) with local authorities and increase accountability in keeping with the value for money requirement.

Overall the 1990s marked a turning point in the development of Community Care policy. It was a period when policy reform in healthcare exerted a strong influence on the development of policy in community care. This was shaped by adherence to the mixed economy of welfare with a pluralist approach to provision, strong emphasis on cost containment to meet centrally determined targets, and notions of partnership working with the aim of creating a 'seamless service' at the interface between health and social care (Wistow, 2000). The community was seen as potentially self-sufficient once its informal resources had been mobilised. Those urban communities with few or inadequate resources continued to be viewed as dysfunctional and targeted as suitable for area-based projects such as Sure Start.

By the end of the 1990s, the general picture that emerges, based upon a number of research studies, is that there had been significant progress in some areas. For example, there is evidence of improved inter-agency co-operation (Glendinning *et al.*, 1998) and good practice to provide creative packages of care for those requiring intensive support (Challis *et al.*, 2002). However, more worrying has been evidence of increasing pressure on resources, tighter eligibility criteria leading to reduced levels of service for some groups (Henwood, 1995). Also a 'reductionist' approach, such as tick box assessments and too much time spent on paperwork that has a tendency to oversimplify the complex reality of living in the community or caring for a vulnerable person (Postle, 2002, cited in Thompson and Thompson, 2005, p. 15). Hence user and carers still have significant misgivings that 'empowerment and choice remain more rhetoric than reality' (Connolly and Johnson, 1996) – see also Social Services Inspectorate and NHS Executive (1995).

The impact of community care on women, especially in their role as informal carers continues to cause concern matched only by the failure of government to acknowledge the full extent of the problem and to provide the necessary support (Becker, 2004). This is despite evidence from the 2001 census on the extent of caring that women do – put simply, a woman has a 1 in 4 chance of becoming a carer when she is in her 50s (ONS, 2003). When one adds in the number of women who report that they are combining their caring role with work in the labour market, not to mention support to neighbours and friends in the community, then the implications for policy makers hardly needs spelling out. Similarly, ethnic minority groups have not benefited from community care consistent with their cultural needs. For far too long there has been an assumption that ethnic minorities 'look after their own' and therefore do not require the full range of community care services (Gunaratnam, 1997). Fortunately, such attitudes are now being replaced by recognition that ethnic minorities should be accorded high priority for assessments and support.

When resources are adequate community care can clearly deliver good outcomes through the deployment of co-ordinated services. However, apart from resource issues, research suggests that much depends on the geographical area of the country (post code lottery) and the partnership arrangements in place (Lewis and Glennerster, 1996). According to Blakemore (1998), in looking back at community care in the 1990s two main impressions stand out: first, 'the lack of any clear public endorsement or popular acclaim, if the new arrangements are working they are doing so in a very quiet way' (p. 179). Second, there has been 'widespread dissatisfaction with the gap between official rhetoric of a needs-led policy and the reality of stringent control upon resources' (p. 179).

Contemporary Issues in Community Care

Three brief examples are discussed concerning financial constraints and fair access to care, partnership between health and social care and the new and expanding role for the voluntary sector. These examples reveal some of the issues faced by practitioners, users and carers in community care. They also illustrate that whilst progress has been made in some areas there are still significant problems that remain to be solved.

(i) Financial constraints and fair access to care
Financial pressures and efforts by central government to control local authority spending, combined with increasing use of the market, has created enormous problems for staff and services users and carers alike. The end result has been pressure on staff to achieve the most cost-effective outcome rather than meet professionally desirable objectives. Allied to this has been an increase in the level of charging for all services.

Assessments should be multidisciplinary and 'needs led' rather than 'service led'. But as we have noted, this has frequently become resource-led in practice and limiting choice in the process. In England, Social Services now undertake a financial assessment to establish the clients' contribution towards the cost of their care. Here savings and the capital asset of the home are taken into consideration. This is something which many older people resent, having paid tax and National Insurance contributions all their working lives. The loss of savings penalises those who have been thrifty and, despite a 3-month embargo on house selling confirmed in the government's response to the Royal Commission on Long Term Care (Department of Health, 2000), older people in England may still be required to sell their own homes to pay for care in a residential or nursing home. The situation is somewhat different in Scotland and Wales as a result of decisions made by the Scottish Parliament and Welsh Assembly, particularly in relation to nursing care, which is 'free' and funded from taxation.

In a climate of increased user-financed services, charging creates particular difficulties for older people, especially for those whose income is marginally above the level of income support. Vulnerable people in this category may require considerable support but can only afford to pay for perhaps a couple of hours home care per week. This effectively leads to rationing of services and inevitably puts more pressure on informal carers (Blakemore, 1998).

The concern about wide variation in the way local councils determined eligibility led to the Department of Health (2002) issuing policy guidance on Fair Access to Care Services (FACS) in circular LAC(2002)13. The policy guidance provides a framework for local authorities setting eligibility criteria based upon assessment of need and risks to independence. The framework has four eligibility bands – critical, substantial, moderate and low. However, Councils have been permitted to draw the line of eligibility in accordance with local resources, with many setting the threshold for services at the level of substantial need and above. Anyone assessed as having moderate or low needs is unlikely to receive a service at all. Hence, the rationing of services will continue but paradoxically under the guise of a national framework designed to end the postcode lottery. Recently, Walsall Council in the West Midlands, with a projected overspend of £4 million in 2006/2007, was forced to redraw the line of eligibility and only provide direct services to those assessed as 'critical' which clearly created serious difficulties for everyone in the community (Walsall Council, 2007).

Thus, questions about eligibility, who pays for care and levels of charging, to name but a few issues associated with the financial pressure on local authorities, will undoubtedly remain highly contested political issues.

(ii) Partnership between Health and Social Care

At the time when the community care reforms were being formulated, health-care policy was undergoing a significant change in emphasis towards a more cost-effective and curative service. Wistow (1995) argues that the driving force within the NHS has been the introduction of 'an efficiency index which measures responsiveness to patients needs' in terms of relatively crude indicators of apparently increased activity and waiting list targets' (p. 234).

One consequence of redefining healthcare in terms of short-term, curative medical treatment has been the passing of responsibility for much routine caring, convalescence and rehabilitation onto social services. This has implications for funding and meant that the boundary between 'free' healthcare and means-tested social care shifted significantly. At the present time, research evidence suggests that this has created considerable tensions especially around what has been referred to as 'continuing care' (Henwood, 1996) and more recently 'intermediate care'

(Department of Health, 2000). The changing role of district nurses along-side home-care workers and the discharge of older people from hospital to residential or nursing care are other related areas of concern (Clarke *et al.*, 1996; Ford and Stepney, 2003; Godfrey and Moore, 1996).

Wistow (1995) reminds us that social services have become the purchasers of nursing and residential care in the community. However, acute downward pressure on budgets is forcing managers to compare the relative cost of residential provision with a domiciliary care package, and go for the cheapest option even if this is a care home. This creates a situation where people could be moved 'along the acute sector conveyor belt to the community care warehouse' (Wistow, 1995, p. 237). However, the 'warehouse' may increasingly look like a large, smart, purpose-built, functional chain-hotel if corporate providers continue to make advances into the residential homes market (Kendall and Knapp, 2001).

Health Policy and legislation including the 1999 Health Act, New NHS Plan 2000 – including provisions for 'intermediate care' – Health and Social Care Bill 2001 and the Community Care (delayed discharges) Bill 2003, all reinforce the movement towards partnership working. However welcome these developments are for promoting joint working within the new Care Trusts, they will operate at the cutting edge of an increasingly marke-tised and managerial welfare state. More recently the government has sought to introduce a choice agenda (DoH, 2006a) on the basis that choice will increase competition and lead to improved performance. Partnership working remains important but with an emphasis on more flexible services, prevention through earlier intervention and an (optimistic) assumption that the majority of people will take responsibility for their own care and exercise healthier lifestyle choices.

This shifting policy boundary will have implications for the nature of partnership working between health and social work professionals. The term partnership has become somewhat over used in New Labour's programme of policy reform – see Chapter 6. At the level of prac-tice there is clearly a need for professionals to work more effec-tively together from across the public, voluntary and independent sectors, as well as with users and carers. Partnership working has emancipatory potential that can be contrasted with the more tradi-tional medical model where there was deference to professional judge-ment (Thompson and Thompson, 2005, p. 30). However, there are a substantial number of barriers to be overcome, including status differ-ences, confidentiality, professional tribalism, issues of trust, sector rival-ries, different accountability structures and resource allocation systems (Rummery and Glendinning, 1997). Not withstanding these problems there are significant benefits to be gained in terms of developing holistic ways of working, mutual support, empowerment and creating a more open and learning society (Thompson and Thompson, 2005, pp. 31–32).

(iii) A new and expanding role for the voluntary sector

The policy reforms in community care have had a significant impact on the role of the voluntary sector. Historically, its role has been rooted in philanthropy, charity and self-help. After the post-war welfare settlement was being re-examined in the harsher financial climate brought about by the 1970s oil crisis, the Wolfenden Committee (1978) were charged with reassessing the future of voluntary organisations. They suggested that voluntary agencies existed to fill gaps and provide alternatives to state services, as well as identify new needs and find new ways of meeting them (Wolfenden, 1978, cited in Harris *et al.*, 2001). This stressed their innovative and complementary role in what was seen as an evolving pluralist welfare society. However, as the state moved away from being the sole provider of care during the Thatcher years the voluntary sector was subject to two contradictory forces. First, the sector was thrust into a more central role in welfare provision, whereupon it was directly exposed to market forces and managerial influence. Second, it found itself often the junior partner in relationships with state agencies competing for contracts (rather than grants) and subject to substantial downward pressure on costs. The business culture had duly arrived and began to influence the mission and day-to-day operation of all NGOs.

During the 1990s the voluntary sector expanded in an era of contracting and service agreements. This made it more vulnerable and likely to be 'buffeted by the fiscal winds of change blowing through the public sector' (Kendall and Knapp, 2001, p. 121) and sometimes 'pinned down in ferocious price negotiations' with social services over contracts (Scott and Russell, 2001, p. 57). This signified the more volatile financial climate in which voluntary agencies became significant providers of community care. The increased market share brought fresh problems in that the funding for new work frequently did not match the full cost of providing the service (Scott and Russell, 2001). For example, there was fierce competition between agencies in many areas to win the bloc contracts to provide domiciliary care services for older persons. In the residential care market, many small family-run homes found themselves unable to compete on price with the large corporate providers, and began to be squeezed out as the latter gained an increasing market share (Kendall and Knapp, 2001). One of the unintended side effects of this market competition was the return of institutional styles of care masquerading as consumer choice in the large, functional, chain hotel homes of the corporate providers.

Research evidence highlights both the problems and potential advantages facing the voluntary sector given its new, more central role in promoting diversity of provision and choice but at a reduced cost. Earlier research appeared to support a welfare pluralist position that voluntary organisations were local, responsive, participatory and empowering (Hadley and Hatch, 1982). However, subsequent studies argued that many of the claimed advantages were not measurable and the empirical evidence inconsistent (Knapp *et al.*, 1990). More recent research adopts a more balanced view that whilst small NGOs face distinctive organisational challenges (Harris, 1998b), they may be able to exploit a comparative advantage over other sectors in the social-care market (Billis and Glennerster, 1998). For example, in the care of older people the small voluntary sector organisation, such as Age Concern, can offer four functions that may be difficult to replicate in either the public or private spheres:

1. an expressive function that attends to service user and carers feelings;

2. an innovation function in setting up new day-care and home-visiting services;

3. a community building function that has potential to strengthen informal networks to enhance prevention; and

4. an advocacy function in debates about policy and planning.

However, the same research noted that voluntary agencies typically revealed weaknesses, such as, chronic resource problems, particularism leading to an uneven distribution of services, latent paternalism dependent on whether the agency was run in a professional or rather amateurish way and accountability problems (Kendall, 2003).

In the new millennium the voluntary sector has high visibility and has had unprecedented expectations placed upon it. All the major political parties in the UK now promise to nurture and support the voluntary sector (Kendall, 2003), as clearly it has become rather fashionable to do so. This recognises the contribution voluntary agencies can make to increasing diversity, choice and social capital building. It also reflects some disillusionment with both private market-based care, now increasingly dominated by corporate providers, and mistrust of politically driven initiatives from government seen as pushing the responsibility back onto the community. However, one unsettling question remains concerning whether the new, more central yet diverse role for the voluntary sector has been achieved at a political cost. To oversimplify some complex arguments, have NGOs lost their capacity for dissent? This question must be located within the nature and direction of wider policy change in community care and will be addressed in the final section.

The Way Forward – Community Care in the New Millennium

Under the premiership of Tony Blair, New Labour came to power in May 1997. Once in government, they set out a modernising agenda to improve standards by setting new performance targets for public services, seeking to transform the benefit system around work, and tackle exclusion through a combination of incentives, penalties and new opportunities. This is the legacy inherited by Blair's successor, Gordon Brown, 10 years later in June 2007. In terms of community care provision, according to Langan (2000) 'the world of social services was still reeling under the impact of the community care revolution of the early 1990s' (p. 153). Further, a series of scandals (see Butler and Drakeford, 2005b) and well-publicised problems have focused public attention on the weaknesses in community care rather than its many strengths. The message from government was that something must change under a regime informed by the 3 m's – modernisation, managerialisation and more marketisation (Clarke *et al.*, 2000b). The voluntary sector was brought in centre stage to increase diversity and choice and then subject to the same pressures and costs. Services in the field of mental health were subject to particular criticism from ministers (cf. Frank Dobson, Department of Health, 1999, p. 24) reinforcing the view that 'community care had failed', in contrast to New Labour's successful modernising project and 'joined up' policy with the voluntary and independent sectors to promote inclusion.

Discourses of community in community care are instructive, as they offer representations based on shared expectations. They also provide a way in which meanings of community can be remade and constructed around the belief that a caring community can be created . . . if not today then tomorrow around a new spirit of caring. Such representations may recognise inequalities of gender, race, class, disability and so on, but do so in ways that underplay and conceal the impact such divisions have on the experience of community care. In the process, as we have noted, the work of women in their role of informal carers may be made invisible. The community in community care has been constructed as harmonious, a unifying entity where social differentiation and conflicts of interest along with power differentials may be set aside and the oppression of minorities ignored. The appeal to community is thus largely symbolic and ideological, which helps to explain why involving the community in community care policy and giving the voluntary sector a more central role has proved to be problematic.

Summary and Conclusion

The focus of this chapter has been on community care and the reforms in social policy that resulted from the movement away from the Victorian institution and the development of services to support people in the community. It has been argued that the apparent universal support for community care was as much a reaction against institutionalisation as a commitment to establishing genuinely needs-led and empowering local services. As a result, the reforms introduced by Margaret Thatcher towards the end of her tenure contained many positive but potentially contradictory intentions – on the one hand they were intended to empower users to make informed choices and support people to live independently, whilst on the other they were designed to contain costs and achieve better value for money by use of the market.

Not surprisingly, these tensions help to explain why there has been progress in some areas, for example, to provide intensive support for those with high care needs, whilst there is evidence to suggest that pressure on local authority resources has resulted in inadequate levels of support for those assessed as having low or moderate care needs. It would therefore seem that community care remains resource driven and that 'empowerment and choice remains more rhetoric than reality' (Blakemore, 1998). New Labour came to power in 1997 and have continued the marketised and managerial approach that they criticised the Conservatives for when in opposition. However, there has been greater emphasis on collaborative working especially between health and social services, with the establishment of new care trusts, and partnership with the voluntary and independent sectors.

There has also been movement towards greater user consultation in policy as outlined in the White Paper (Department of Health, 1998a). However, this has revealed that appeals to community, however well intentioned, may be misjudged and of more benefit to government than community members. Pollitt notes the dangers of tokenism and 'manipulative managerialism' in superficial consultation exercises that have little effect on practice (Pollitt, 1996). So targets, contracts and control along with regular audits of performance ('the audit society') seem to be the order of the day not just for social services but voluntary agencies as well in the new millennium – with community care very much in the front line here. Lymbery (1998a) suggests that we will have fewer professional social workers providing services for older people in the future as they will be required to undertake the high-risk assessment work with vulnerable adults. In this scenario, community care may become equated with 'social warehousing' and the return of institutional style care in the community from large corporate providers, financed by the community itself – a legacy of nineteenth century social policy (Wistow, 2000). If this were to happen, it would ultimately weaken the moral economy of New Labour's new and modernised welfare state, which is the subject of the next chapter.

6

Remaking Community: Communitarianism and the Modernisation of the Welfare State

neo Liberals may have sought Hayek but they found Etzioni
(Williams, 2003, p. 6)

Introduction

The aim of this chapter is to explore the rise of communitarianism, both as an ideology and a social movement, and assess its impact on social policy. The concept entered policy debates during the 1990s and quickly gained widespread appeal especially, as the above quote suggests, for those on the political right seeking to make communities more receptive to market-based reform. Communitarian ideas have also been taken up by New Labour and translated into the 'third way' project to modernise the welfare state. In offering a critique of communitarianism a brief outline of an alternative discourse based upon transformative action will be set out – this perspective will be taken up and developed further in the chapters concerned with community-based practice in Part III. The remaking of community, with a greater emphasis on partnership and collaboration, has since 1997 become central to the reforms and provides a clear moral message for both welfare professionals and service users alike. The impact of policy on practice will be illustrated with reference to altering the balance between protection and prevention in child care (Stepney, 2006a), and more generally in the reconstruction of social work as 'tough love' (Jordan, 2001).

The Rise of Communitarianism in a Global Context

Communitarian ideas began to exert a decisive influence on social policy at a time when there was widespread disillusionment with both the excesses of free-market liberalism, with its rampant individualism, and bureaucratic state socialism. The former associated with the New Right, which had been in the ascendancy in both the US and Britain throughout the 1980s and early 1990s, and the latter equated with the old Labour Left. Whilst the hegemony of the right was undermined by growing inequalities and a recession across Europe, a return to a universal welfare model was made virtually impossible by the imperatives of economic globalisation. This required nation states to increase international competitiveness in global markets by reducing social costs and securing a better return on welfare expenditure (Mishra, 1999). This is not to infer that globalisation is a distinctive entity producing a new world order characterised by capital mobility and the information superhighway, but rather a dynamic concept formed by different social, political and economic processes. It is therefore likely to be marked by partial, contradictory and conflictual tendencies (Clarke, 2000). The dynamics of globalisation has unsettled the ability of welfare states throughout Europe to manage socially differentiated populations, and has impinged upon existing social divisions of class, race, gender, age and disability in the community (Clarke, 2001).

Assessing the impact of globalisation at the local level is far from straightforward and could be a chapter in its own right. Take a walk down the high street of any sizeable town and city in Europe and we soon notice that it begins to look very similar with the same kind of international multi-stores selling the same branded products (often made in the Far East), with small local businesses closing down in the face of global competition from large corporate players, and in the process transforming the character and identity of local communities – what human geographers refer to as a global sense of place (Massey, 1991). The local versus global connections reflects these processes as in many of the old urban areas the formal economy has collapsed, as jobs have gone elsewhere, leaving people dependent on the informal economy and living at the edge of the welfare state. The state's ability to develop any more than safety net social protection services has been compromised. Divisions and tensions in the community have increased with a widening gap between the young and affluent euro-winners, living, for example, in new canal side apartments, and losers, epitomised by the poor, older people and the most vulnerable members of the community. Globalisation has therefore impinged on the ability of the welfare state to manage existing inequalities at the local level, forged new inter-dependencies that are cultural as well as social and economic, and produced new relationships that taken together destabilise the social cohesion of the community.

The impact of local versus global issues at the level of the community reflects a certain paradox. On the one hand, the global market appears to operate with little concern for local communities with decision making about investment, planning and so on taken in financial centres, board-rooms and gatherings of political leaders spread around the globe. Even nation states outside the G8 may have little more than a consultation role. On the other hand, global markets have become dependent upon the community for selling their products and cultural ideas, and remind us that people still matter because the economy cannot operate as a disem-bodied entity.

The community has also become the site where the contradictions and costs associated with globalisation may be revealed and worked out. The escalation of global conflicts in Africa and the Middle East has led to a dramatic rise in unplanned migration throughout Europe. New migrants, including refugees and asylum-seekers, arrive as vulnerable and dispos-sessed citizens and after surviving the trauma of living in reception centres for many months are displaced into highly differentiated and fragmented communities. Tensions emerge with indigenous groups around compe-tition for jobs, cultural space, access to welfare and use of community resources, exacerbated by different cultural traditions and an indigenous and latent racism. These tensions can quickly spill out onto the streets in racist incidents, begging, hustling, prostitution and petty crime. At the same time, the global market also creates enhanced opportunities and rewards for those in well-paid corporate employment. Such euro-winners may feel the need to reside in gated enclosures to protect themselves from members of the dangerous classes outside who are prone to throw things.

The dynamics of globalisation has undermined the welfare states' capacity to protect vulnerable groups and modify how communities are differentiated. Whatever the benefits of globalisation these differences produce inequalities that superimpose themselves on existing divisions creating new patterns of 'exclusion and inclusion, hierarchy, marginalisa-tion and subordination' (Clarke, 2001, p. 2). Social workers get caught up in these processes in seeking to protect and support the most vulnerable members of the community, even when they seek to work autonomously on negotiated terms as outreach workers (Jordan, 2007). Thus the way local versus global conflicts are resolved may intensify existing social divisions by disturbing the interventions by the state for the reproduction of social differences and the management of problematic communities.

Communitarianism as a social movement came to the fore at this time of uncertainty and growing discontent that, whatever its benefits, glob-alisation left many mainstream citizens feeling disconnected from their community. But rather than align itself with movements on the left with a socialist agenda, communitarianism offered a route to social harmony through individual responsibility, active citizenship and more recently respect for the well-being of the community (Jordan, 2007). It should be added that disillusionment with socialism was reinforced by the weakening of the political Left in Europe immediately after the collapse of the Soviet bloc following the fall of the Berlin Wall and subsequent re-unification of Germany. Thus, a historical turning point had been reached that created conditions for a new set of ideas to emerge, concerning how to provide welfare without compromising efficiency or enterprise. Enter Etzioni (1994) and the communitarian platform in the US that influenced the Clinton Administration. Communitarian ideas applied to social policy quickly spread across the Atlantic and received an enthusiastic reception in London from across the political spectrum, particularly from New Labour theoreticians. They were also well received by SPD politicians in Germany and centre left groups in other European countries including the Nordic welfare states (Stepney, 2006b).

Communitarian ideas are not in themselves new but derive from a number of distinct philosophical and sociological sources. They can be traced back to Aristotle and Plato who debated the basis for a civic republic in ancient Greece as well as finding expression in the work of Tönnies, Owen and Ruskin. More recently the work of MacIntyre (1981), Bell (1993) and the British Council of Churches (1985) report *Faith in the City,* to name but a few writers amongst many, all articulate communitarian principles. The key themes of communitarianism are represented by a strong appeal to the core moral values of the community, such as, mutual respect, adherence to collective rules, self-reliance and social responsibility. These set out the relationship between the citizen, the state and the wider society. For example, the relationship between citizen and state should be governed by reciprocal obligations whereby rights must be balanced by responsibilities. Communitarians share with those on the political right the belief that in modern Western society too much emphasis has been given to rights producing 'a strong sense of entitlement and a weak sense of obligation' (Etzioni, 1994, p. 3). They argue that moral authority derives from coherent communal and cultural traditions rather than any abstract notion of individual freedom as Liberalism has claimed (Lenard, 2004; Smith, 1996).

The implications for welfare reform are quite clear as communitarians 'claim to reject the market-led ideology of the New Right... and top down approach to welfare from the state' (Hughes and Mooney, 1998, p. 74). Welfare should encourage and enable individuals to actively pursue solutions to common problems in collaboration with their fellow citizens rather than maximise individual freedom. There is a concern to ensure that welfare promotes the core moral values of personal responsibility, justice, integrity and in the US respect for the constitution. In the UK such concerns have found expression in the campaign to re-establish traditional family values as a touchstone for the remoralisation of society. Controversially, Etzioni's (1995) notion of a 'parenting deficit' with parents held to be failing in their duty to children and equated with a range of problems such as delinquency, crime and the breakdown of community demonstrate how communitarianism can feed into a neo-conservative political agenda about moral decline. This has been accompanied both in UK and Europe with attempts to reduce welfare dependency though workfare and job activation policies (Stepney, 2000, 2006b).

Governments throughout Europe found communitarian ideas an attractive option as they sought to create a new welfare consensus or 'third way' to balance the freedom of the global market with a commitment to social justice (Stepney, 2000). This consensus stressed the obligations of the citizen to the collective rules and moral values of the community to become more independent and less reliant on state welfare except as a last resort consistent with the subsidiarity principle. It offered the prospect of establishing a new social glue that could potentially seal the scars of fragmentation and division that characterised so many urban communities and so much of the contemporary welfare landscape. Hence as Hughes and Mooney (1998) note the 'popular political appeal of the communitarian discourse is unsurprising' (p. 75).

Communitarianism – A Critique

Before moving on to examine how communitarianism was translated into New Labour's modernisation project, it is appropriate to note that as a coherent manifesto for change it can be criticised on a number of grounds. First, the generalised wish to achieve a new social consensus in the community based upon justice and mutual responsibility makes no mention of the need for wider economic reform or any changes to the social structure. The health of a community more than ever before is influenced by economic forces stemming from the global market and the absence of such an analysis seriously limits the communitarian message. Similarly, recognition of wider divisions of class, race, gender and so on and the oppression which flows from them is also missing. The communitarian message may be more suited to middle England than those who it is intended to influence – namely, dispossessed groups struggling to survive in the most marginalised and run down inner-urban areas.

Second, the appeal to the core values of the community would appear to be based upon a somewhat romantic vision of a past golden age of community that was orderly and harmonious. Such visions are highly contested and overlook the conflicts that existed between different groups, such as squire, parson and labourer, and the divergent value systems represented in modern plural societies like Britain. The core values of the community then as now are likely to be disputed and the experience of different groups socially and culturally constructed.

Third, the vision of the family in the communitarian discourse appears to be heavily overlain with traditional patriarchal assumptions reinforced by Etzioni's (1995) views about the 'parenting deficit' in modern society. This has strong echoes of the radical Right's condemnation of lone parents and fatherless families (see Murray, 1996) and becomes a manifesto for middle England. Although Etzioni has sought to distance himself from such views (Smith, 1996), there appears to be insufficient recognition that the traditional two parents family is no longer the dominant family form. Communitarians also appear to overlook evidence that the traditional family can be the site of women's oppression and that domestic labour is exploitative. Further, as feminist writers have argued (see, for example, Fraser and Lacey, 1993) policies designed to strengthen the family may inevitably involve cutting benefits to those who do not conform to this image, such as lone parents and gay and lesbian couples. And indeed this is exactly what has happened during New Labour's first term of office (Vaux, 2004).

Fourth, the inequalities that exist between communities stemming from the variable impact of global forces are seriously underplayed in the communitarian discourse. For example, the subsidiarity principle may work perfectly well in affluent communities with significant levels of social capital, but not among the most marginalised and disadvantaged. Similarly, support for local environmental campaigns to increase recycling and tackle litter problems is to be welcomed; however, comunitarians have not extended their analysis to address wider issues such as the environmental impact of unbridled economic growth and the need to promote fair trade with the Third World. Again it is the global economic analysis that appears to be off radar. Further, communitarian logic may acknowledge the local versus global connections but place them in an uncritical framework. This fails to recognise the full impact of globalisation on the community and the way in which a persons' relationship with their environment has become increasingly tenuous and disconnected.

Fifthly (and implicit in other criticisms), communitarians appear to be ambivalent to say the least about the need to try to regulate the market and seriously tackle the structural inequalities that spring from it. In fact, once elected, New Labour appears to have embraced the global market and introduced market mechanisms into welfare with considerable relish. It was argued that this was necessary to modernise the welfare state, secure inward investment in the face of international competition and the best way of influencing capital to develop more ethical and responsible policies on trade. Whether this represents the responsible face of capitalism under New Labour or what Hall (1993), referring to an earlier communitarian approach (John Major's 'Back to Basics' campaign), describes as an attempt to 'combine the impossible – respectability and enterprise' (p. 24), is a pertinent question. This will be explored further after a brief examination of an alternative discourse.

An Alternative Discourse of Transformatory Community Action – The Collective Struggle for Communities

As we noted in Chapter 5 about competing discourses on community care, an alternative to communitarianism and its voluntary self-help ethos does exist. This discourse draws on Marxist and Feminist theory concerning the potential in communities for promoting solidarity through the collective struggle against oppression. The work of Freire (1972) and Gramsci (1971) epitomises this tradition associated with transformative community action, which will be examined in greater depth in Part III, Chapter 8, thus it is only briefly sketched out here. Finding an inclusive name to capture this oppositional discourse is in itself problematic as clearly there are a number of divergent strands that can only be loosely grouped together. Hughes and Mooney (1998) use the term radical left pluralism whilst other writers, for example, Smith (1996) propose an alternative communitarianism, whilst both Popple (1995) and Mayo (2002) refer to transformative action. We have adopted the latter term here.

This discourse is concerned with drawing collectively on the resources of the community and experience of marginalised groups in organising for change. The experience of the labour movement, women's groups, disabled peoples' movement, survivors of the psychiatric system and community organisations from the voluntary sector will be very relevant here. This demonstrates a key distinction with communitarianism, in that this discourse moves the debate beyond the idea of one cohesive community to the collective struggle for communities, which are likely to be characterised by considerable social and cultural diversity. Transformative action implies a strategy of inclusion centred around collectively organised action in the community concerned at a wider level with the re-democratisation of civil society. The interests of the diverse groups involved will clearly influence the particular focus for tackling oppression.

Even from this brief resume it will be evident that the transformatory action discourse may be inherently problematic and can be criticised in a number of ways. First, although the impact of the global economy is recognised, the ability to influence powerful multinational corporations and governmental agencies through localised action may be seriously over-estimated. Although there have been some notable successes such as the campaign by Greenpeace against Shell and the pressure by disabled people over the direct payments scheme, there have been countless messy failures. In other words, local versus global issues may become somewhat romanticised. Second, unlike communitarianism, transformative action does not have a unifying set of principles and its ideological position is constructed and will necessarily be actively contested. There is thus no social glue that binds people together. Third, the divisions and conflicts between groups on the Left are not easily resolved and may undermine effective strategies for action ever developing beyond radical theorising around the coffee table. Fourth, there may be a disjuncture between the views of intellectuals and activists on the left and marginalised groups who may be understandably wary of engaging in political action given their limited resources and restricted citizenship rights. Fifth, members of indigenous local communities may reveal highly oppressive racist and sexist views that are directed at local minority groups and new migrants, especially refugees and asylum-seekers from central and Eastern Europe. These must be challenged and worked through before transformative action can be considered.

Smith (1996) in considering the values an alternative discourse might require, examines postmodernism and offers a critique of its 'pick and mix culture' as being barren and lacking 'any firm ethical base or notion of social justice on which social and political action might be built' (ch 9, p. 5). Instead he sets out five values for an alternative communitarian discourse that starts from a community-based challenge to the established order and offers 'a degree of liberation from enslavement to market forces and political vested interests' (ch 9, p. 5). The five values are

1. the sacredness of the human person, whose dignity should not be subordinate to market forces;

2. solidarity, but without resorting to romanticise or absolutise notions of community;

3. neighbourliness or fraternity to the neighbour modern society has lost;

4. justice and equality however utopian it has become; and

5. peace and social harmony between people.
   (Smith, 1996, ch 9, pp. 5–6)

These issues and how they might be translated into positive strategies for action will be explored further in the chapters on practice in Part III. According to Hughes and Mooney (1998), these competing discourses on community viz. communitarianism versus transformative action 'are part of the struggle for a new moral economy' (p. 99), which is reflected in policy reform. New Labour's programme of welfare reform seeks transformation of the community but within a discourse of moral communitarian and therefore merits closer attention.

New Labour's 'Third Way' Project to Modernise the Welfare State

During the 1990s a new 'third way' model of social policy was formulated by governments in the UK, the USA and Germany. This approach created conditions for a new form of social work to emerge: one which demanded more from those who received its services, including a requirement for better behaviour and greater contributions to the common good (Lorenz, 2001). As already noted, this development owed much to communitarian ideas as well as the intellectual influence of Anthony Giddens (Giddens, 2000). This in turn led to a modernising programme of welfare reform by Tony Blair's New Labour government in the UK and former Reich Chancellor, Gerhard Schröder in Germany, following the lead given by Bill Clinton in the US (Blair und Schröder, 1999).

The new approach to welfare reform has been characterised by three elements:

1. pro-global market, where capital remains largely unrestricted and able to move relatively freely throughout the globe;

2. pro-modernised state, cast in an image suitable for new and vibrant economies (new Europe) and free from excessive bureaucratic regulation (said to be a characteristic of old Europe); and

3. pro-welfare, once it has been successfully reformed and modernised.

(adapted from Clarke et al., 2000a; see also Jordan, 1998;
Fitzpatrick, 2001)

Giddens placed the emphasis on the integration of such factors as 'equal opportunities, personal responsibility and the mobilising of citizens and communities' (Giddens, 2000, p. 2). These were important communitarian themes that struck a resonant chord with Tony Blair and convinced him that the broader aim was to 'accelerate the move from a welfare state that primarily provides passive support to one that provides active support to help people become independent' (Blair, 2000, p. i). This meant that as a policy formula the 'third way' quickly demonstrated its communitarian credentials by reminding citizens about their social obligations and responsibilities rather than rights (Jordan, 1998). However, in terms of economic policy New Labour's 'third way' embraced the global market in a way more reminiscent of the neo-Liberalism of the New Right, resulting in 'the incorporation of critical concepts into a hegemonic discourse' (Lorenz, 2001, p. 606). Such a policy paradigm became attractive to governments across Europe who were seeking to uphold social protection and maintain solidarity, but at a lower social cost. This included the Nordic welfare states, hitherto seen as the last stronghold of universalism and solidarity (Stepney, 2006b).

In terms of practical policy, three identifiable elements can be identified

1. a moral–political communitarian crusade against irresponsibility and deviance in the community;
2. the creation of a strongly conditional welfare state based upon inclusion through labour market activation – using welfare as a trampoline to bounce people off benefits and into work or training;
3. US-style enforcement – this entails 'zero tolerance' towards 'cheats, yobs, bullies and deviants of all kinds' including 'binge drinkers' revealed in the policing of inner-city areas. Accompanied by tough responses to such problems as benefit dependency, street begging, drug abuse, truanting from school, as well as a '3 strikes and you are out' approach to crime, with an automatic prison sentence for those committing their third offence within a specified period.

According to Jordan (2000), Tony Blair 'tried to tell UK citizens a new story about themselves, one that turned their frustrations and resentments into positive action'. This story has recently been given a communitarian gloss to argue that the liberal consensus of the 1960s, which had shaped the reconstruction of the welfare state, did not give sufficient priority to the need for individual responsibility and social obligations to balance the enhancement of citizenship rights (Blair, 2004). The UK government sought to renegotiate a new social contract with 'middle England' (the hardcore supporters of the previous conservative administrations of Margaret Thatcher and John Major) telling them that their hard-earned taxes would be put to good use in a modernised and improved range of public services. In return, the individual must become a more active, responsible and self-improving citizen.

The 'third way' approach reinforces the growing emphasis on individualism rather than collectivism in social policy (Jordan, 2004). Politically it has enabled the government to claim that they could achieve better outcomes in welfare to meet improved performance targets without throwing money at the problem (Powell, 2000; Stepney *et al.*, 1999). It should be noted that within the 'third way' discourse, social justice has been redefined in communitarian terms associated with opportunity and inclusion rather than redistribution and transformation. It follows that New Labour's approach to tackling poverty through social inclusion (the latter talked of more favourably), based around labour market activation, is also promoted as a means for achieving a self-improving form of citizenship which is seen as the basis for developing responsible communities (Jordan, 2001; Powell, 2000). This is communitarian social policy and economic Liberalism operating in tandem. It has been argued elsewhere that by denying the structural basis of inequality such an approach will do little to tackle the problems in disadvantaged communities or do more than ameliorate the difficulties experienced by oppressed groups (Lund, 1999; Stepney, 2000).

In summary, the 'third way' reforms contain elements of populism and pragmatism (Powell, 2000), which as we have noted avoids a direct assault on the causes of structural inequality (Lister, 2001). It tries to capture the moral high ground of politics: combining fiscal prudence in economic policy with tough social policies to appease the political right, whilst attempting to win over the left with policies to tackle disadvantage and exclusion. However, the performance of welfare agencies has been at the cutting edge of policy reform and, whatever the political rhetoric, the government was keenly aware that it would be judged by the public on whether it could deliver.

Although New Labour committed itself to increased spending on the personal social services, along with education and health, this was made conditional on raising standards. Whilst few would dispute the need for change to improve quality and tackle problems of inefficiency, the White Paper *Modernising the Social Services* (Department of Health, 1998a), was highly prescriptive about how standards could be raised. It used reforms in education and the NHS as a template to establish a new regulatory landscape for social services with the use of performance indicators, league tables and external audit (Jordan, 2002). The problem is that whatever the league tables may say about social services performance, public perceptions are likely to be more decisively shaped by high profile cases, such as the death of Victoria Climbié. This is addressed in the next section.

'Third Way' Communitarian Policy in Action: An Attempt to Readjust the Balance Between Protection and Prevention in Child Care

The question of how to improve the care and protection of children is a topic that has understandably occupied the minds of policy makers, social work practitioners and communitarians for some considerable time.

Finding a more effective approach combining protection alongside prevention has been made more urgent by the recent tragic case of Victoria Climbié. In this section, recent policy initiatives in the area are critically assessed.

In the White Paper (Department of Health, 1998a), social services were sharply criticised for failing to promote independence and not developing sufficient preventive services. However, the White Paper was confusing about the whole question of prevention – a concept with multifaceted meanings (Hardiker *et al.*, 1991). It has been defined in relation to child care as 'the stopping or hindering of deprivation and neglect, admission into care, appearance before the courts, family breakdown and child abuse' (Hardiker *et al.*, 1991, p. 342). More recently it has been associated with an expansion of broader family support services in the UK (Pinkney, 2000), early intervention programmes which are much more developed in the US (Davis *et al.*, 2000; Nichols, 2004) and an enhanced role for the state (Clarke *et al.*, 2000a). It follows that there is a tension between two discourses on prevention:

1. one that stresses the need for carefully targeted intervention with high-risk clients where prevention is often subjugated to protection and the medical model of child abuse (Department of Health, 1998a; see Corby, 2000 for a critique); and

2. the other is a social and ecological model concerned with establishing wider support in the community to tackle problems of poverty and disadvantage at source (Jack and Jack, 2000; Holman, 1998).

In the UK, the first discourse has become the more dominant and, for example, under the 1989 Children Act, resulted in more and more resources being devoted to the child protection system at the expense of family support in the community (Jack and Stepney, 1995). This is a high profile area where ostensibly neither communitarian nor transformative action discourses appear to have exerted very much influence on policy, although clearly they are relevant if policy makers were to adopt the second discourse.

The dominance of the protection discourse has also invaded adult care services where research evidence on the high value of low level preventive services (Clark *et al.*, 1998) appears to have been misinterpreted in recent modernising policy documents as being largely suitable for high-risk clients. The broader vision concerning the need for prevention alongside protection to promote more sustainable communities is only superficially addressed. This is unfortunate as there is a strong literature in community social work of meeting this challenge through a range of local initiatives both in adult care (Cooper, 1983; Hadley and McGrath, 1984; Henderson and Thomas, 1987; Popple, 1995; Smale *et al.*, 2000), as well as child care (Department of Health, 1995; Holman, 1981, 1999; Jack and Jack, 2000; Southwell, 1994).

The balance between preventive work and child protection has recently been subject to a fundamental reassessment. This follows Lord Laming's enquiry into the death of Victoria Climbié (Laming, 2003), and a major review of services resulting in proposals for a new more holistic and better co-ordinated approach outlined in the Green Paper, *Every Child Matters: Change for Children* (Department for Education and Skills, 2004), which forms the basis of the 2004 Children Act.

The Laming inquiry highlighted a series of missed opportunities and a systematic failure by a number of agencies to prevent the death of Victoria (Laming, 2003). In *Every Child Matters,* prevention is presented as a central statement of policy intent with early intervention in the community required before a crisis point is reached. The *Every Child Matters* agenda sets out five outcomes for children that will drive child care policy in the UK: being healthy, staying safe, achieving the most out of life, making a positive contribution to the community and achieving economic well-being.

These outcomes reveal a significant communitarian influence, although they clearly resonate with the aspirations any reasonable parent or caring society would want for their children. However, they require a commitment from all key stakeholders if the preventive intentions and a more collaborative approach are to be realised (DfES, 2004). At this stage a number of concerns can be raised. First, it would appear that *Every Child Matters* is not being entirely true to its name as it is not being recommended for every child, in particular, those whose needs have already been identified and services set up. This may be driven by concern for the resource implications of adopting a more universalist approach than the need to widen good practice. Second, there is some confusion about whether the intention is better co-operation rather than dismantling the barriers to genuine collaboration (Anning, 2001; Leiba, 1996). The third concern relates to the role of the voluntary sector, and changing the approach of statutory agencies could undermine the sector's partnership role (www.zerotonineteen.co.uk/articles/May2005). For example, the role of Sure Start and other local community projects could be relegated to tendering and delivery only. Allied to this is a fourth concern about the continuing use of the market and whether the independent sector can fully embrace a culture of prevention given the limited experience of this approach in that sector and its uneasy fit with commercial imperatives.

Overall, there is a genuine fear that although the structures for a more preventive approach have been established by the *Every Child Matters* programme and guidance on the 2004 Children Act, in practice prevention will still be prioritised in terms of children assessed as being most at risk. The structural changes proposed will place prevention centre stage but the potential for transformation might be tempered by agencies continuing to operate within a protection discourse. Communitarian and to a lesser extent transformational ideas have clearly helped to shape the new policy in child care, for example, by setting out the nature of mutual obligations. However, the preventive potential has been undermined by other political realities associated with limited resources, ambitious performance targets, restricting access only to those considered high risk and the continuing emphasis on the market. The reshaping of social work in line with these requirements has also been occurring and this will be explored in the next section.

The Reshaping of Social Work – A Paradox at the Heart of the 'Third Way'

A number of questions can be raised in response to this analysis about the extent to which social work has been reshaped by New Labour's 'third way' modernisation project. One way of approaching this issue is by recognising a central paradox at the heart of the 'third way' – how to balance measures for inclusion in the community, with those for enforcement through acti-vation, social protection and raising standards. As we have already noted, the enforcement of moral standards and inclusion measures, whilst osten-sibly strengthening communitarian obligations, can in fact weaken them if these are enforced in a punitive and authoritarian way.

This paradox points to a more fundamental reworking of the relationship between the state and its citizens underpinning the movement towards the new modernised but conditional welfare state. Social workers have been placed very much in the front line (or firing line) required to balance communitarian inclusion with enforcement and protection. According to Jordan (2001), the old universal welfare state in the UK was 'bureaucratic, regulated and rule bound, whilst New Labour's modernised welfare state is concerned with throughput, achievement (measured by meeting targets) and change. The old relied on control to try and restrain class conflicts, the new is built on motivation and mutual respect. The old claimed but failed to treat everyone equally, the new is premised upon choice, opportunity and responsibility (adapted from Jordan, 2001, p. 540).

The paradox highlights something of an Achilles heel in the 'third way' modernisation project and one that has already produced a serious problem with a very practical cutting edge. For example, in the UK the government soon found that it could not fully trust professionals working in the public sector or the trade unions. Many social workers were sceptical about the reforms, and some were seen to be too closely associated with the old order (commitment to old Labour-style socialism) or too sympathetic to transformational change and thus prone to question and challenge the new neo-liberal/communitarian orthodoxy. In the event, fragmentation and constraint became a by-product of reform, and the problem of professional autonomy was addressed by the introduction of performance targets, national service standards and a league table culture. Social services departments, where the majority of UK social workers are employed, were subject to periodic appraisal and awarded star ratings. Failure (signified by a zero star rating) could ultimately result in state services being taken over and run by a private company. This not unnaturally created tensions and further resistance from staff, resulting in variable compliance. Staff in the voluntary sector were subject to parallel scrutiny through the introduction of contracts and service agreements (Scott and Russell, 2001).

This problem according to Jordan with Jordan (2000) is that it produces yet another paradox where non or partial compliance creates an 'implementation gap' in 'third way' policy. At the heart of this gap is a more fundamental crisis of solidarity within the welfare state (Lorenz, 1997), which expresses itself as a more visible identity crisis amongst front-line social workers. Social work traditionally promoted 'the moral message of adjustment and integration... upon which the stability of society depended' (Lorenz, 2001, p. 606). However, that moral message has now been weakened paradoxically by exactly the new neo-liberal and communitarian methods used to promote it. In the UK, social work has been systematically reshaped and repositioned during the past decade by market and managerial imperatives (Stepney, 2000), including US-style care management, such that 'the capacity for professional discretion and judgement has been replaced by routinised procedures... dominated by business plans and budgets' (Jones, 1996, p. 1).

The effect on front-line practitioners and managers, as practice 1 below illustrates, can be interpreted as one of deskilling to meet financial priorities producing feelings of ambivalence and a sense of uncertainty (Stepney and Ford, 2000). Not surprisingly many staff feel overworked and undervalued – with modest pay and demanding working conditions identified by the significant number who leave not only social work, but allied professions such as nursing and teaching within a few years of professional training (Salt, 2001). Top-down regulation and targeting imposes a false consensus rather than creating conditions for negotiation and mutual respect and, therefore, in the long term seem destined to failure. The reshaping of social work has been achieved by the imposition of a rather

---

Practice Focus 1

I am supervised by my manager but the person I need to see most, and this is no reflection on my manager, is the Finance Officer. As the culture and nature of my work has changed, so 'my speak' and my attitude has changed. At the end of the day the last thing I want on my epitaph is 'he filed the last invoice', because that is what it feels like, you know. Before you could measure someone's worth as a team leader . . . by the quality of supervision and things like that which we had and would talk about. Now you feel that you are your own kind of business unit, your own enterprise.

(views of a front-line UK social services manager, cited in Harris, 2005)

What is your immediate response to the views of the manager cited above?

If you reflect on your own practice, can you identify points of commonality and difference with the manager's position. What steps do you feel social workers can take to prevent practice from becoming dominated by budgets and business plans?

---

simplistic and conservative moral communitairian logic. And yet hitherto professional staff have been unable to suggest any convincing alternatives that will improve performance.

The result of this reshaping of welfare priorities, very much in the mould of new labour's 'third way', has been a movement towards creating more 'lean and mean' welfare states across Europe. The reconstruction of social work in the mould of being 'more demanding, more controlling and more coercive' (Jordan with Jordan, 2000), the parameters of 'tough love' practice, becomes a necessary part of this development.

The Reconstruction of Social Work as 'Tough Love'

The modernisation and reform of the welfare state, as set out above, has had far-reaching consequences for all UK citizens irrespective of whether they are practitioners, service users or carers. New Labour's adoption of moral communitarianism as a policy pill means that it now treats the majority of citizens in ways that are quite similar to how social work treated its clients in the universalist heyday of the post-war welfare state. According to Ducklow (2003), 'promoting individual responsibility, self sufficiency and choice to promote a self-improving form of citizenship' (in Jordan, 2004, p. 9). If communitarian logic is imposed in an authoritarian way through centrally determined targets rigorously enforced and the message is 'self-improvement or be damned', then it quickly becomes self-defeating.

Not everyone will find it easy to become one of New Labour's self-improving citizens. For example, poor and marginalised groups, like new migrants especially refugees and asylum-seekers, and many service users in the fields of mental health, substance abuse and child protection now receive much harsher and more conditional forms of treatment (Dominelli, 2002). This highlights that social work is now very much associated with risk assessment and resource management, and the protection of vulnerable adults and children at risk (Parton *et al.*, 1997). It is ironically no longer directly involved in the more enabling and preventive work in the community associated with cultural processes of inclusion (Holman, 1998). In short it may be argued that social work has at best lost its way, and at worst effectively had its soul stripped out (Butler and Drakeford, 2001). This new form of practice may be referred to as 'tough love' (Jordan, 2001).

'Tough love' as a prescription for a new style of practice has emerged in recent years and reflects a slogan which is consistent with this more demanding form of social policy (Jordan, 2001). However, it is not quite as clear-cut as its name suggests. The 'tough' element in tough love requires social workers to be challenging, assertive and more demanding of those that seek their help. But this is not something new. In fact practitioners have always balanced their caring and support role with the need for monitoring, protection and where necessary control, what might be termed managing the 'social' (Donzelot, 1988). What has changed under the guidance of 'third way' policy makers is the style of intervention and the extent to which the policing function dominates practice objectives at the expense of other priorities.

Here New Labour has once again looked to the US for a model and found merit in the communitarian approach designed to turn passive service users into independent, responsible and active citizens. Public sector social work has had to toughen-up, but unlike in Wisconsin, where black single mothers might be persuaded to give up their rights to social benefits in return for something like a one-off payment of US$1000 (Stepney, 2000), hitherto in Europe the state has rather modest returns to show for its efforts to change practice. The 'love' dimension is more closely associated with social work's historical befriending tradition, and reminiscent of a story or critical incident concerning a young hospital social worker:

Practice Focus 2

one day I was called down to a ward where an elderly gentleman, to be precise – a vagrant, someone who would now be referred to as a rough sleeper – had come into the hospital out of the cold, found an empty bed and climbed in for a sleep. He had been later discovered by a nurse and the doctor had been called and . . . fearing that he may prove troublesome the duty social worker was called. I was on duty that day and went down to the ward. I went over to the bed, pulled the curtains around to give some privacy and attempted to gently wake him. He stared into my eyes, smiled and asked me what my profession was. On hearing that I was a social worker he took my hand and whispered that he remembered the time when social work could be described as 'the comfort of strangers' and promptly went back to sleep.

(The young social worker was of course one of the co-authors) Please consider a story or critical incident from your own practice . . . something perhaps that made you stop and think because it raised moral–political issues.

At this stage just describe the incident in a similar way to the story set out above. Can you begin to locate the incident in its appropriate theoretical, policy and community context. What theory and policy help to inform the incident? What aspects of community come into your story – in the above incident was the vagrant in search of community and found some comfort and security in the hospital? How is your incident likely be viewed by different stakeholders – your manager, colleagues, other service users etc? These may be termed the dominant discourses surrounding the incident.

Please keep your notes as they will be helpful and extremely relevant for the exercise on critical practice, page 172 towards the end of Chapter 9.

Incidents such as this remind us of how social work was once seen as 'the comfort of strangers' and captured beautifully by John Clarke in his analysis of the historical development of the profession (see Clarke and Cochrane, 1998). This has subsequently become a casualty of the policy developments referred to above, such that the concept of 'love' in contemporary welfare may be extremely problematic. Perhaps surprisingly there would appear to be little place for it in New Labour's moral communitarian discourse except in relation to the motto 'love thy civic obligations rather than thyself' and even 'ask not what your community can do for you' (Lund, 1999). Part of the problem is the limited number of contemporary examples of such practice outside of the voluntary sector in the UK and the 'third sector' in other European countries. Further, counselling and non-directive approaches have followed a similar path and been taken up by other professions, such as nursing and psychology. Combining toughness with compassion, street credibility with social concern and integrating different methods to achieve negotiated change are fast becoming qualities that are in rather short supply, in social work as in many other caring professions.

Summary and Conclusion

In this chapter, we have examined the way communitarian ideas have impacted on social policy and informed New Labour's 'third way' modernisation of the welfare state. Communitarianism has been subject to critical appraisal and contrasted with an alternative discourse based upon transformative action. The importation of communitarian principles into contemporary policy debate has led to the remaking of community based upon notions of partnership and collaboration that are designed to help the state manage socially differentiated populations and problematic communities. The communitarian pill is seen as having the potential to heal long established social divisions and conflicts based upon race, class, gender and so on. This has been illustrated in relation to child care, to re-establish the balance between protection and prevention following the tragic death of Victoria Climbié, and more generally the reshaping of social work as 'tough love'.

However, the imposition of moral communitarianism into policy making has created a paradox, in that the values of mutuality, self-reliance and self-responsibility become seriously weakened if they have to be enforced by authoritarian methods of control. And the use of targets and a league table culture creates yet another paradox, where partial or superficial compliance creates an implementation gap and one that ironically coincides with the identity crisis currently being experienced by front-line practitioners. To understand this better, we need to examine the way the policy agenda combined with other trends has impacted on the theory and practice of social work in the community – a central theme that will be examined in greater depth in Part III.

Part III

Social Work and the Community: From Theory to Practice

The third and final part of the book is concerned with practice. It examines how the remaking of community within the new policy discourse provides a backdrop to the theory to practice debate in community-based social work. In Part II it was argued that New Labour's modernisation project has created a policy paradox: on the one hand idealised representations of community have become the basis for promoting a more active, responsible and self-improving form of citizenship, whilst on the other the remaking of community reflects anxieties about disorder, protection and control. It was also noted that in such a bracing policy climate wider concerns about inequality and injustice become displaced by an emphasis on opportunity, inclusion, 'choice' and respect.

Practitioners have been subjected to competing pressures and claims both from policy makers to meet inclusion and efficiency targets, the global market to reduce social costs, as well as service users and community members who justifiably expect high quality services. This contested agenda has reshaped social work practice and influenced the professional culture that sustains it, epitomised by the notion of 'tough love'. The view practitioners have of themselves is now characterised by uncertainty, and their everyday practice has become dominated by the need to manage risk rather than promote social justice (Fitzpatrick, 2001). More generally social work reflects the dilemma of being unable to resolve many of the problems it identifies in the community, in its theory and practice (Hugman, 2005). Community-based practice must compete for recognition and resources on professional agendas and develop its theoretical approach. The chapters in Part III will explore this within an international context.

In Chapter 7 we examine the current identity and status of community social work. There has been a reawakening of interest in community-based intervention methods across the spectrum of health and social care.

However, in the post-Climbié climate of *Every Child Matters* (DfES, 2004) and more recently *Our Health, Our Care, Our Say* (DoH, 2006a), practitioners will be required to give greater emphasis to prevention and collaborative working, but balance this within increasingly proscribed protection protocols. Chapter 7 explores how this might be achieved in practice drawing on a range of theory and research evidence. However, it is argued that the creative use of theory and a continuing commitment to justice in the community may be more important than reliance on protocols and technical skills.

Chapter 8 focuses on community work, its theory and practice. There have been many new developments and projects in the field where community workers have played a key role in supporting disadvantaged communities to tackle exclusion. However, meeting centrally determined inclusion targets may create a familiar dilemma for workers – how to balance this requirement with the expressed needs of increasingly diverse local communities. Further, the traditional change agent role may be compromised by too close adherence to the modernising policies of the state and its neo-liberal agenda. The chapter will examine how community work, in its theory and practice, seeks to reconcile such competing expectations and retain a wider commitment to justice, diversity and change.

Finally, Chapter 9 assesses future possibilities for community-based social work in an international context. As we move further into the twenty-first century not for the first time social work appears to be at the crossroads. Hence, making predictions about its future direction is likely to be a particularly hazardous exercise. Drawing on the work of Hugman (2005), the chapter explores this in the context of two competing responses to the current dilemma: on the one hand has been the 'search for certainty' in evidence-based practice designed to increase effectiveness, whilst on the other is the 'search for uncertainty' in postmodernism that captures the growing fragmentation and difference found in so many communities. This theoretical debate provides the backdrop to the development of what is referred to as critical practice. In Chapter 9 two versions of critical practice are explored – one combining a structural analysis with elements of critical postmodernism (Fook, 2002) and the other based on critical realism that seeks to be sensitive to subjective experience but views this within the context of dominant social structures (Houston, 2001). By drawing on research findings from the international literature it is argued that critical practice offers a progressive and emancipatory way of working in the community and managing the contradictions that emerge – responding to concrete problems and community needs whilst being critical of the structures that contribute to the production of those problems.

7

The Theory and Practice of Community Social Work

Community is back in vogue as a context, method and as a level of intervention.

(Mizrahi, 2001, p. 176)

Introduction

There is a certain ambiguity about the current identity and status of community social work (CSW). This in part reflects a paradox concerning limitations in the predictive capacity of social work to resolve many of the problems it identifies in the community, in its theory and practice (Hugman, 2005), at a time when, as the above quote notes, methods of community intervention are being brought back into use. CSW has undergone a transformation from the pioneer days of small patch teams being set up by local authorities in the 1980s (Cooper, 1983) alongside preventive projects in the voluntary sector (Holman, 1981), to become part of a process of social inclusion and neighbourhood renewal (Popple, 2006a). However, underlying such development is a tension about the changing relationship between the state and its citizens. In particular, whether the modernised state can promote change at the local level in favour of marginalised groups, and develop preventive policies for collaboration and inclusion whilst resisting pressure for more enforcement and control (Stepney, 2006a).

This tension points to a paradox at the heart of CSW. On the one hand, it has sought to foster a sense of social responsibility reflected in its professional culture and commitment to social justice – such as, setting up new services and promoting initiatives for inclusion and change; whilst on the other, it is working at the front line in local agencies where ultimately opportunities for meeting such aims may be limited and highly proscribed. It follows that problems of inadequate resources and support

in the community, poor infrastructure services, fragmentation of community networks and so on, may all come within a workers' remit but often
remain frustratingly beyond their capacity to solve. This contradiction
has traditionally been resolved by stressing the innovatory nature of the
work, its emphasis on prevention and commitment to empowerment
through the mobilisation of community members. However, another path
to resolving this dilemma is revealed by evidence that in the last 25 years or
so community-based approaches have come of age and become a respected
activity moving 'from outside to inside the citadel' (Popple, 2000, p. 113).
This raises a fresh dilemma associated with social legitimation and the
incorporation of CSW's more radical agenda for change, suggesting that
development has been largely conditional and dependent upon the politics of the state (Popple, 2006a).

As social work entered the new millennium, there has certainly been a
reawakening of interest in the development of community-based interventions, especially for health and social-care professionals (Mizrahi, 2001).
This is reflected in proposals to enhance partnership working and develop
more sustainable communities. Collaboration with health professionals
and partnership work with staff in voluntary agencies and a range of
community members increasingly shape professional agendas. Nonetheless, as noted above, practitioners must now practice in a policy paradox
and balance measures for prevention with procedures for risk assessment,
protection and control (Jordan, 2004). As policy has become more prescriptive and target driven, reflecting managerial and marketised imperatives,
there is an increasing need to find creative solutions and establish new and
more inclusive partnerships with a diverse range of community members
(Heenan, 2004). The practitioners' dilemma is that the creative potential of the latter may be undermined by an overemphasis on the former,
with practice becoming increasingly shaped by efforts to meet government
targets.

One of the essential appeals of CSW is that it has the potential to match
the aspirations of those in the community, who want to be empowered
and participate in local decision making, with those in government seeking
ameliorative reform. Although there is clearly some common ground here,
the former is ultimately concerned with emancipatory change, whilst the
latter draws on the more conservative tradition of restoring or rebuilding
community. The result perhaps inevitably is often disappointment on
both sides. Thus the development of CSW, following publication of the
Barclay report (Barclay Committee, 1982), has been littered with high
hopes, modest achievements and some messy failures (Sawdon, 1986).

In this chapter, a rigorous attempt will be made to set out the theoretical
knowledge base, methods and models of CSW, acknowledging that the
way theory informs social work practice is necessarily contested. The key

themes, issues and dilemmas facing the practitioner will be analysed in the context of developing collaborative working partnerships with other professionals, local service users and community members. Policy provides an important context and influence on the theory to practice debate and this will be briefly considered first.

The Policy Context

As has been noted in Chapter 6, economic globalisation, combined with the increasing marketisation and managerialisation of public services, creates new patterns of exclusion and inequality in the community. However, rather than tackle exclusion direct New Labour's modernisation policy constructs idealised notions of community where collective concerns about inequality give way to arguments about individual responsibility, opportunity and choice. Individualism and subsidiarity have all but displaced collectivism and universalism as principles of policy making in the UK, and this clearly has important implications for CSW.

In theory, such a policy context still provides scope for social workers to promote inclusion by moving beyond the modernising rhetoric and developing

- the preventive potential of public services (Hadley and Leidy, 1996);

- work in collaborative partnership with health professionals and other public sector staff, voluntary agency workers and community members; and

- encourage initiatives to support and enhance informal community development and work alongside a range of community members.

However, in practice this may prove quite difficult unless practitioners understand the nature of this wider policy paradox and are able to exploit opportunities whilst simultaneously managing the constraints now imposed on all welfare agencies. This will mean practitioners orientating themselves more clearly in the direction of community initiatives, so that they become proactive about community development and resist the tendency to reproduce regimented, residualised and reactive services (Heenan, 2004). It is therefore essential that practitioners do not uncritically embrace New Labour's 'performative policy rhetoric' (Mann, 2006, p. 85), and make over-optimistic assumptions about the nature of 'community' but appreciate the difficulties alongside the potential of integrating formal services with informal resources at the local level. Collaboration has increasingly played an important role both in policy making as well as practice.

The move towards greater collaborative working can be situated within a much longer policy shift associated with de-institutionalisation and de-segregation (Payne, 1995). The change from institutional to community-based care (Barr *et al.*, 1999; Sibbald, 2000) meant that the demarcations and hierarchical relations between professions were neither sustainable nor appropriate. New more collaborative ways of working that crossed professional boundaries had to be created, in order to allow a more flex-ible approach to care delivery in the community (Malin *et al.*, 2002). Some commentators have referred to the task of collaborative working as analoguous to building social capital and contributing to the stock of mutual understanding and values that help bind the social fabric of a community together (Putnam, 2000). But as was noted in Chapter 6, such communitarian ideas remain contested and do not adequately acknowl-edge the structural dimension of community problems. As part of the task of setting out the theoretical knowledge base and methods under-pinning contemporary practice, it is important to examine the road taken following the publication of the Barclay report (Barclay Committee, 1982). In the early 1980s an attempt was made to move social work practice deci-sively in the direction of CSW, to produce a more integrative and inclusive approach, and this will be the focus of the next section.

The Development of Community Social Work Post Barclay – Seeking the Less Travelled Road?

Although community-based interventions can be traced back to the nineteenth-century settlement movement, CSW as it emerged post Barclay revealed a number of key features that were highly contested. For example, the Report recommended that CSW should become a central feature of social services provision and social workers should seek to integrate formal services with informal networks of support. However, subsequent research quickly exposed a serious weakness in the analysis informing this central recommendation, in that those in greatest need frequently had inade-quate or non-existent informal networks of support (Abrams *et al.*, 1989; Oakley and Rajan, 1991) or in the current vogue, low levels of social capital (Putnam, 2000). Thus, a compelling case for implementation was under-mined by inadequate research evidence. This was quickly seized upon by opponents who saw CSW as misguided, naïve and romantic, and ulti-mately trying to swim against the rising tide of social change (Pinker, 1982). From this perspective communities low on social capital would need more than 'a kiss [from a CSWer] to be awakened' (Van de Veen, 2003, p. 580).

In seeking a definition of CSW, comparisons are sometimes made with community work, as both appear to share common theoretical assumptions, methods and core skills. However, it is important to acknowledge a fundamental difference in orientation. Community work is concerned with tackling injustice and inequality by organising people and promoting policy change at the local level, all of which is likely to find expression in collective action (Popple, 1995, See also Chapter 9). On the other hand, CSW is concerned with developing more accessible and effective local services (Smale *et al.*, 1988) and attempts to find alternative ways of meeting the needs of individual service users. Both approaches, of course, seek to build on indigenous skills and utilise a range of local resources rather than import them from outside the community (Mayo, 1998).

The Barclay Committee recognised that the vast majority of care in the UK is provided informally and much of this work, about 65% according to recent survey data (OPCS, 2002), is provided by women in their role as informal carers. It is difficult to determine how much this saves the state. In the case of frail older people in the Gateshead care scheme, research has estimated that the average cost per case incurred by social services, the NHS and society as a whole was about £8800 per year (at 1981 prices), of which something like £5000 represented the costs borne by informal carers, resources consumed by the older person themselves and included a housing allowance (Challis *et al.*, 1991). Consequently, the potential for CSW to reinforce a discourse of care informed by traditional gender roles and a cost-saving imperative has been a continuing point of concern (Twigg, 1998). In other words a patriarchal discourse has shaped not only models of care but frequently forms of support as well.

The Committee advocated new forms of collaborative partnerships between formal service providers and community members in the provision of care, but surprisingly underestimated the need for basic community development (Batten, 1967; York, 1984). As noted above, without attention to such detail it would prove impossible to distinguish between those communities where a CSW approach might work, by building upon existing networks, and those more fragmented areas where this would be much more difficult to achieve because no such networks existed. Predictably, there is often an urgent need for CSW in neighbourhoods like the latter. However, these ideas have always been contested. At the time when the report was being written, the Committee was fraught with tensions between Robert Pinker (Professor of Social Work at the LSE and a traditionalist), who was very sceptical and dismissive of CSW, and Roger Hadley (Professor from Lancaster University and a more radical thinker committed to community action), who argued that the report didn't go far enough in terms of devolving responsibility and power (Barclay Committee, 1982). The essential difference between these two visions of social work is captured in Table 7.1 below.

Table 7.1 A comparison of traditional and community-oriented approaches to social work

Characteristics of traditional approach	Characteristics of community approach	Changes required for community approach
Reactive Practitioner reacts to demands for service made when the situation has deteriorated and the user's network can no longer cope	*Preventive / proactive* Practitioner intervenes before a service is demanded and before the situation has deteriorated and the user's network can no longer cope	1. Reduction of reactive responses, replaced by proactive intervention 2. Reduction of case-by-case approach based on work of individual professional 3. Close interaction with the local community
Services at arm's length Professional practice is influenced by bureaucratic and institutional norms, is often predefined by department programmes and is completely monopolised by numerous and pressing demands of individual clients.	*Services close to the community* Professional practice is defined by the living conditions and environmental situation of service users, community members and their social surroundings.	1. Variability and flexibility in the method of conceiving, realising and evaluating local programmes 2. Individuals are considered in the round, not compartmentalised by programme 3. Recognise importance of informal networks 4. Sharing of professional responsibilities
Based on professional responsibility The practitioner is entirely and exclusively responsible	*Based on shared responsibility* The practitioner shares responsibility with	Practitioners replace, in part, their direct responsibilities by activities supporting

for the solution to the user's problems	citizens and / or natural helpers	others who assume part of these responsibilities
Centred on the individual client The only target of intervention is the individual client. Evaluation is directed mainly at his/her internal problems and the degree of pathology	*Centred on the social network* The target of intervention is the social network, including the client's. Evaluation centres on the distribution of responsibility and capacities to adapt	The practitioner needs to develop skills to evaluate the weight of responsibility experienced by the principal carers, to support them and to identify and elicit the support of potential users and non-users.

Translated and adapted from training documents prepared by Professor Jerôme Guay, Université Laval, Quebec.
Source: Hadley *et al*., 1987, pp. 8–9.

As Hadley, Holman and others have noted, CSW as it developed during the 1980s was a loose knit collection of different interest groups that took a variety of forms. However, the above table reveals that community-based approaches have a number of common organisational features, for example, a stress on working with people to develop their informal networks; emphasis on early intervention; a concern with preventive action; the desire to utilise and enhance local resources; and ultimately the empowerment of community members for the common good (Hadley *et al*., 1987; Holman, 1993; Smale *et al*., 1988).

During the 1980s the state began to experiment with CSW projects included decentralising services into small 'patch' teams, developing more integrative services and promoting a degree of community (and user) participation. One way of implementing this approach was to adopt a patch system of locally based staff serving relatively small populations of say 12–15,000 people. Various patch models emerged in such places as Normanton in West Yorkshire, East Sussex, Islington and Humberside (see Beresford and Croft, 1986; Cooper, 1983; Smale *et al*., 1988). The staff in a patch team were likely to include two or three professional social workers, community care workers, occupational therapists as well as local people employed on a paid and unpaid basis, as carers, street wardens, home helps and so on.

Despite evidence of effectiveness (see later), by the early 1990s CSW staff began to experience the same forces of fragmentation and exclusion that had been affecting the communities in which they worked. According to Hadley and Leidy (1996), this was a consequence of 'the conjunction of central government policies which combined to reduce local authority autonomy, cap spending, prescribe essential separate services for children and other users and introduce market mechanisms into social care' (p. 825).

Holman (1993) suggests three reasons for the marginalisation of CSW from mainstream practice:

1. first, the media focus on child abuse post-Cleveland (the inquiry controversially brought the issue of child sex abuse and problems of diagnosis into the public eye – see Jack and Stepney, 1995) and persuaded social services departments to concentrate resources on statutory interventions;

2. second, the belief that CSW would undermine efforts to improve the status of the profession; and

3. third, the growth of managerialism which promoted a more centralised and marketised approach.

It is significant to note that during the 1990s the debate about CSW was also influenced by two further developments. The movement for enhancing citizenship rights and promoting user involvement on the one hand, and the emergence of care management with the social worker redesignated as a care manager on the other. Whilst in theory these two developments were mutually reinforcing and consistent with producing a needs-led service, in practice they have been fraught with contradictions. This is principally because the system of care management developed by local authority social service departments in the UK contained an inbuilt tension between empowerment and cost containment (see Chapter 5 for a more elaborate account of this). To understand the situation CSW found itself in, we need to develop a more extensive theoretical framework, and this is the focus of the next section.

A Theoretical Framework for Community Social Work

At one level CSW might be said to be informed by a very broad range of theory associated with systems theory, community networking and theories of empowerment. CSW does not owe alliegence to any one theoretical model but rather uses theory in an integrative and somewhat eclectic way. CSW is not the only method that uses theory in this way, and as Payne (2005a) notes, similar views have been advanced about task-centred practice. However, it is worth looking at the theoretical elements in a little more depth.

Systems theory appears to have wide applicability to practice and an ecological approach seems especially relevant to working with different groups in the community. Unlike earlier unitary versions of systems theory (Pincus and Minahan, 1973), eco-social work 'incorporates analysis of structural causes of disadvantage and includes full consideration of wider support networks beyond the nuclear family' (Jack and Jack, 2000, p. 93). An eco-systems approach encourages the practitioner to recognise that problems arise out of 'a poor fit between a person's environment and her/his needs, capacities, rights and aspirations' (Germain and Gitterman, 1996). Community-based practitioners will seek to focus on transactions within and across systems and seek more sustainable rather than 'quick fix' solutions (Henriques, 2005). In practice, this means working holistically with service users recognising that change in one part of a system will influence activity in another – for example, strengthening the support network is likely to have a positive impact on a users' home situation or micro system. If as Henriques (2005) notes, 'individuals and their environment can never be understood separately' (p. 5), then the application of an eco-systems model leads logically towards the theory of networking.

A network may be seen as a 'system or pattern of links between points which have particular meanings for those involved' (Seed, 1990, cited in Payne, 2005a, p. 156). It is often helpful to identify a service users' network in the community and links with various agencies as a basis for assessing the right blend of formal and informal support. Social workers may be required to engage with networks in one of three ways: 'identify them, consult with them and, cynics might say, they will have to create them' (Coulshed and Orme, 2006, p. 276). Smale argues that it is the quality of the relationship between people in a network that is important and the processes the worker engages in which determine the objectives of CSW (Smale *et al.*, 1988).

One approach to networking which seems particularly applicable is referred to as network construction. A brief case example (Henriques, 2005) will illustrate what is involved, where the social worker has produced a geneogram and helped Eric draw an eco-map in the diagram below. Key people are positioned according to the nature of the relationship, which may be strong, weak or stressful. Eric has a strong relationship with his foster carer and school club, a weak relationship with his parents, a conflictual relationship with his teacher and stressful relations with friends. Clearly such information requires further exploration and evaluation, but may help the practitioner assist the child and their carer to assess the quality of different relationships, and importantly, identify potential sources of help and support. The practitioner might then consider organising a meeting of the network to discuss particular issues, assist key members to draw up an action/protection plan and identify sources of further support. It is important that the practitioner understands theories of empowerment to ensure the network does not become dependent upon her/him.

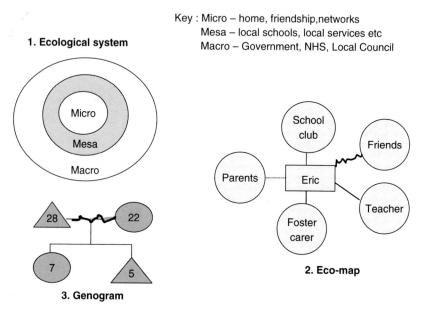

Key : Micro – home, friendship, networks
Mesa – local schools, local services etc
Macro – Government, NHS, Local Council

1. Ecological system

2. Eco-map

3. Genogram

Figure 7.1   Ecological models

Henriques (2005) based upon the work of Bronfenbrenner (1979) and Meyer (1983).

Community empowerment is a strong element in CSW and as Dominelli (2000) notes has become a 'trendy catchword that has aquired resonance across the political spectrum . . . making it an intellectually messy concept' (p. 125). It follows that empowerment is a contested term concerned at one level with societal transformation (Rees, 1991) and 'changing the relationship between rich and poor' (Berner and Phillips, 2005, p. 26), whilst at another level it is concerned with the psychology of liberation and personal change (Riger, 1993). As a multi-level construct, it may be concerned with individual development, group processes and organisational change (Forrest, 1999). However, whilst personal change may be a by-product of wider collective political action (Dominelli, 2000), CSW tends to work through individuals and groups for the wider benefit of the community as in the example of network construction above.

But empowerment theory offers us a broader context for practice and raises questions about social justice, diversity and equality that must also be addressed.

At the societal level, theory has the potential for providing a framework which connects personal experience with empowerment and 'collective action for a more just, equal and sustainable world' (Ledwith, 2005, p. 61). It must therefore offer a paradigm for practice that addresses issues of justice, difference and change. The ideas of Freire (1972) and Gramsci (1986) are relevant to both community work and CSW and helpful for constructing such a paradigm as they offer a 'critical way forward' (Popple, 1995, p. 102). However, given that a Freirean–Gramscian pedagogy is more central to community work rather than CSW practice, this will be examined more thoroughly in Chapter 8. CSW generates responses to local problems and uses Freirean–Gramscian dialogical methods of empowerment in partnership with service users and community members, although hitherto it has tended to work at the self-help/service reform end of the continuum using a range of intervention methods.

Methods of Intervention in Community Social Work

Drawing on both the authors' practice experience and the wider literature, three methods will be examined here – collaboration for community empowerment (Yoo *et al.*, 2004), eco-social models (Matthies *et al.*, 2000b) and CSW process models (Stepney and Evans, 2000). It will be found that there are points of overlap between each approach, as all are concerned with developing a more holistic, integrated and empowering model of practice. When these are taken together they provide elements of what might be termed critical practice, and this will be taken up in Chapter 9.

(i) Collaboration for community empowerment
This approach uses ideas drawn from research on collaborative practice in health and social care (Callwood, 2003; Lymbery, 1998b; Rummery and Glendinning, 1997) and community empowerment (Dominelli, 2000; Yoo *et al.*, 2004). Taken together they provide a model of collaborative practice that can be applied in various settings. Leiba (1996) states that 'Professional cultures which are shaped by long tradition and where specialists skills are

practised, can become enclaves where like-minded people reinforce shared perceptions and sustain working methods unresponsive to change' (p. 6). To counteract this practitioners will work more effectively where there is a 'process based on shared goals and philosophies, mutual respect, trust, a willingness to share knowledge, adapt, manage change, communicate openly and to take on board the realities of status, authority and power differentials.' (Leiba, 1996, p. 9). This is clearly a challenging agenda, and one where it is necessary to be confident in one's own professional knowledge base and to respect the knowledge base of others (Clatworthy, 1999).

At a policy level as noted above, collaborative working has gained the status of being '...the common sense approach...the joined up solution to the joined up problem' (Callwood, 2003, p. 2) and thus becomes 'naturalised' as part of an ideology of collaboration (Department of Health, 1998b). For it to become a reality, common understanding needs to replace tribalism and self-interest. There is a broad consensus that collaboration represents an ethical method of practice where differences are respected and used creatively to find solutions to complex problems. This concurs with Gray's vision of collaboration as 'a process through which parties who see different aspects of a problem can constructively explore their differences and search for solutions that go beyond their own limited vision of what is possible.' (Gray, 1989, p. 5). However, a number of barriers and in-built resistance may have to be overcome, such as different resource systems, accountability structures and professional tribalism (Rummery and Glendinning, 1997). For example, social workers will need to overcome role conflicts in multidisciplinary teams (Carpenter *et al.*, 2003), whilst nurses may need to throw off an 'alleged misogyny intrinsic to oppression theory and...stop acting as insidious gatekeepers to an iniquitous status quo' (Farrell, 2001, p. 32).

Translating these ideas into concrete and effective practice clearly represents a challenge. Yoo *et al.* (2004) have written about collaborative community empowerment as a six-step process in health promotion using a social–ecological model, and Lee (2001) has developed a model of empowerment in relation to working with women and children in poverty. The benefits of a community-based approach is that it can increase the capacity of a community (skills, transferable knowledge and resources) as well as empower individuals and improve the well-being and overall health of a community. Yoo *et al.* (2004) outline one example that draws upon a social–ecological model first developed by Goodman (2000). The model, as noted above, revolves around the various interactions between people and their environment at four different levels – the family/individual, community, agency/organisation and policy. This approach was applied to community organisations in New Orleans, Louisiana in 2001 in the form of a six-step process (NB: a seventh step has been added by the authors).

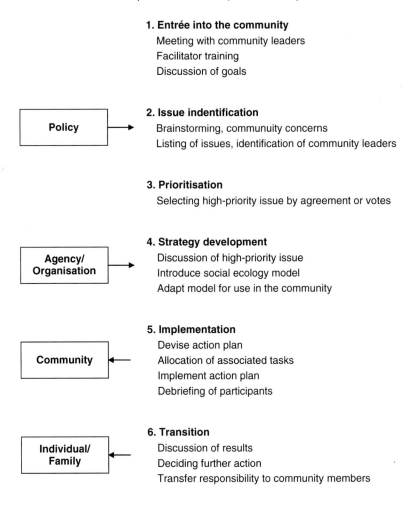

1. Entrée into the community
Meeting with community leaders
Facilitator training
Discussion of goals

2. Issue indentification
Brainstorming, communuity concerns
Listing of issues, identification of community leaders

3. Prioritisation
Selecting high-priority issue by agreement or votes

4. Strategy development
Discussion of high-priority issue
Introduce social ecology model
Adapt model for use in the community

5. Implementation
Devise action plan
Allocation of associated tasks
Implement action plan
Debriefing of participants

6. Transition
Discussion of results
Deciding further action
Transfer responsibility to community members

7. Research/Evaluation from participants and wider community

Policy

Agency/
Organisation

Community

Individual/
Family

Figure 7.2 Six step process of collaborative community empowerment
(Adapted from Table 1, Yoo *et al.*, 2004, p. 260).

The six steps of the model are fairly self-explanatory, although at each stage professional judgement and creativity will be needed to determine how to put such a plan into action and adapt it to suit the precise needs of the community in question. This will undoubtably require good communication, organisation and groupwork skills and the worker will almost certainly need to undertake other tasks in addition to those iden-tified. For example, at step 1, the initial entrée into the community, how the social worker establishes trust and credibility with different community members and groups will clearly influence subsequent developments including which issues are taken up during step 2. Making a credible job of this may literally make or break a project. Much will depend upon the nature and orientation of existing groups – in New Orleans these were well established and quite influential, whilst in other more fragmented communities the opposite may be the case. Step 2 is very much the 'storming' stage in classical groupwork processes (Tuckman, 1965), when issues are identified and leaders or potential leaders emerge sometimes as friends but also as enemies (Sawdon, 1986).

At step 3 the task of prioritising what issues are to be taken up could prove conflictual and highlight existing divisions in the community as well as points of consensus. At step 4 the introduction of a theoretical model could prove problematic unless the worker can clearly demonstrate its relevance and the benefits of using it. Step 5 involves the implementation of the action plan and may involve a combination of task and problem-solving techniques in addition to the community-organising methods identified. At step 6 the issue of transition involving an evaluation of the progress made and supporting community leaders to develop their own future action plan will indicate whether the process has succeeded in empowering the community rather than giving it a temporary boost. For this reason a seventh step, research and evaluation, not included in the original model has been added.

The four rectangles on the left hand side of the table represent the four levels of interaction identified by Goodman (2000). Policy and the organisational procedures of the agency are likely to impinge on the project and must be taken account of, which is the reason for the inward-facing arrows. The impact of the project on individuals, families and the local community is designed to enhance their capacity and thereby raise the level of social capital in the community, hence the outward-facing arrows.

In discussion of the application of the model in New Orleans, Yoo *et al.* (2004) argue that the model was well received and effective in creating the conditions for empowerment and community group facilitation. The introduction of a social–ecology model 'was well received by community members... and left a significant impact in terms of developing comprehensive and systematic strategies' (p. 264). Three out of four of the groups involved achieved their desired goals and were said to be sustained by involvement in the project – thus demonstrating that much can be accomplished in a relatively short time frame.

A number of factors can be identified which reinforce community empowerment and these can be contrasted with those that challenge it (adapted from Yoo *et al.*, 2004, p. 263).

Reinforcing factors	Challenging factors
Sound theoretical framework	Inadequate resources
Understanding of context	Slow progress due to lengthy process
Consistent purpose at meetings	Low participation
Supporting staff and community leaders	Concerns about safety
Open communication	Non-promotion in community
Staying focused and on task	Insufficient ability to respond to new information during the project
Good informal networks	Rigidity and inflexibility
Regular discussion and debriefing of staff	

These findings are consistent with those in the wider literature (Hadley and Leidy, 1996; Ohmer and Korr, 2006; Popple, 1995) and provide a useful checklist against which CSW practice interventions can be evaluated.

(ii) Eco-social models: Towards eco-criticality

Whilst ecological systems theory situate individuals in their community and sees them as interdependent with each other in a reciprocal relationship with wider environmental systems, eco-social models are much more political and highlight how ecological ideas have transformative potential (Payne, 2005a). In short, ecological ideas and the systems which support them must be placed in a wider policy context concerned with social exclusion if change for marginalised groups is to be realised (Matthies *et al.*, 2000b). This enables the environmental impact of ecological policy initiatives to be assessed including the influence on different social groups – for example, eco-feminism would assess the environmental impact on women and how social systems may proscribe certain roles in the community that are inherently oppressive.

The issue of sustainability has been addressed by a number of writers (Coates, 2003; Payne, 2005a) where our relationship with the environment may become more tenuous and disconnected in an age of globalisation. Eco-social models seek to combine diversity with social responsibility not just for the local environment but for the future of the planet. In other words, this is where social capital building, community action and Green politics potentially collide in an attempt to develop more sustainable communities. Lifestyles, jobs, relationships, housing, health and community well-being are all brought into the equation, and social work practice must rise to the challenge of relating such environmental concerns to the situation that clients and poor people generally find themselves in. In the past, the green agenda has tended to be the preserve of the middle classes, who could afford to promote and display sustainable lifestyles, but eco-social models help to highlight its relevance for marginalised groups.

In an important contribution to both comparative research and practice knowledge, Matthies *et al.* (2000b) develop an eco-social approach for tackling exclusion based upon research in three European cities – Jyväskylä (Finland), Magdeburg (Germany) and Leicester (England). The research had three broad aims:

1. to develop practice methods that enable citizens to improve their environment through community participation;

2. to provide social impact assessments drawing on social work knowledge to influence planning and political decision making around issues of sustainability; and

3. to incorporate an eco-social approach to the problem of exclusion in different European contexts and thereby contribute to the theoretical knowledge base of social work

(Adapted from Matthies *et al.*, 2000b, p. 44)

Although the research designs and strategies in each city were different, involving elements of locality development, social planning and social action, the level of collaboration encouraged 'the development of a new European model against social exclusion' (Matthies *et al.*, 2000b, p. 44) based upon social work practices in each locality. The model draws on the policies of the Green movement in Germany designed to achieve ecological sustainability, environmental sociology from Finland and the social action tradition from the UK. This produces an eco-social model of social work that may be characterised as:

● holistic in its analysis of the living environment and the local/global connections;

● practical in involving people in decision making about local policy and planning;

● theoretical in incorporating sustainability in its conception of social work practice;

- developmental in understanding exclusion as a multi-dimensional problem relating to segregation from a range of systems, relationships and environments; and

- respectful of the position of marginalised people and community members including a commitment to empowerment through social action.

What the research teams found was that instead of producing one clear-cut and universal European eco-social model applicable to any context, a number of approaches emerged with a mixture of common elements (set out above) and unique local features. So the model by definition must be flexible and adaptable without compromising its core values and commitment towards producing a fairer and more sustainable environment.

The application of an eco-social model to practice can be illustrated in relation to work with young people (Sanders and Munford, 2005); children (Henriques, 2005); children with disabilities (Jack and Jack, 2000); and older people (Stepney and Evans, 2000). The use of eco-maps and social network maps allied to a sensitivity for community development offer a valuable set of resources for working with each group and understanding the nature of the social landscape. As Sanders and Munford (2005) note, 'being able to describe all the different dimensions of relationships gave us a rich understanding of the complex and sometimes delicate balancing young people needed to engage in as they positioned themselves in their relational landscapes' (p. 201). Such insights can be supplemented with life story work, use of toys, books and pictures in direct work with children (Henriques, 2005), cultural and historical artefacts in reminiscence work with older persons, as well as more traditional methods involving interviewing.

Practice Focus 1 – Direct Work with Children (can be adapted for reminiscence work with older people focussing on a period, such as the 1930s, or when participants were 18)

Recall the family home you lived in as a child when you were 8-years old. Draw a floor plan of the living room and what you remember about the key features of the room. What do you remember about your family and the character of the people you lived with, also your best friends. Do you remember your favourite TV/radio shows, books, music and the sporting or film stars of the day?

What do you recall about the local community in which you grew up and the people who lived in it? Draw an eco-map of the local community and what you remember about its most important features.

(iii) Community social work process models

The following model draws on the work of Vickery (1983), Smale *et al.* (1988), Sawdon (1986), Mayo (1998) and can be applied to virtually any community setting. The main circle in the diagram shows the CSW process and some of the activities which might spring from it.

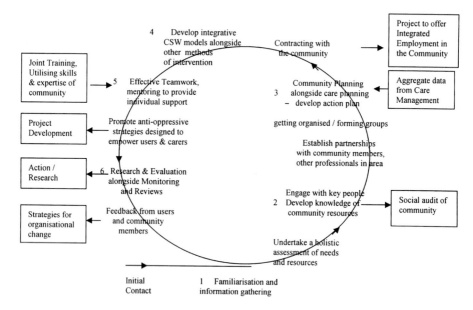

Figure 7.3 A six phase model of the community social work process
Source: Stepney and Evans, 2000, p. 113.

There are six phases to the model which to some extent overlap and may not follow in precise sequential order – for example, phase 6, the research to evaluate effectiveness, would clearly need to be set up at the outset. The six phases are

1. familiarisation and information gathering;

2. engagement and assessment;

3. organisation, planning and partnerships;

4. intervention in collaboration with community members;

5. mobilising team resources for empowerment (users and staff); and

6. research and evaluation.

The practitioner will need to adapt the model to particular situations, noting that at each stage in the process there are additional opportunities or requirements depicted by the seven rectangles, which open up new possibilities for constructive action – for example, after phase 2, it may be useful to carry out a social audit of the wider community to map out the full range of needs and resources; after phase 3, opportunities for contracting could involve setting up a project to provide employment for local people (Stepney and Davis, 2004); during phase 5, training strategies might include planning joint sessions with user groups and other community members. In certain respects the CSW model can be seen to have similar features to the six-step process introduced by Yoo *et al.* (2004) above, as well as elements of the care management process (see Chapter 5). However, there are important differences, especially the introduction of additional elements designed to assist community development and promote a more integrative model of practice.

Practice Focus 2 – The Case of Mr Beasley Alongside Peggy and Ruth Lyle

Mr Beasley is a man in his 50s with mental health problems who suffers from depression with memory loss due to earlier alcohol abuse. He stopped working about 2 years ago after the death of his wife, and now attends a horticultural project run by a local ASW one day per week. He lives alone in a high-rise flat in an area of town which suffers from environmental decay, with boarded up houses, a derelict factory and few shops and infrastructure services.

Apart from attending the project, Mr Beasley hardly goes out as he fears that he might be mugged after an incident involving some local youths last year. He is quite isolated and hardly knows any of his neighbours. The other neighbours in the block of flats include Peggy and Ruth Lyle who are disabled and also quite isolated (see Stepney and Evans, 2000, p. 107 for further details of this case) as well as a number of refugee families offered short-term emergency accommodation by the council. A Housing Association have recently taken over the management of the flats and would like to upgrade them. The council have plans to regenerate the area and funds are available to support community group activity.

How might a community social work/eco-social approach be used to good effect here?

What kind of model would you use and which local people would you seek to involve?

Do you think it would be appropriate to treat the case of Peggy and Ruth separately from Mr Beasley or could they be tackled using a combined strategy? If the latter, how might this work in practice?

Research Evidence Concerning the Effectiveness of Community Social Work

A review of the literature by Ohmer and Korr (2006) found that there were 269 journal articles published between 1985 and 2001 that focused on community-based practice. The vast majority were from the US literature and many employed qualitative designs including a rich array of case studies and ethnographic accounts. A quantitative methodology was adopted by 20 studies and only nine used an experimental design to evaluate the effectiveness of community practice interventions which were invariably found to be 'complex with multiple locations, goals and activities that makes them difficult to evaluate' (Coulton, 2004, cited in Ohmer and Korr, 2006, p. 143).

In a majority of the US studies a consensus emerged indicating that CSW practice interventions were more effective 'on the pscho-social aspects of communities, especially influencing citizen participation... and its effect on participants in terms of increasing self awareness and self esteem' (Ohmer and Korr, 2006, p. 142). The impact on the physical and economic environment was found to be mixed with some studies reporting improvements whilst many did not. These findings are by and large supported by UK research.

In the UK, although CSW appears well suited to operating in conditions of uncertainty and conflict, it has proved quite difficult to provide robust empirical evidence of effectiveness. Many initiatives were by definition small scale and localised. For example, research in Yorkshire by Hadley and McGrath (1984) suggested that if CSW initiatives were properly resourced then the long-term outcomes could be impressive. The Normanton patch team was investigated and compared with a traditional social work fieldwork team in nearby Featherstone. It was found that crisis work, including the use of emergency protection orders, were similar in both teams in year one, but reduced significantly during the second and third years of the Normanton project. In Normanton 40% of clients officially referred were known to the team as opposed to only 3% in Featherstone (Hadley and McGrath, 1984). It emerged that working with older people, using local residents as street wardens or homehelps, resulted in a lower proportion entering residential care; as well as leading to increased satisfaction with the services and improved life expectancy – findings which importantly correspond with influential research carried out in Kent during the same period by Challis and Davies (Davies and Challis, 1986; see also Chapter 5).

According to Holman (1993) partnerships based on availability, local knowledge and joint action are the essence of CSW. Social workers need to find ways of developing more effective partnerships between statutory service providers, voluntary agencies and informal carers (Holman, 1993). Research by the Children's Society, based upon its work in different child-care projects and family centres also demonstrate that this approach can be preventive – preventing crisis through strengthening communities as well as cost effective in terms of reducing the number of official referrals and statutory interventions (cited in Holman 1995). Further, research by the Department of Health (1995) suggested that families without adequate community support were being drawn into the child protection system (Gill, 1996). It is also known that economic and environmental deprivation act as 'powerful stress factors which . . . make it more difficult to be an effective parent' (Utting *et al.*, 1993, cited in Southwell, 1994). There is also evidence that families referred to family centres by social workers as a child protection strategy, have similar problems to other families from the same community and therefore should have access to the same facilities (Southwell, 1994). Moreover, there is evidence that variations in rates of child mistreatment are associated with the strength of social support networks and general poverty levels (Garbarino and Kostelny, 1992, cited in Jack, 1997).

Research evidence is an increasing requirement of government funding against a backdrop of effectiveness research provided by the movement for evidence-based practice (Sheldon and MacDonald, 1999). As we have noted, effectiveness research in community settings has tended to adopt qualitative methodologies utilising soft outcome measures, such as, changes in the attitude of participants, strength of informal networks and so on, rather than hard outcome measures to do with jobs, skills and qualifications that can be more easily quantified. Paradoxically, as Ohmer and Korr (2006) note it 'may be easier for community practice interventions to positively effect citizen participation and its effects on participants, than it is to improve complex social and economic problems in poor communities' (p. 142). This view is supported by Barr (1997) who suggests that there are few instances where CSW has solved the problems of disadvantaged communities, but many examples of increasing the self-confidence, self-respect and skills of local people. However, passing over the problems inherent in using mixed methodologies, evidence of the impact of citizen participation, although not easy to measure, may be supported by other data relating to referral trends and numbers using particular services. Further, CSW is not generally suited to experimental methods of evaluation such as random controlled trials both for ethical and practical reasons. What is critical is that, as noted in each intervention method outlined above, a research or evaluation component should be integrated into practice from the outset. The challenge is to use the models in ways that can address structural problems alongside enhancing the knowledge and skills of community members.

Summary and Conclusion

In this chapter we have explored the current identity and status of CSW. Encouragingly, since the mid-1990s, there has been a reawakening of interest in CSW, partnership working and notions of ecologically sound community empowerment in Britain, Europe and the USA. This is in part a response to the limitations of market-led, centralised services but also to a general disenchantment with new managerial methods. However, we have noted that CSW now operates in something of a policy paradox: competing for priority on professional agendas that are increasingly shaped by a centrally driven emphasis on risk assessment, protection and control of resources. Whilst collaboration with community members to achieve inclusion through the development of locally run services has received official sanction, this is unlikely to satisfy those who call for the genuine empowerment of marginalised groups. The tension between these two visions or paradigms of change has parallels with an earlier debate – between those who saw community participation as an inherently ineffectual response to the problems of poverty and disadvantage, and those who saw it as a valuable contribution in its own right (Piven and Cloward, 1972). Professionals who embrace partnership working may work on the inside to promote change and try to counteract the trend towards 'de-professionalisation, downsizing and privatisation' (Mizrahi, 2001).

CSW continues to develop, albeit in the shadow of the market economy, and Bob Holman (1999) reports the continuing relevance of this approach in Glasgow. Hadley and Leidy refer to CSW experiments in Pennsylvania State, USA (Hadley and Leidy, 1996) while Mizrahi (2001) reports on 'practitioners struggling to find creative ways to create community driven, client centred structures and infuse business orientated, social entrepreneur roles with socially compassionate and socially just agendas' (p. 183). This reminds us of both the wider context and the professional challenge. CSW uses theory in an integrative and eclectic way and has developed a range of models – with three approaches to practice explored in this chapter. The effectiveness of CSW has been demonstrated by a strong literature informed by largely qualitative research (Ohmer and Korr, 2006). This suggests that CSW increases levels of participation, whilst improving the self-confidence and self-esteem of community members. The impact on the physical and economic environment has been less clear-cut both in the US and UK.

In Europe, community-based social work as part of efforts to regenerate communities in ecologically sound ways remains popular and importantly supported by municipal agencies (Matthies *et al.*, 2000b). CSW can promote the notion of a diverse and critical community, opening up possibliities for the inclusion of marginalised groups as part of a wider struggle against oppression and exclusion. For this to happen, social workers must be prepared to travel where influential figures may fear to tread – into the cold and troubled side of the community and grapple with a complex array of messy problems and everyday realities. In undertaking such work, critical thinking in the Freirean–Gramscian tradition, the ability to reconnect theory with practice and a commitment to justice may be more important than reliance on any specific technical skills.

8

Community Work and Community Action

Introduction

The focus of this chapter is the consideration of the location and role of community work and community action in contemporary UK society. In doing this we will make links with both the historical development of social work and community work and community action's current context.

In his text *Social Work and Community Care*, Malcolm Payne makes the observation that 'Community work has a long history as an aspect of social work' (1995, p. 165). It is true to say, however, that although social work and community work address common issues and share similar themes, community work and community action are distinct and different forms of practice compared with social work. Moreover, community work and community action has been informed by a discrete body of knowledge and theory (Ledwith, 2005; Popple, 1995). Nevertheless, as we will observe social work and community work do share a common evolution and there are specific historical and contemporary links with and between the two areas.

Before moving forward it would be helpful to briefly consider what we mean by community work and community action.

Community work is a term used to describe a wide range of activity and interventions that take place in a variety of settings and usually in neighbourhoods. However, most paid community workers describe themselves as community development workers. At the same time New Labour, through a plethora of different and diverse funding streams, has increasingly been using the term community development in place of community work in order to emphasise the *developmental* aspects of the work. Both terms are used interchangeably here.

Since New Labour was elected in 1997 there has been an expansion of locally based interventions in communities and neighbourhoods and an increase in the employment of paid community development workers.

For example, the government has created the £800 million Neighbourhood Renewal Fund, available to the most deprived local authorities. In addition, the government is providing £400,000 over 3 years from a Community Empowerment Fund (over £35 million in total) for communities in each of these areas, specifically for community involvement in Local Strategic Partnerships. Further, the government has set aside £50 million to be spent over 3 years to provide small grants for community organisations in deprived areas. All these will be utilising the skills of community development. In particular, community development has been given a key role in assisting deprived communities in capacity building and in securing valuable resources. The establishment in 2006 of the Department of Communities and Local Government headed by a Secretary of State with a cabinet seat underlined the government's intention of addressing the need for cohesive communities. One of the key intentions of this department is to 'see empowered and confident communities, with higher levels of democratic participation and citizen engagement' (www.communities.gov.uk.index.asp?id=1165628 accessed 28 January 2007). Community work and community development are seen as important tools in delivering this target however they might be measured.

Community action, on the other hand, is a term that refers to activity that has evolved from communities themselves often taking an oppositional position to wider developments which affect them but which are outside of their immediate control. Examples of community action include attempting to curtail planned closures of public facilities or services such as swimming pools and schools, the redevelopment of particular areas and neighbourhoods and to prevent the development of housing and industrial plant on green field sites (Popple, 2007). A good deal of community action has taken a conflict approach to the resolution of issues, but this is often as a prelude to, or is working in tandem with, attempts to reach a negotiated position by discussion and persuasion. Tactics that are frequently deployed in community action include public meetings, demonstrations and using the media to highlight the issues of concern. The role of the paid community development worker in this scenario is more problematic. The worker who is employed by public funded bodies is likely to be required by his/her employer not to directly engage in community action that may bring them into conflict with those who pay, regulate and supervise them (Popple, 2002). It is local residents that usually undertake community action, or activists that are working for NGOs or in the voluntary sector. However, many NGOs and voluntary sector organisations receive central and local government funding and this can act as a brake on employees' activity.

There is in community work an inherent paradox where the practitioner uses a good deal of dedication and skill, not to mention charisma to balance the competing demands we have outlined. Bob Holman represents a good example of the process of this. In the process this elevates community workers to a 'different level from the expertise in individual practice' (Jordan, 2007, p. 118).

The Development of the Practice and Theory of Community Work and Community Action

Early Developments

To understand the development of the practice and theory of community work and community action, we need first to make connections with the early evolution of social work. According to Payne (2005b), the roots of social work are in nineteenth-century organisations and charities that were concerned that welfare should not create a 'dependence culture' amongst the working class. An important role undertaken by these organisations was the assessment of families and individuals in order to consider their eligibility for charity disbursements and support. For example, Octavia Hill of the London housing movement was instrumental in establishing the role of female visitors who would make assessments of families' entitlement to housing. The visitors would also assist families' plan and organise their budgets. According to Payne (2005b, p. 36), this was the beginning of 'assessment' as a bedrock of social work practice.

Particularly important at this time was the activity of the Charity Organisation Society (COS) which, founded in April 1869, was a strategic response to the increasing overlap and lack of co-operation of organisations engaged in delivering welfare. Prior to the COS there was evidence that there was in certain areas a degree of competition between charities in the intervention in neighbourhoods.

> It was said, for instance, that some churches competed with each other in gifts and food tickets, in order to increase their congregations; that such was the competition among the relief societies working with the homeless that John Burns decided to clear the Thames Embankment of all charitable societies distributing relief there.
>
> (Young, 1956, p. 93)

The COS and its affiliated organisations were the forerunners of modern-day social work (Roof, 1972). However, a number of key people within the COS became increasingly dissatisfied with the organisations' inability to satisfactorily address the need to improve the living and working conditions of the poor. One of these critics was Canon Samuel Barnett, a founder of the COS. As the Vicar of St Jude's, in Whitechapel, east London, Barnett argued that it was necessary to live and work alongside the poor in order to better understand and address the problems they faced. For Barnett, this meant undertaking the Christian mission in the areas of greatest need. Barnett argued that this intervention could best be undertaken by establishing neighbourhood settlements, which would offer educational and recreational opportunities, and certain limited welfare services to local communities. The intention was that these settlements would provide accommodation for those (usually undergraduates) who wanted to engage in face-to-face work in the communities. Following in the wake of the work of an Oxford undergraduate, Arnold Toynbee, and his colleagues, who had spent their summer vacation of 1883 living and working in Whitechapel in order to study poverty, Barnett formed the University Settlement Association. A year later he established Toynbee Hall in Commercial Road, east London, which became the first settlement in the UK.

Barnett established a trend that has continued to the present day with socially committed individuals living and working in areas of economic deprivation. Probably one of the best known of contemporary workers is Bob Holman who until a few years was employed by the Children Society, in Easterhouse in Glasgow. Holman lived and worked as a community social worker and local resident in one the most economically deprived estates in Western Europe. A Christian socialist, he has written extensively on his work with residents in the area in which he lives arguing for a society based on equality, democracy and an end to social divisions (Holman, 1976, 1988, 1998, 2000, 2001, 2003; www.community-links.org.02Holmanpp2635, accessed 23 May 2007).

Returning to the influence of Samuel Barnett, the philosophy of Toynbee Hall was one that if the poor were treated as having equal worth and respect as the rich, class barriers would cease to exist and material improvement increased. Barnett reviews the possibilities of settlement life in an article published in 1898 and recalls the influence of T. H. Green upon the 'men at universities' who were asking whether these institutions could do more for the poorest in neighbouring areas.

> They heard the 'bitter cry' of the poor; they were conscious something was wrong underneath modern progress; they realised that free trade, reform bills . . . had made neither health and wealth. They were drawn to do something for the poor.
>
> (Barnett, 1898, p. 12)

Toynbee Hall was designed to accommodate up to 14 university students and graduates, and offered those living in the neighbourhood a range

of facilities and educational classes including art and music. The Settlement proved to be influential in the early development of community-
based intervention in poor areas and had amongst its student residents
the author of the seminal 1943 Report *Social Insurance and Allied Services*,
William Beveridge, who worked at Tonybee Hall from 1903 to 1907, and
the 1945–1950 Labour Prime Minister, Clement Atlee, who worked at the
Settlement from 1909 to 1910 (Harris, 1977, p. 43). American students also
stayed at Toynbee Hall and in1887 they formed the College Settlement in
the United States of America (Rimmer, 1980, p. 2).

Within 14 years some 30 settlements based on the model of Toynbee
Hall had been established, many in university cities. The settlements were
usually residential and students and others were able to spend some of
their free time living and working in poor neighbourhoods offering a range
of educational classes and welfare services (Thane, 1996, p. 23). Under the
influence of Barnett's wife, Henrietta, women's settlements were established replicating the practice of separate university colleges for men and
women. It is more accurate to state, however, that there were mixed settlements and women's settlements. In the early days of the settlement movement, the men regarded their work in the settlements as a brief interlude
before developing a career in another sphere. Women, however, who were
faced with significant career restrictions saw settlements as offering opportunities for self-enhancement (Seed, 1973 p. 29; Walton, 1975, p. 50). As
a result, women's settlements linked with the COS in establishing for the
first time, professional social work training courses (Parry and Parry, 1979,
p. 25).

An example of a mixed settlement was that established by Waldorf and
Nancy Astor in Plymouth in 1925. Nancy Astor was the Conservative MP
for the Plymouth Sutton constituency, which included the Barbican area,
a small area of streets nestling close to Sutton Harbour at the entrance
to the River Plym. In the early twentieth century, the Barbican was a
busy fishing port, with its residents dependent on the vagaries of the
market for fish, and the catch that could be made in the English Channel
and beyond. With no welfare state, Barbican residents were constantly in
fear of poverty and destitution. Virginia House Settlement was to provide
Plymouth people, and in particular those living in the Barbican, with
education and social facilities which focused on supporting women, and
in providing assistance to children and adolescents (Popple, 2006b).

The settlement movement, which was part of a wider response to a range
of social, economic and political difficulties facing neighbourhoods in
Victorian and Edwardian Britain, contained within it the early stages in the
development of community work. The main architects of this activity were
the Anglican and Nonconformist Churches, the universities and members
of the upper and middle classes. As we have noted, charity giving and

voluntary work, such as that carried out in developing and running the settlements, was becoming established in a manner not previously seen. For example, by the mid-1880s the income of London charities exceeded that of the Swedish state and in the period between '1818 and 1840 there were 28,880 endowed charities, with a total income of £1.2 million' (Horner, 2006, p. 21). Further, a study of middle-class homes in the 1890s estimated that on average, middle-class families gave a larger share of their income to charity than any other item apart from food (Prochaska, 1980).

At this time the British social structure was dominated by two major themes: the ascendancy of the bourgeoisie and the development of the new industrial working class. The settlement movement reflected these key themes with a number of influential upper and middle-class social reformers playing a strategic role in the establishment of a new form of community-based intervention aimed at addressing poverty, and to some degree dissolving dissent between social classes. These reformers were concerned with both the social health of the locality in which they were situated, and in encouraging responsible community leadership in order to reduce social unrest. Concurrently, a stronger industrial working class was demanding a greater stake in society and through the newly established Labour Party (founded in 1900) began making inroads into the parliamentary democratic system. While it can be seen that early settlements were a pragmatic response to growing social unrest, this form of community work was in essence an example of benevolent paternalism by socially concerned philanthropists. Craig *et al.* (1982), for example, describes the Settlement movement as being

> concerned to reform and improve the character of the poor by example; it was believed that the presence of upright, articulate members of the more prosperous classes might simultaneously provide role models for the poor and help to engineer some cautious social reforms.
>
> (Craig *et al.*, 1982, p. 1)

Whilst Craig *et al.*'s view is a valuable one, it can be argued that Barnett and his fellow reformers did not fully accept the dominant orthodox explanations of poverty and were driven by a wish to collectivise provision for the poor. Simultaneously, the Settlement movement influenced the thinking of some key social and political reformers like Atlee and Beveridge, who had spent some time working in Settlements and were later to help establish the framework for the workings of the post-war welfare state.

Although a schism emerged in the late nineteenth century between early forms of social work and the launch of community work, there continued a close link between the two during the twentieth century. We mentioned in Chapter 1 the prominence given to development in the reports by Younghusband (1959) and Seebohm (1968). Both of which emphasised the benefits of the notion of community and the role of community work in delivering a more comprehensive service to disadvantaged communities and individuals.

The Colonial Influence

It was the role of community work and in particular community development in the developing world that was to raise the profile of the activity in the UK during the mid-twentieth century. In the early part of the century, the British Ministry of Overseas Development and the Colonial Office had deployed Mass Education (the forerunner to community development) as a way of spreading the influence of Britain in the far-flung colonies. The purpose was to act as a bulwark to the growth of communism and to assist the maintenance of the British economic and political imperialist agendas. However, there is evidence that in some areas, and in particular the Gold Coast (now Ghana), these strategies had the reverse effect and fired up the independence movements (Mayo, 2008).

By the 1960s a group of leading educators such as T. R. Batten (1957, 1962, 1965, 1967) employed in community development by the Ministry of Overseas Development had returned to the UK and were engaged in shaping British community work. In 1966 this group had established the international quarterly *Community Development Journal* that continues today as arguably the leading journal in this field and which has done much to contribute to the theory and practice of community development internationally (Popple, 2006c).

The Developing Competing and Contested Theoretical Base

With post-war reconstruction and development gaining momentum, and the need to address the issues thrown up by urban renewal and redevelopment, community work had, by the late 1960s, begun to establish itself as a recognisable form of state-funded practice. In parallel, the activity was developing a competing and contested theoretical base. It was clear by then that the theories informing community work were falling into two broad camps or approaches, which have continued until the present day.

One approach can be interpreted as the reformist approach. This approach, which has links with communitarianism (Tam, 1998), argues that power in the UK is exercised by the mass of the people rather than a small elite group or class. No one group or individual has complete or full control since there are a plethora of individuals, groups and political parties that can in different ways, exercise competing pressure and power. The reformist view is that voting at parliamentary and local elections are key to determining polices. If elected representatives fail to deliver what the electorate demand, they can be dismissed from office at elections and replaced by others who either promise to deliver, or have a proven record of delivering effective polices and services. Community groups and pressure groups have an important role to play here as they can influence political decision making, although it is also recognised that these groups, who have different levels of funding and influence, are often competing against each other to secure the attention of decision makers. Reformists argue that this form of democracy is healthy for society as it encourages active participation and prevents power being concentrated in the hands of the few. Community work in this approach has a valuable role in advocating on behalf of communities, and as a form of practice that can assist people to develop the skills and confidence to challenge for their voice to be heard and responded to.

The other approach that has influenced community work can loosely be described as the elite and potentially transformative community action (TCA). Unlike the reformist approach, the elite or TCA approach argues that power in the UK is concentrated in relatively few hands. They argue that a small but influential elite, predominately white and male, run the country through systems that are intended to further their own power base and to block or dilute the interests of the majority who it is claimed are passive and disinterested in politics. George Orwell described the situation of the elite in England in the 1940s in the following way:

> England is the most class-ridden country under the sun. It is a land of snobbery and privilege, ruled largely by the old and silly.
>
> (Orwell, 1982, p. 52)

This group that Orwell argues is 'old and silly' is drawn from what is commonly termed the 'Establishment' whose economic and social power shapes the political agenda so that their interests are served before those that represent the areas or groups that may challenge their own position. Members of the establishment are drawn from highly privileged backgrounds and tend to occupy elite and powerful positions in Britain. The elite approach argues that 'Establishment' is made up of smaller elites that are located in the political system, the judiciary, higher civil servants, major financial institutions and the directors of large corporations. According to Haralambos and Holborn (1995, pp. 518–519), 'there maybe some degree of cohesion within and between the various elites'.

In more recent times researchers' attention has moved to the emergence of elites that operate on a global level. In particular, commentators have examined the power of particular individuals such as Bill Gates and Rupert Murdoch, and the role of transnational power networks and elites including the United Nations, the International Monetary Fund and the

World Bank, as well as major corporations such as Wal-Mart, General Motors, Exxon Mobile, Ford Motors, Citigroup and Royal Dutch Shell.

Community work that has been influenced by the elite or TCA approach is not dissimilar to that pursued by those influenced by the reformist approach. However, those who have adopted the elite approach are arguably more aware of the limits that small-scale initiatives can achieve. They argue that in a system where there are varying and competing groups the status quo can move to dismiss, co-opt, weaken or play one group off against another. In this approach the way forward is for groups to work in collaboration to achieve their goals. There is also some scepticism within the elite approach as to whether political parties are sufficiently responsive to views or opinions that do not coincide with their own position. Therefore, community work is more likely to adopt a radical approach that advocates far-reaching and widespread changes in the political, social and economic system. Radical community work argues that the inequality and disadvantage within society is perpetuated in order to sustain the divisions between people in order that the elite remains powerful and privileged. What is distinctive about community work here is that it promotes autonomous ways of working through collective action to address moral and political issues (Jordan, 2007). We discuss the discourses of communitarianism and TCA in more detail in Chapter 6.

Two theorists that have influenced both approaches are Paulo Freire and Antonio Gramsci. At the societal level theory has the potential for providing a framework which connects personal experience with empowerment and 'collective action for a more just, equal and sustainable world' (Ledwith, 2005, p. 61). It must therefore offer a paradigm for practice that addresses issues of justice, difference and change. The ideas of Freire and Gramsci are relevant to community work and community action and helpful for constructing such a paradigm as they offer a 'critical way forward' (Popple, 1995, p. 105) Although Freire developed his ideas working as an adult educator with oppressed groups in South America, they remain relevant to the situation facing community workers in many European welfare states. Freire (1972) suggests that large numbers of people are effectively disenfranchised by the dominant ideology and divisive social relationships that exploit them. A theme that connects with Gramsci's (1986) notion of hegemony and the power of ideas that permeate all relationships and shapes reality to achieve consent. Some of the more individualistic and competitive elements of what Freire referred to as 'the banking system of education' remain in place. Here the learner is essentially seen as a passive and empty vessel waiting to be filled with factual knowledge. Further, banking education may be reinforced by the current 'league table' culture and emphasis on meeting centrally determined targets. For ethnic minority and other marginalised groups, the concept of cultural invasion remains significant and refers to the way the dominant culture imposes its values on subordinate groups and in doing so creates a 'culture of silence'.

Practice Focus 1

Consider the different types of community work initiatives that take place in the town or city you are most familiar with. Attempt to distinguish them in relation to the two approaches we have identified above.

The Changing Context

By the late 1960s the UK was facing a mixture of an economic downturn and rising unemployment; the post-war industrial restructuring which was leading to the decline of older industrial areas and further increasing unemployment and hardship; the impact of immigration and the settlement of people from the Commonwealth and accounts of rising racism; the identification of 'disruptive' and 'difficult' communities; and the increasing awareness of failures in the welfare state (Midwinter, 1994). All this led to the Labour government escalating its intervention in urban areas.

One of its major initiatives was the Urban Programme that was launched by the Prime Minister Harold Wilson in 1968 as a response to Enoch Powell's 'Rivers of Blood' speech. Powell, who was a Conservative front-bench speaker, argued that racial tension in UK cities would emulate that witnessed in the United States (Powell, 1968). Although set in motion as a response to Powell's inflammatory speech, the Urban Programme did not specifically target areas of high immigrant density partly 'for fear of provoking accusations of favoured treatment for immigrants' (Loney, 1983, p. 34). Instead areas for targeting additional resources were based on a range of poverty indicators including unemployment, overcrowding, large families, poor environment and children in care or in need of care. An immigrant concentration was only one of these indicators. However, through substantial funding over several years the Urban Programme was to stimulate the growth of community work projects and the employment of community workers as community-based intervention was seen as both a valuable preventive and ameliorating approach to what were considered to be local problems. The Inner Area Programme, which included the Inner Area Partnership Schemes and the Free Enterprise Zones evolved from the Urban Programme and by the late 1970s the Urban Programme was recast to reflect increasing recognition of the need to economically regenerate the inner cities, often with a mixture of private and public finance (Boddy, 1984). These area-based policies are considered further in Chapter 4.

In 1969 the government established 12 Community Development Projects (CDPs) in areas identified as requiring specific additional resources and improved co-ordination of local services. Using finance from central government and from local authorities, the hope was that by intervening in these localities, the Projects would address internal community and individual personal problems. The aims of the CDPs rested on three assumptions.

> Firstly that it was the 'deprived' themselves who were the cause of 'urban depri-vation'. Secondly, the problem could best be solved by overcoming these people's apathy and promoting self-help. Thirdly, locally-based research into the prob-lems would serve to bring about changes in local and central government policy.
> (Community Development Projects, 1977, p. 2)

The CDP staff, however, brought to their work a structural analysis and in doing so they dismissed the government's traditional explanations of poverty that centred around the ideas of a 'cycle of poverty' and personal inadequacy. Instead the practitioners and researchers attached to these projects argued that it was the unequal distribution of resources and power in society that was at the root of the creation of areas in which the poor resided (Loney, 1983). This radical critique, which can be placed within the elite approach to community work theory, was to influence community work thinking well beyond the time the last CDP had its central govern-ment funding withdrawn in the late 1970s. We consider the work of the CDPs in more detail in Chapter 4.

The Seebohm Report on local authority social work in 1968 was similarly influential in the development of community work as the Report encour-aged social work departments to focus on preventive work, and creating local area offices in order to be more connected to the communities they claimed to serve. This led to many social service departments appointing community workers to 'stimulate local voluntary and community sector development' (Payne, 2005b, p. 87).

Whilst there was a good deal of activity in the state-sponsored sector, community action was also in evidence during the 1960s. Much of it evolved from the activities of residents in opposing and challenging the redevelopment schemes that were in evidence in most cities in the UK. Whilst some consultation was undertaken with residents groups and individuals, there was considerable concern by many community action groups that their wishes were not satisfactorily addressed. In some cases this led to major 'stop the bulldozer' campaigns, whilst other protests were more low key, but nevertheless significant for those who felt threatened and intimidated by the major changes occurring in urban communities.

The Rise of Neo-liberalism

By the mid-1970s community work had begun to rethink its role in response to the economic recession that was due in part to the aftermath of the Arab–Israeli war of October 1973 that led to Arab oil producers to reduce their supplies and increase the price of exported oil. Soon afterwards Britain's oil import bill had quadrupled, which further weakened its already disappointing trade balance. The 1974 incoming Labour governments (elected in February and October of that year) began to reorder public sector priorities and commenced a pruning of welfare services. However, the recession continued with a devaluation of the pound sterling so that in 1976 the government was compelled to request a loan from the International Monetary Fund (IMF) that was agreed on the condition of further cuts in the UK's public sector expenditure. At the same time, a growing group of influential monetarists and neo-liberals, primarily informed by two academic economists, Milton Friedman and Frederick von Hayek and the work of the right-wing think tanks, the Institute of Economic Affairs, the Social Affairs Unit, the Centre for Policy Studies and the Adam Smith Institute, were calling for a much greater role for the market and the private sector in the delivery of public services. They were also demanding that the state should be 'rolled back' and personal and corporation taxes reduced so releasing more resources for an enterprise culture. The view of the neo-liberals was the market should govern supply and demand, managers should be given clear and unambiguous authority to mange staff and resources and the consumer was sovereign. The outcome would be that the poor would benefit from a 'trickle down' from this invigorated 'enterprise culture'.

In 1979, after what was termed the 'winter of discontent' when local authority workers were engaged in strikes in a protest to protect public services and their own living standards, the Conservative Party, under the leadership of Margaret Thatcher, was elected to power. Thatcher and her Cabinet were to drive forward neo-liberal policies leading to the biggest political change in post-war Britain as the Conservatives promised to reverse the relative decline in the UK economy, address what they considered to be fundamental problems in welfare, health, education and housing, and to control and target public spending. Margaret Thatcher herself was inspired by the Victorian period.

> I never felt uneasy about praising 'Victorian values'... The Victorians had a way of talking which summed up what we were now rediscovering – they distinguished between the 'deserving' and the 'undeserving poor'. Both groups should be given help, but it must be a very different kind if public spending is not just going to reinforce the dependency culture.
>
> (Thatcher, 1993, p. 627)

Community workers, many of whom were influenced by anti-statism philosophies (Lees and Mayo, 1984) had by then turned their attention from attacking the state, as it had done in various ways during the 1960s and early 1970s, to one of defending public services, whilst highlighting the oppressive nature of the relationships that the state had with its citizens (London to Edinburgh Weekend Return Group, 1980). Interestingly, however, community work enjoyed something of an expansion during the 1980s. A survey undertaken in 1983 of community workers showed that 5000 practitioners were employed, whilst little more that 1000 were working in the 1970s (Francis *et al.*, 1984). Many of these new workers were employed to facilitate schemes aimed at 'shifting the burden of welfare work from public collective to private individual shoulders' (Craig, 1979, p. 12).

There was no doubt the 1980s was a difficult period for community development. The United States Republican administration under President Ronald Regan was forcing its demand for structural adjustment on less wealthy countries that required American financial and political assistance through the work of the World Bank and the IMF. In doing so the USA became increasingly powerful in the world both economically and politically. In the UK, the accelerating speed of change that accompanied the impact of neo-liberalism was in contrast to the inadequacy of a clear political understanding by Left wing intellectuals and politicians of the phenomenon sweeping through the country. One notable exception to this were the writings of the cultural commentator and Professor of Sociology at the Open University, Stuart Hall (1988) whose analysis was to both depress and inspire those who wanted to see an end to the increasing wealth and income gap; the erosion of the 'social wage' which protected working-class communities from the excesses of the social and economic restructuring; and the conflict approaches taken by the Tories over most matters of state. Hall's writings were addressed to the Left which sought increased solidarity to tackle structural problems and the 'hard policing' of inner-city communities.

During this period of restructuring and increasing polarisation of political approaches, community work was faced with the problem of how to effectively engage with a reactionary state that was cutting public services, and encouraging self-help schemes that were intended to replace public-funded schemes but which did not satisfactorily meet people's needs. Paid community workers were frequently in conflict with their employers as they tried to represent and advocate on behalf of community members (Waddington, 1983). However, there were local authorities, and in particular the Greater London Council, which were prepared to challenge the Conservative government and to support their local communities with the funding of creative and democratically run community development projects, and promoting local economic development in some of the UK's poorest areas.

Community action during this period was often in response to the major adjustments made by a regressive state. The closure and reduction of industries such as coal mining, an increase in unemployment from 1.5 million in 1979 to around 3.2 million in mid-1985, the imposition of the poll tax and the placing of American nuclear missiles on British soil, all led to local and national action. In fact it is considered by many that the anti-poll tax campaigns, including the refusal of large numbers of people to pay the tax, which allied with Conservative splits over Europe, the resignation of Cabinet ministers, a weakened economic position in 1990 and a series of poor election results, led to the Conservatives to remove Margaret Thatcher from the role of Prime Minister (Burns, 1992). Similarly, the campaign in the early and mid-1980s to prevent the siting of American nuclear weapons at Greenham Common in Berkshire was to bring together local and national campaigns that linked feminism and anti-war protests. Finally, during the 1980s urban unrest simmered in many British cities as a mixture of high youth unemployment, racism, poverty, distrust of the police, and the feeling of political exclusion and powerlessness led to violence and riots in various inner-city areas, such as Brixton in London, St Paul's in Bristol, Toxteth in Liverpool, Handsworth in Birmingham and Mosside in Manchester. Whilst this opposition cannot be considered to be a 'conventional' form of community action, the encounters between black youth and the police were similar to community action in that the events were sporadic and relatively short lived, and did focus attention on wider themes of racial and economic disadvantage at a time when opposition to Thatcherism at the party political level was weak.

In concluding remarks on this period we can state that neo-liberalism as pursued by the Conservatives up to their general election defeat in 1997 was to lead to Britain to experiencing greater social and economic inequality than at any time since before the Second World War. Although the election in 1990 of John Major to the leadership of the Conservative Party, and hence Prime Minister, was to lead to 'capitalism with a caring face' with the replacement of the poll tax with the council tax, the launch of a Citizen's Charter, and a renewed plea of 'Back to basics', fundamentally there remained Thatcherite polices in place. Furthermore, restricted trade union rights, increased social exclusion, weak and compliant regulatory regimes in the private and corporate sectors and incompetent handling of the economy were to mark the period as one of bitterness in the divide between the 'haves' and the 'have nots' (Hall, 1998).

New Labour and Social Cohesion

The election of New Labour to government in May 1997 led to the new administration continuing with the Conservative government's neo-liberal economic policies, and harnessing these with their Third Way social policies. According to Jordan the Third Way was

> an alternative to Margaret Thatcher's free-market model of the neo-liberal state, and to old-style socialism, both of the undemocratic Soviet, command-economy kind, and the Old Labour variety (with a mixed economy and universalistic, collectivist welfare state)
>
> (Jordan, 2000, p. 20)

In practice this meant greater intervention in the social sphere, together with the modernising of public services. (See also Chapter 6 for a detailed elaboration of the Third Way which one of us has described as an attempt to 'balance the freedom of the market with a commitment to social justice' (Stepney, 2000, p. 6)).

After the defeat of the Conservatives, one of the key issues for New Labour to deal with was addressing the growing disadvantage of large numbers of already poor communities. The neo-liberal agenda and market operations were increasingly leaving people in poverty, without employment, and more importantly without any significant hope of escaping a life on welfare benefits. Almost immediately New Labour legislated for a minimum wage, and introduced a philosophy of 'welfare to work' with incentives to assist those on benefits to move from unemployment to paid work. Launched in its first budget of July 1997 with funds of £5.2 billion (almost wholly financed by a windfall tax on the profits of the utilities privatised by the Conservative government), the 'New Deal' for the unemployed was created to ensure that those who are unemployed are promptly integrated into the labour market. As the Prime Minister said soon after New Labour's election in 1997,

> the greatest challenge to any democratic government is to refashion our institutions to bring [the] workless class back into society and into useful work
> (Tony Blair's Speech, Aylesbury Estate, Southwark, South London,
> 2 June 1997)

Although New Labour has not openly concurred with the view that social exclusion is the result of the pursuit of the neo-liberal agenda, it has been aware that failure to address some of the outcomes of these policies will alienate large numbers of its electoral power base, what Hall (2003) calls its 'traditional working-class and public sector middle-class support'. Similarly, New Labour knew that if it was to make the neo-liberal agenda workable they had to increase market competition for jobs and to ensure through direct targeting of social policies there would not be too many people objecting to the rampant pursuit of economic growth and inequality (Paxton and Dixon, 2004).

Evidence of the economic polarisation that is taking place in the UK can be seen from the *Sunday Times* Rich List. Ten years into New Labour's period in office in 2007, the wealth of the richest 1000 people in Britain had more than trebled. The 260% rise in wealth of Britain's richest people from 1997 to 2007 compared with a 120% average wealth increase for the population as a whole (Woods, 2007). According to Kate Green, the chief executive of the Child Poverty Action Group, New Labour has lost confidence in its ability to tackle levels of poverty in the UK and has blamed 'the poorest for their own misfortune, hardening existing public misconceptions' (Green, 2007). She points to evidence that one in four children are growing up below the poverty line, and that the UK's child poverty is one of the highest in Europe. Official figures released by the government supports Green's view and shows that New Labour has failed to reverse the significant inequality that took place under Margaret Thatcher and John Major.

> Under Labour changes in the distribution of income have become more complicated than they were under the previous conservative government. But the very rich are still getting richer
>
> (Chote and Sibieta, 2007)

It against this sort of evidence that New Labour's commitment to poor communities needs to be judged. The government's funding of a wide range of community development initiatives can be viewed as attempts to address social cohesion rather than to tackle inequality, a move reinforced by the introduction in 2006 of the 'respect agenda' to tackle anti-social behaviour (Blair, 2006). According to the 2007 Office for National Statistics report, it is cash benefits that have played the biggest part in reducing inequality with the poorest two-fifths of households receiving 59% of the total. Nevertheless, poor families paid a larger share of their incomes in tax than rich families.

If state-funded community development is primarily about social cohesion and not tackling inequality which Polly Toynbee (2007) argues is 'splitting and damaging our society', then practitioners will need to consider if their intervention are more than papering over the cracks.

Whilst community development has been developed by the state in what one of us has described as 'conditional development' (Popple, 2006d), there has at the same time been a good deal of community action at the neighbourhood level that has not been funded by local or central government. For example, a community action group Nomast (www.nomast.org.uk, accessed 20 May 2007) has been protesting against the siting of a 40-foot mast, which will serve G3 phones in the London Fields area of

Hackney, north London. If erected the mast would be close to a school, a lido and a children's paddling pool. The community action group is protesting against the phone company, T-Mobile and the London Borough of Hackney, which they argue, have reneged on agreements not to site the mast in the area. This sort of community action is not unusual as local people engage actively in their communities. In the case of Nomast, we can witness local authorities under pressure to assist large corporations secure maximum profit whilst local people who elect the council consider that their views are not being properly valued and responded to.

Practice Focus 2

A community development project, located in a neighbourhood of considerable deprivation, and funded by the local authority has received deputations from local residents reflecting their worry that a team of 'loan sharks' are operating in the area. The community development workers have heard that these 'loan sharks' are offering local people, and in particular single parents and families with several children, loans that have extremely high rates of interest. It is reported that those who find it difficult to repay these loans, or are unable to make final payments, are often offered further loans at high interest payments so increasing their indebtedness. It is also said that people are physically threatened and in some cases physically attacked by these loan sharks.

What role can the community development workers play in addressing this problem?

What kind of action might follow this?

What methods might the community development worker adopt? (refer to the models in Chapter 7)

An area that community development could have a role is assisting action at a local level to stem modern slavery in the UK. According to a disturbing Joseph Rowntree Foundation report published in 2007, various forms of slavery can be identified in the shape of people who are coerced into an abusive relationship that involves them being trafficked and/or smuggled for the purposes of forced labour and other forms of slavery including debt bondage, sexual slavery and child trafficking and labour. The report's authors (Craig *et al.*, 2007) identify the severe economic exploitation of migrants who travel to the UK often legally but become subject of forced labour through a mix of intimidation, enforced debt, the removal of documents and an inadequate understanding of their rights. Often these slaves first contact in their attempt to appeal for help are local community groups and social work agencies either in the statutory or voluntary sector. There is a real need here for a community-based approach to address this appalling situation that blights the UK and all other countries where this takes place. This approach could involve local public awareness campaigns, the coordination of the work of community development organisations and the statutory sector and the involvement of church groups, housing bodies, advice agencies and trade unions.

Summary and Conclusion

As we have noted, community work developed as an offshoot from the work of the COS in the late nineteen century. Social work's role of assessing the 'deserving' and 'undeserving' ran counter to the approaches adopted by community work, which was to offer support and services to as wide a group as possible. Since then, although social work and community work have developed separate and distinct forms of practice, the two interventions have been linked at different periods of their evolution.

We have considered the development of community development and community action over the last century and noted that the style and focus of their interventions are closely linked with changing political, economic and social formations. Both community development and community action are likely to continue to make their different and distinct contribution to community life in the UK. Community development is presently enjoying a renaissance with its main funder the state using the practice to further its social cohesion agenda. Tackling social deprivation and increasing social capital in targeted poor estates and neighbourhoods is a key platform in New Labour's Third Way approach to dealing with the fallout from its adherence to neo-liberalism. At the same time, community action, which like community work has a long and noteworthy history, provides people with the opportunity to address the issues and problems they face at a locality level. A tension has always existed between community development, community action and the state and this is unlikely to disappear. The sign of a healthy and vibrant democracy is the tolerance of this tension and demands of practitioners' high levels of skill and political nous.

9

Future Possibilities for Community-Based Social Work in an International Context

Introduction

As we move further into the twenty-first century, not for the first time, social work appears to be at the crossroads. It has become abundantly clear that social work now operates within the context of the global economy and is increasingly shaped and critically judged by the criteria of the market, in terms of its performance, efficiency and outcomes. It would seem that the day of the universal welfare state is over. Practitioners in the developed world face a vast array of similar problems whilst their governments have been developing a diverse range of policy responses to manage socially differentiated populations. Paradoxically, such responses may still result in quite similar practice outcomes (Stepney, 2006b). This is despite the fact that there are significant differences among European welfare states – for example, in the proportion of GDP devoted to spending on social protection (see Table 9.1 below), the range of municipal priorities and percentage of the population at risk of poverty both before and after social transfers (see Table 9.2 below).

There are also distinctive organisational arrangements in the way social workers are employed and provide services at the local level. However, as we search for explanations to such policy to practice conundrums, it becomes necessary to situate the debate in its wider socio-economic, cultural and community context.

The focus of this final chapter is on exploring future possibilities for community-based social work in an international context. However, making judgments about the nature of contemporary practice, let alone predicting where it is heading in the future seems a particularly hazardous exercise. One of the reasons for this is the growing feeling of uncertainty surrounding the role of social work more generally in society. Fundamental

Table 9.1 Total expenditure on social protection as a percentage of GDP

Total expenditure on soc protection %GDP	1993	1997	2000	2003
Germany	27.8	28.9	29.3	30.2
Czech Republic		18.6	19.6	20.1
The Netherlands	32.3	29.4	27.4	28.1
Finland	34.5	29.0	25.3	26.9
Sweden	38.2	32.9	31.0	33.5
United Kingdom	29.0	27.5	27.0	26.7
EU 15 (ave)	28.7	27.9	27.2	28.3

(European Communities, 2007, p. 126).

Table 9.2 At risk of poverty rate – percentage of population in 2003

Country	Before social transfers	After social transfers
Germany	23	15
Czech Republic	21	8
The Netherlands	23	12
Finland	28	11
United Kingdom	29	18
EU 25 (ave)	25	15
EU 15 (ave)	26	15

(European Communities, 2007, p. 117).

questions about whether social work is still relevant to the problems it confronts (or increasingly irrelevant), and a force for progressive social change seem as important today as when they were first raised more than 30 years ago (Pearson, 1975). This is especially the case given what Hugman (2005) refers to as 'limitations in the predictive capacity of [its] concepts and techniques' (p. 612). Social work reveals this uncertainty quite acutely alongside the dilemma of being unable to resolve many of the problems it identifies in the community, both in its theory and practice.

In the UK, community-based social work has had a tenuous relationship with mainstream practice (Heenan, 2004). And whilst the latter, as was noted in Chapter 6, has been reconstructed as 'tough love', the ideas underpinning community social work have either been co-opted by the state in areas such as partnership working to facilitate community involvement or have slowly migrated to the voluntary sector (Stepney, 2006a). This is not to infer that the state has reaffirmed a genuine commitment to social work, rather it has merely borrowed and adapted the language of social work and used this to legitimise certain aspects of welfare reform. One of the important effects of borrowing from the language of the profession is that it has made its 'third way' inclusion policy concerning the mobilisation of citizens and communities, and more recently the respect agenda, sound remarkably like social work (Jordan, 2004).

The state has sought to form a new partnership with its citizens, whereby the vast majority of potential service users (except the most needy and vulnerable with high care needs) must take responsibility for their own welfare and effectively care for themselves. Only more complex or high-risk clients will receive support (DoH, 2006a). This is revealed in an extract from a recent policy document, euphemistically subtitled 'Empowering and enabling individuals to take control':

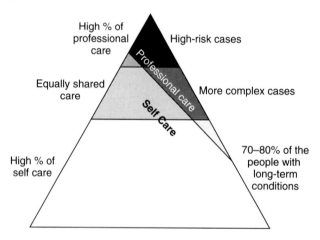

Figure 9.1 Empowering and enabling individuals to take control
(DoH, 2006a, Figure 5.2 p. 111).

Thus, in the UK the New Labour government has become skilled in the art of 'performativity' (Mann, 2006), and their policy initiatives, promoted in the name of cultural inclusion, enablement and social capital building, have communitarian rather than genuinely community empowerment motives. Here 'third way' communitarianism, whatever its merits, has been described as 'reactionary politics dressed up as progressive community stakeholding' (Robson, 2000, p. 14).

The impact in communities throughout Europe of this cultural shift in policy, practice and values has been quite dramatic. As capital has gone elsewhere, either to Central and Eastern Europe or to the developing world in search of lower labour costs, it has left behind areas of high unemployment, where an increasing number of mainstream citizens live without any welfare support. This social and economic disinvestment has taken place in the shadow of the market and occurred at a time when multinational corporations have seen their investments yield record profits (Jordan, 1998). Added to this is a growing underclass of homeless people, refugees, asylum-seekers and other marginal groups, who survive through the informal economy and end up living on the edge of welfare systems through a combination of petty crime, hustling, short-term work for cash and support from NGOs working in the community.

The scale of this tactical retrenchment from universalist forms of welfare has left many urban communities with deep scars that intensify existing social divisions. These have recently been gilded with the artefacts of the 24-hour economy that has taken over some inner-city areas. The Mailbox and Gas Street Basin area of central Birmingham in the UK represents a good example. This was once a busy canal side area of warehousing and commerce at the height of the industrial revolution that subsequently fell into disuse. The regeneration of the area has led to the creation of new mixed tenure housing, including smart apartment blocks and some social housing. Alongside this, the influx of new bars, hotels, restaurants, boutiques, business units, supermarket and leisure complex has given the area a long overdue makeover. However, more generally the transformation of the urban wastelands has been achieved at a huge social cost, for while the young and affluent become active participants in the night-time economy, the poorer sections of the community are more likely to experience the transformation in terms of alienation and exclusion (Ferguson and Lavalette, 2004).

At the same time the welfare state is no longer able to offer much support to those excluded from this commercial makeover. Disadvantaged communities have been effectively dislocated from mainstream welfare, excluded from commercial market-based development and become reliant on special community projects or area-based initiatives (see Chapter 4). Responding positively to this agenda and making social work relevant to people from excluded communities and those living in the shadow of the market is one of the stark challenges facing practitioners today.

This final chapter will examine the way community-based social work has responded to this challenge. On the one hand it has had to recognise the new cultural context and adapt to the modernising policy discourse (see Chapter 6), whilst on the other seek to develop more distinctive community-based approaches. The theoretical debate between postmodernism, critical realism, Marxist and feminist theory alongside evidence-based practice (EBP) will be examined as this provides the context for the development of a more critical community-based approach. This will be illustrated with reference to practice examples from different international contexts including

- working with service users in different areas of the UK to promote inclusion;

- an eco-social work project to tackle exclusion in three European cities; and

- critical practice as a basis for community-based research in Australia and the USA.

European Policy Context

A detailed analysis of the wider policy context is set out in Part II above. The dynamics of globalisation has led to greater fragmentation, differentiation and competition in the labour market, creating new patterns of exclusion and inequality in the community. New Labour's modernisation policy addresses concerns about exclusion and well-being, but seeks to balance individual responsibility and opportunity with market freedom and choice. This 'third way' approach, based upon individualism and subsidiarity, has been exported to other European welfare states and held up as a model for social reconstruction in the enlarged EU. It has even surfaced in Scandinavia, until recently the last stronghold of universalism and solidarity (Stepney, 2006b). The election of a new centre-right government in Sweden in Autumn 2006 has led to the further modernisation of its welfare system. The prime minister Fredrik Reinfeldt, an admirer of Tony Blair and Bill Clinton, was elected on a platform of greater efficiency in public services and welfare reform.

The adoption of a modernising discourse has shaped the development of tougher policies that front-line staff must now implement (Jordan, 2006). For example, there is a surplus of unskilled labour in all European welfare states as employers take advantage of the global market by recruiting workers from central and eastern Europe and using labour power more flexibly especially in the service sector, including social care. Welfare regimes across Europe compete for international investment as much in terms of low social costs as high levels of social capital. With the influence of the US ever present, the UK has led the way in social deregulation and modernisation in line with these requirements.

In a global market the mobility of capital has put European nation states on the defensive about welfare and led to a growth of the private and voluntary sectors to offset restraints on public spending (Jordan, 2006). However, this has been at a cost of greater inequality and the reform of social services to meet market-driven imperatives and targets. Further, in the UK the 'choice agenda' and more recently 'respect' are now beginning to invade all public services, to such an extent that collaboration, partnership and community involvement, for so long the flagship aims of policy, remain significant but have become subordinate to this search for well-being (Jordan, 2007). This is because choice is now seen as one of the mechanisms that will create greater competition in a global economy and thereby improve the performance of public sector staff like social workers, nurses and teachers (DoH, 2006a). In the Nordic welfare states, for example, despite adopting elements of 'third way' reform, there remains a greater degree of consensus and commitment to solidarity and equality (Lorenz, 2001). This means that hitherto choice has remained relatively underused as an instrument in formal policy making (Stepney, 2006b). Such trends are particularly evident in Sweden which has moved from a public to a more pluralist welfare system (Stepney, 2006b). According to Jordan (2006), welfare regimes have all 'tried to adapt human resources to the requirements of mobile capital, while protecting their most vulnerable populations' (p. 143).

Social work has been placed in the front line of policy reform as it occupies contested territory and provides a legacy of services that were once the hallmark of an earlier approach. Social Works' perceived attachment to the old welfare order is one of the professions enduring strengths, but ironically one that is viewed by government as its principal weakness. Social work in the UK, despite adapting to dynamic global pressures, is still seen to be too closely allied with Old Labour style socialism, with practitioners prone to question the neo-liberal orthodoxy underpinning the modernising discourse. The problem of professional resistance that this creates has been addressed within public services by the introduction of performance targets and a league table culture. This clearly has important implications for the future development of social work and the community.

Theoretical Developments in Social Work: Postmodernism Versus Evidence-Based Practice

The translation of policy into practice requires very careful analysis. It was not very long ago that the profession was accused of political correct-ness for supporting marginalised groups (Butler and Drakeford, 2005b). However, since New Labour took office there has been a gradual submer-sion of anti-racist and anti-oppressive objectives into a project to address exclusion and promote social diversity and more recently the respect agenda. Whilst ensuring services are sensitive to cultural differences is more than justifiable, what it has meant is that critical questions about the social division of oppression have been essentially de-politicised in a more modernising agenda. However, in 2006 this debate took a bizarre twist with ministerial condemnation of Muslim women for wearing a veil, dubbed a mark of separation. Suddenly New Labour's diversity strategy has been re-branded and exposed as euro-centric and heavy handed. The wider issues raised by the veiling debate in the Muslim community against a backdrop of fear and anti-terrorism are beyond the scope of this chapter. Notwithstanding the debate about diversity, the development of social work since 1997 has reflected the shifting sands of policy reform in a highly contested political arena.

In an authoritative contribution, Hugman (2005), looking at contemporary developments across the globe from an Australian vantage point, identifies two alternative responses to the current concern about social disadvantage, disrespect and difference. On the one hand is the contribution of postmodernist ideas and post-structural theory, epitomised by the notion of searching for and working with uncertainty. On the other is the rise of the evidence-based practice (EBP) movement, which may be characterised as an attempt to impose certainty in unsettling and deeply troubled times. The tension between these two approaches and the implications for community-based social work are worthy of more detailed consideration.

From a postmodernist perspective, the world is seen as characterised by uncertainty, relativism and contingency exemplified by the twin concepts of fragmentation and difference. Postmodernism adopts an interpretivist approach to knowledge production and highlights the importance of values and context in constructing meaning. Thus, a plurality of meanings are possible all potentially valid even if they are ultimately contradictory. The scientific (positivist) view that universal truth exists and underpins an objective reality has been abandoned in favour of a diversity of truths. Here all knowledge is seen as socially constructed and, as such, partial, fragmented and encoded with contested meanings and cultural values (Parton, 1996). Identity is not seen as 'fixed' and derived from social position and status based upon class, race, gender and so on, as critical modernist theorists have argued, but is constructed from multiple starting points. In searching for uncertainty (and finding it alive and well in the archives of social work theory), postmodernist ideas can be said 'to have challenged the certainties of structural analysis and ways of understanding the aims and methods of social work' (Hugman, 2005, p. 615).

By contrast the development of a more evidence-based approach has gained momentum during the past decade and complements the modernising discourse. Best practice, it is argued, comes from a rational and objective assessment of the evidence and this logically leads to the adoption of the most appropriate course of action. Ignoring for the moment the complexity of reasoning and the problems inherent in a rational model of decision making, evidence-based practice should be the approach where 'there is the most clear and robust evidence of effectiveness' (Hugman, 2005, p. 615). These ideas originated from the natural sciences, in particular medicine, through the Cochrane collaboration, and adopt a neo-positivist epistemology. Here knowledge is reliant upon scientific measurement and observation that are viewed as contributing to general laws that underpin an objective reality. These laws are seen to be independent of sectional interests, politically neutral and developed on the basis of social facts as absolute truths.

The proponents of EBP favour the use of research methodologies, such as random controlled trials (RCTs) that are seen as the gold standard in research (MacDonald and Sheldon, 1992). It is significant that little mention is made of interpretive or qualitative research methodologies, such as ethnography, case studies, observational studies and so on, presumably because these 'are considered either too subjective, lacking in cost-effectiveness or the disciplinary prestige of the medical sciences' (Webb, 2001, p. 63). This in turn has led to the favouring of practice methods that can be subject to systematic evaluation and measurement, such as cognitive behavioural therapy (Sheldon, 2000) and, to some extent, task-centred practice (Marsh and Doel, 2005). By implication methods that utilise qualitative evidence may be viewed as inferior. According to Healy (2005), it also reinforces a 'top-down' model where theory is handed down to be used by practitioners and they become 'the user of knowledge, not the maker of it' (p. 99).

While few practitioners would dissent from the need to become more research literate and evidence based (Healy, 2005), the question of what constitutes the best methodology remains contested. Here social work has been influenced by criticism from the social sciences that positivism represents an inadequate basis for understanding complex social phenomena. In particular, it fails to recognise the limitations of knowledge based upon 'facts' and truths derived from observation. Such knowledge cannot achieve certainty, as observation is theory driven, contextual and value laden (Kuhn, 1970; Popper, 1959). Scientific knowledge is at best probabilistic knowledge as what is known today may be replaced tomorrow (Kazi, 2003). The social world cannot be known independent of theoretical constructs and stripped of its political and ideological representations and structures. This is one of the reasons why evidence is frequently contested and requires careful interpretation. Practitioners are understandably perplexed when faced with an array of research findings that leaves them uncertain about which to follow (Healy, 2005).

The assumption in EBP that rational decision making is a relatively straightforward task can be shown to be problematic. Research in social psychology has identified that motivational and cognitive biases influence human judgement irrespective of the available evidence (Webb, 2001). Even Sheldon (2000) has acknowledged that people 'have a strong tendency to find what we expect or have been told to find' (p. 66). And science far from providing a way out of this connundrum may be seen as creating evidence that is not always readily useable. According to Nisbett and Ross (1980), 'people are unmoved by dry statistical data that are dear to the hearts of scientists and...the information that the scientist regards as highly pertinent and logically compelling are habitually ignored by people' (cited in Webb, 2001, p. 65). It is therefore necessary to understand the conceptual filters that people employ and the values they use to determine their actions, rather than concentrate exclusively on the way evidence is processed.

EBP can be further criticised for being part of the managerial agenda, consistent with the search for greater efficiency and value for money services (Harris, 1998a). While practitioners accept the need for the efficient use of resources and public accountability, an overemphasis on evidential processing, taken to its logical conclusion, may eventually lead to the 'Macdonaldisation of social work' (Harris, 2005). There is a genuine fear that in such a managerial climate the moral–political dilemmas faced by social workers in their everyday practice will be submerged within the technical–rational task of processing evidence. This has echoes of an earlier debate about the end of ideology thesis and reform of the welfare state, suggesting that the problems of politics have become the problems of administration (Habermas, 1978).

Notwithstanding such criticisms, Hugman (2005) suggests that there are positive as well as negative reasons why social work is searching for certainty at the present time. Practitioners naturally wish to justify their actions and demonstrate why particular kinds of intervention are necessary. This is one of the most positive aspects of the academisation of social work, which has been reinforced by the introduction (in 2003) in UK universities of the new degree in social work. Graduate studies in social work have generally been established much earlier in the USA, Australia and many other European countries. For example, in Finland the introduction of a doctoral programme in the early 1990s helped to promote a strong research culture, which in turn enhanced professional status (Karvinen *et al.*, 1999). The search for certainty (even if this is contentious) by ensuring best practice is supported by good research evidence may also be viewed as an opportunity for social work to develop a more critical, research informed and community-based practice.

Towards a More Critical and Community-Based Practice

A major impediment for critical social workers seeking to incorporate postmodern understandings is how universal ideals like social justice can be upheld simultaneously with an inclusion of multiple and differing perspectives.

(Fook, 2003, p. 126)

From the two approaches set out in the previous section, it would appear that postmodernist ideas combined with a structural analysis offer in theory a more useful basis for what might be termed critical community-based social work than EBP. However, four observations can be made at this stage:

1. first, postmodernist ideas will need to be adapted sufficiently to complement the structural modernist critique of policy that justifies CSW's change agent role. Balancing a universal commitment to justice with multiple perspectives, as Fook notes in the above quote, represents a major epistemological challenge that will be addressed below;

2. second, the issue of ontological coherence must be addressed;

3. third, critical community-based practice will need to have a practical cutting edge to ensure its relevance to the lives of service users and acceptability to community members; and

4. fourth, the foregoing observations do not rule out the more progressive aspects of an evidence-based approach making a contribution to critical community-based practice, for example, by encouraging social workers to incorporate a research dimension into their work.

The epistemological and ontological challenge of combining the multiple perspectives of postmodernism with a structural critique as a basis for developing critical community-based practice is perhaps the most ambitious task to be addressed. The starting point here is to recognise that from a structural modernist analysis, much of New Labour's modernising policy reform has tended to reinforce rather than challenge dominant market-based discourses. The reform of practice in line with such requirements seriously undermines the capacity of social work to promote emancipatory change and compromises the preventive role of the state. Further, the regulatory framework constructed around protection and risk management would appear to leave little room for a critical and more empowering practice that will challenge and change dominant power structures (Fook, 2002). Consequently, a structural critique can easily produce a fatalistic view that nothing much can be changed (Morley, 2004).

There are two potential ways out of this dilemma that lead to different versions of critical practice:

1. The first is offered by Fook (2002) who draws upon elements of critical postmodernism as a way of revitalising structural theories under conditions of globalisation (Leonard, 1997).

2. The second might be called critical realist practice that aims to provide a deeper understanding of human agency located in the context of dominant social structures (Houston, 2001; Pease, 2007).

Let us look at these two approaches in more detail.

Critical Postmodernist Practice

Postmodernists believe that reality is not something fixed and handed down to people but can be shaped by language and different meanings through contemporary discourses (Healy, 2005). Reality can therefore be 'understood to be a reflection of both external structures as well as internal constructed ways of thinking' (Morley, 2004, p. 299). And it is the latter that offers scope for the practitioner to reject dominant discourses, examine (and deconstruct) wider contexts and formulate alternative constructions through new language and practice (Fook *et al.*, 2000).

The belief that language (and knowledge) is power is relevant here (Lukes, 1974). The concept of power is seen as embedded in language, relationships and importantly practice, rather than a commodity derived from external structures (Foucault, 1984). The implication of this is that power may be seen as 'exercised rather than possessed' (Sawicki, 1991, cited in Healy, 2005, p. 203), productive rather than repressive and may be analysed in local interactions. It follows that if we adopt a bottom-up approach we must begin with practitioner/service user interactions at the local level. The practitioner through critical reflection is able to unpack dominant discourses and the assumptions that sustain them to ensure that through participation in a discourse, oppressive relationships may be resisted rather than inadvertently reproduced. As Morley (2004) notes, 'this highlights the transformative capacity of critical postmodernism to improve practice and facilitate social change' (p. 299).

Although this model of critical practice may be seen as central to a project for change, three specific criticisms can be made

1. This version of critical practice results from a 'shotgun marriage' that involves the fusion of two theoretical perspectives: Foucault and neo-Marxist theory (Webb, 2006).

2. The interpretation of Foucault as the basis for critical postmodernism derives from a particular reading of power based upon binary oppositions that is contested. In other words, Foucault's work offers the potential for a more complex reading of power that should not be avoided even if the results do not rest easily with the critical practice agenda (Webb, 2006).

3. The implications for social work need very careful consideration and this approach may be over-optimistic in offering itself up as an emancipatory route to another 'leftist road to utopia' (Healy, 2001).

The theoretical perspectives underpinning this version of critical practice represent two schemes of thought that derive from different epistemological traditions rather than one unified theoretical position. It should be acknowledged that this has the advantage of allowing for various engagements with critical theory at different levels of analysis – for example, Marxist/Feminist theory can be employed in the analysis of wider institutional structures and macro policy, whilst critical postmodernism is helpful in understanding the rich diversity of experience in the community and unpacking the forces of exploitation and oppression. However, the disadvantage is that the researcher/practitioner will find it extremely difficult to construct a coherent ontological position (somewhere between the relativism of postmodernism and the objectivism of much neo-Marxist theory) and be able to justify this. There is thus a danger of slipping into a pluralist ontology that can easily become a recipe for confusion and muddled thinking.

Social work derives its power and legitimacy from the state and in many respects the authority vested in professional staff can be seen as an extension of state power. Postmodernists draw upon the work of Foucault to stress a more flexible, dispersed and pervasive micro-analysis of power. Foucault did not see power as being located within the state apparatus or indeed 'localised in a particular type of institution' (Foucault, 1977, p. 26). He offers a more complex account of power, tracing, for example, the growth of the medical profession since the nineteenth century and their increasing influence over the body of the citizen. What he found was that over time power became looser and de-centred, but paradoxically more controlling and pervasive. In a contemporary world characterised by postmodernism's twin concepts of fragmentation and difference, power may be conceptualised 'as an unfolding flow of differentiation' (Webb, 2006, p. 11). In other words, it is in a constant state of flux and disconnection and as a result cannot easily be linked to an emamcipatory project for change in critical practice. Postmodernists have been sharply criticised for providing rich textual and critical insights but no clear moral message – such that the inherent relativism in postmodernism may undermine the structural analysis, its critique of globalisation and commitment to social justice (Noble, 2004). Hence, rather than being a complementary perspective, there is a danger that postmodernism could be seen to temper and dilute the case for transformative action.

While a postmodernist perspective can help to contextualise our understanding of social conditions characterised by fragmentation and difference, and the discourses of power that flow from them, it is based upon an epistemological theory about ways of knowing not a moral theory for political action (Fook, 2002). Therefore when postmodernism is combined with Marxist/Feminist theory it becomes relatively unstable and ontologically incoherent. And although these two perspectives may be harnessed to tackle common concerns (Mullaly, 2007), critical realism offers an alternative way forward that would appear to be more ontologically coherent.

Critical Realist Practice

Moving along the ontological continuum, between the objectivism associated with positivism and the relativism related to interpretivism, is an important position called realism (Sheppard, 1998). Critical realism draws upon critical theory and adopts a realist ontology that maintains that an external reality exists and can be approximated in research, albeit imperfectly (Kazi, 2003). Drawing upon the work of Bhaskar (1978), critical realism has three basic premises operating at different levels: First, it is assumed that a reality independent of human experience exists and so all events in the world (actual level) can be distinguished from those that are directly perceived (empirical level). For example, we can directly experience poverty and discrimination in our own lives as well as being aware of its existence in other communities that collectively contribute to a wider reality of structural disadvantage. And this reality is not dependent on individual perception, although clearly it shapes our experience. Second, reality is a dynamic process that draws upon subjective knowledge and understanding. Third, reality cannot be understood without critical thinking about theories of causation (causal level), which involves an analysis of structures, mechanisms and contexts, linking human agency with social structure (Pease, 2007).

Critical realism seeks to be sensitive to the multiple realities of subjective experience but views these within the context of dominant social structures. It shares with postmodernism the view that knowledge is socially constructed and, as such, partial, fragmented and encoded with contested meanings and cultural values (Parton, 1996). However, while a plurality of subjective meanings are possible, it rejects the 'abyss of relativism' in postmodernism that all meanings are equally valid even if they are contradictory, and sees knowledge as partial, provisional and shaped by wider social structures. Hence, critical realism offers an alternative to the inherent relativism of postmodernist positions and can thus provide a more viable basis for critical practice (Houston, 2001).

Critical realism gives access to a deeper understanding and explanation of human agency to counteract the current tendency in much social work to offer surface explanations rather than depth (Howe, 1996). Analysis should be at the causal level complemented by observation and measurement. It follows that a bottom-up approach is favoured beginning with service user experiences and identifying the causal mechanisms and structures that lead to discrimination and oppression. Participatory methods are preferred drawing upon a variety of knowledge, practice wisdom and theory, set in the context of relevant policy and community resources. This enables strategies of prevention alongside protection to be deployed, particularly significant in such high-risk fields as child care and mental health (see Stepney, 2006a). By integrating methods, such as task-centred, eco-systems and community social work, hybrid models of practice may be produced. In this respect, critical practice becomes reflective, preventative and anti-oppressive, designed to raise critical consciousness (Houston, 2001) through enhanced understanding, theoretical explanation and emancipatory action (Pease, 2007).

The community represents a logical site and appropriate context for testing out the validity of ideas about critical practice. In the next section, the application of ideas will be illustrated using examples from a number of international contexts.

Practice Context One – Community Social Work in Two Areas of the UK

This context concerns contributing to processes of inclusion and justice in the community. Community social work in the UK has a long history of working with local groups to achieve change and interweave statutory services with local networks of support (Hadley *et al.*, 1987; Smale *et al.*, 1988). Social workers have considerable qualitative knowledge about the local community often accumulated over many years alongside their professional expertise. However, this knowledge has become a victim of the dominant discourses referred to above and fallen into disuse. Practitioners need to relearn the community social work skill of utilising local knowledge in a culturally sensitive way, and respond constructively to identified problems and areas of unmet need (Smale *et al.*, 1988).

In taking up community-based issues that cannot be adequately tackled on a one-to-one basis, we are often concerned here with tackling structural issues of poverty, racism and exclusion, and how these feed into problems of inadequate facilities, ill health, isolation, relationship breakdown and so on. The internal response to such problems from service users is frequently informed by a sense of powerlessness that nothing much can be done. By adopting a critical approach, the practitioner can begin the process of challenging dominant discourses both about the definition of specific problems and the belief that the local community are either apathetic or content with existing arrangements. This can then help in reconstructing the problem in a more empowering way as part of a strategy for change (Heenan, 2004; Stepney and Evans, 2000). The following practice focus is taken from a real life scenario in a Lancashire town to the north of Manchester and reveal some of the issues that emerge when trying to tackle structural problems in a fragmented community.

Practice Focus 1 – 'Pollution from That Factory Chimney Has Put Holes in My Washing' (Local Resident Speaking at a Public Meeting)

In response to complaints about pollution from a local factory, a group of residents from Westwood (an old industrial part of town), with help from a local community worker, decided to organise a public meeting to discuss the problem and what might be done about it. The meeting was well attended and productive, but when it came to establishing an action group . . . Charles a local artist stood up and argued strongly that this would be a waste of time and could even prove counter-productive. He argued that the residents should leave the matter to the local councillors who could refer the matter to the environmental health department of the council. The residents were divided on this, some agreeing with Charles whilst others said that this had been tried before and hadn't led to any improvement. The residents looked to the community worker for guidance.

What was your initial response to this predicament? Industrial pollution is a structural problem but one that may be tolerated as the cost residents must bear for securing local jobs. The environmental health officers are aware of the problem but have been working with the factory management to make improvements but progress has been very slow. The community worker is also employed by the council but feels that she has a professional responsibility to assist the residents.

What are the advantages of adopting a critical practice approach that challenges dominant discourses about the definition of the problem? How might the problem be constructed differently and with what effect? What other resources and systems in the community could be mobilised to help? How might the community worker engage the support of council colleagues to try and find a way forward? In what way can critical practice offer solutions that are different to other social work methods?

A different example of a community-based project involving one of the authors is a land-based rehabilitation project for mental health service users in North Somerset, UK. This offers 'day care without walls' alongside new pathways to inclusion for people who previously felt disempowered by the psychiatric system (Stepney and Davis, 2004). The research question addressed by the project was whether a programme of 'green' land-based therapeutic work, training and support could produce better outcomes than predicted by either standard support informed by the service users' clinical diagnostic assessment or open employment in the labour market. Critical practice in this context might look different to responses to the pollution problem in the Lancashire example, partly because it began very much as a research project. However, both examples reveal a strong commitment to challenging dominant views of the problem, and using qualitative knowledge to reconstruct it in line with local peoples' experience and community resources as a basis for developing more empowering ways forward.

The rehabilitation project was evaluated by adopting a mixed method approach, incorporating a quasi-experimental design and standard testing followed by interviews and focus group discussion. It produced some unexpected findings, for example, in that no strong correlation was found between diagnosis and performance. A majority of mental health users performed better than had been predicted by their diagnostic assessment. However, the reasons for this remained unclear until the qualitative interviews enabled users to give accounts of the problems they faced in the community, explain what inclusion meant for them and outline how the project had brought gains in confidence, motivation and self-belief.

The data gathered during the research derived from different epistemological positions, including quantitative data that derived from the more empirical evidence-based tests. This can be seen as representing two ways of 'slicing the reality cake' rather than producing one complete view of mental health users' reality. One construction related to how 'the psychiatric system' diagnosed, processed and 'objectively' managed them. The other concerned how service users responded to their situation, utilised the opportunities available through the project and in the community and made 'subjective' sense of their experience. Critical practice here was in finding a more preventive road to inclusion that necessarily started where service users were located but, in the words of one participant, enabled them 'to reclaim their lives'. A further lesson from the evaluation of the project is that critical practice can have an influence on mainstream services. Here it had a decisive influence on the development of day-care services and more sustainable job opportunities in North Somerset (Stepney and Davis, 2004).

The wider implications for developing critical practice are encouraging but it is clearly helpful to draw on evidence from projects elsewhere. Heenan (2004) reports on a preventive community-based approach to providing family support in the Foyle district of Northern Ireland. Community development in Northern Ireland as elsewhere, has received low priority in terms of recognition and resources in comparison to statutory interventions in child protection. As one practitioner put it, 'the management of the [Foyle] Trust can talk the talk about partnership and empowerment but they won't walk the walk' (cited in Heenan, 2004, p. 803). So although the workers wanted to break down barriers and involve clients in decision making, both policy and procedure-driven practice priorities made this difficult.

The findings of the research identified three factors that were crucial before community-based methods could be recognised as valid:

1. first, there was the need for a partnership approach with the local community, including statutory and voluntary agencies;

2. second, community development training was seen as essential if staff were to acquire the necessary knowledge and skills; and

3. third, although such initiatives are inherently preventative they require adequate resources and the backing of senior staff to be effective (Heenan, 2004).

Overall the three examples-tackling pollution in Lancashire, the mental health project in North Somerset and the family support team in Northern Ireland, all illustrate the need for a multidimensional strategy that analyses dominant discourses about the problem, but moves beyond them as part of a co-ordinated and empowering approach. This would seek to combine prevention with protection, whilst enhancing local potential through capacity building to strengthen community networks and increase individual well-being for the common good (Jordan, 2007). One important test of critical practice is whether it is helpful and relevant to mainstream

---

Practice Focus 2 – Mrs Kahn and Her Sons Abdul and Jaz

Mrs Kahn and her two sons Abdul (14) and Jaz (9) have recently relocated to the area following incidents of domestic violence. She is currently in the process of divorcing her husband who lives in another town. The family has relatives nearby but they are unable to offer much help. Mrs Kahn who speaks limited English is currently feeling overwhelmed and unable to cope, especially with Abdul whose behaviour has become increasingly difficult. He has begun bullying his brother and threatening his mother saying he wants to go back to his old school and be with his friends. An uncle has come round and reprimanded Abdul but with little effect. The local School staff have said they are concerned about both Abdul and Jaz because they have not settled well and appear to be struggling with their work.

On visiting with an interpreter you find the family in a state of crisis as Abdul had just hit his brother and was threatening his mother. Mrs Kahn tells the interpreter that she is fearful that her husband might turn up and take both boys away.

The family has been allocated to you as a child protection case. How might your knowledge of critical practice help to unravel the crisis? What kind of intervention might follow from your critical analysis of the situation set in its policy and community context? Could this be integrated with other approaches such as systems theory, crisis intervention and task-centred practice?

practitioners when faced with say a child protection or vulnerable adult scenario, as in practice focus 2, that will be all too common to social workers in field-work teams.

Practice Context Two – An Eco-Social Approach to Exclusion in Three European Cities

In Chapter 7, the work of Matthies *et al.* (2000b) was identified as an example of an eco-social approach for tackling exclusion in the European cities of Jyväskylä (Finland), Magdeburg (Germany) and Leicester (UK). This influential EU-funded action-research project will be examined again here as it raises some important issues for developing critical and community-based practice. The project sought to utilise different European traditions in community social work concerning how to mobilise citizens to tackle exclusion in communities with high levels of disadvantage, unemployment and social stress (Matthies *et al.*, 2000b). The project had three broad aims:

1. to develop practice methods to improve the local environment through community participation;

2. to contribute to social impact assessments in local decision making; and

3. to develop an eco-social approach to exclusion that informs the theoretical knowledge base of social work.

The action-research developed in Leicester epitomised these aims by empowering local people 'to define the agenda, participate in the research, and thus, contribute to meeting their own needs and shaping their environment' (Turunen, 1999, p. 7). The organisational structure of the project is set out in Figure 9.2.

It can be seen that each local network was based upon a partnership between the host university, municipal city council and local people supported by a discussion forum. This helped establish a European research network where knowledge, based on the experience of running and evaluating local field projects, could be transferred across international boundaries. Although the research designs differed in each city, a similar eco-social approach was adopted set in its appropriate local and cultural context. This meant that different eco-social models of practice emerged combining core commitments towards promoting a more sustainable environment with unique local features. A comparative analysis of the project was undertaken by an external Finnish researcher based in Sweden (Turunen, 1999).

MAGDEBURG (GER)

Fachhochschule

Co-ordinator of Project

City of Magdeburg

*Field Projects in

Neu-Olvenstedt

*Discussion Forum

THEORY OF ECO-SOCIAL APPROACH TO SOCIAL EXCLUSION (Matthies *et al.*, 2000a)

European research network

* Exchange

* Comparison

INFLUENCING LOCAL POLICIES JYVÄSKYLÄ (FIN) University of Jyväskylä

SOCIAL ACTION LEICESTER (UK) De Montford University Leicester

City of Jyväskylä
* Field Projects in Huhtasuo, Pupuhuhta, Keltinmäki and Lutakko
* Discussions Forum

City of Leicester
Community Development in Saffron Lane, Leicester
* Discussion Forum

Figure 9.2 European research network: new local policies against social exclusion in three European cities
(Matthies, 1999, cited in Turunen, 1999).

The knowledge transfer across the three networks produced a number of convergent findings:

- in each locality urban development initiatives were already addressing issues of inclusion and eco-sustainability, thus there was a need for the project to build upon this experience;

- there appeared to be a lack of political will to prevent exclusion from key stakeholders, plus a tendency to accept inequalities as almost an unavoidable feature of disadvantaged areas;

- local residents expressed many positive views about their communities often in the face of objective evidence of deprivation;

- the European network exchange led to new practice initiatives in each locality drawing upon the experience of what worked elsewhere;

- social exclusion is a complex phenomena that has complicated causalities involving micro and structural factors that defy simple linear explanations;

- no single strategy can be expected to work, but a combination of macro-political, community initiatives and individual interventions proved to be the most effective; and

- small, well-targeted, bottom-up and flexible projects are better than large-scale top-down interventions (amended from Turunen, 1999, pp. 12–13)

Overall it can be seen that the project was informed by three dimensions:

1. a structural dimension concerned with exclusion and sustainability;

2. a local dimension reflecting the characteristics of the local community; and

3. a personal dimension based upon the stories and experience of local people.

This created some interesting possibilities for critical practice by integrating a structural analysis with elements of postmodernism. For example, at the structural level there were tensions between the views of local influentials, that disadvantaged areas reflected inequalities that were unavoidable, and the views of local people supported by practitioners that the problems were not only avoidable but changeable. This illustrates how critical postmodernist ideas conveyed in the language of local people usefully captures their experience, but a series of fragmented stories will not lead to policy change or new practice without some external collectivising and politicising agent. The project attempted to provide that missing ingredient by bringing a clear policy analysis and practical cutting edge for change backed up by research, as two parts of the same strategy rather than separate initiatives.

Practice Context Three – Using Critical Practice as a Basis for Community-Based Evaluation and Research in an International Context

Gardner (2003) discusses the development of a critical reflection framework for evaluating two community-based projects in Victoria state, Australia. This values 'subjective ways of knowing and the importance of inter-actional processes in the generation of knowledge' and can therefore be used with groups in different contexts (Gardner, 2003, p. 199). The criteria for evaluation embraced a number of dimensions including:

- view subjective histories (often oral histories and personal stories) as legitimate sources of knowledge;

- ensure a diversity of perspectives are included, especially those of marginalised groups;

- explore and manage uncertainty in the quest of seeking deeper understanding through causal explanations (Everitt and Hardiker, 1996);

- concern with process as much as outcomes;

- connect the personal with the structural and issues of power; and

- see participants and community members as potential change agents (Adapted from Gardner, 2003, pp. 200–202).

Critical reflection as a framework for research shares many common features with action-research as well as critical practice. Both have a commitment to social justice and span the divide between objective and subjective accounts that value experience and action as much as insight. Bradbury and Reason (2003) identify the core ideals of action-research as being 'grounded in lived experience, developed in partnership . . . works with rather than simply studies people, develops new [theoretical] ways of interpreting the world, and leaves infrastructure in its wake' (p. 156).

In practice, action-research involves a process of ongoing inquiry as the researcher uses their own inquiring self as an 'instrument of their own research' (Bradbury and Reason, 2003, p. 161). This approach when applied to marginalised communities seeks to establish relationships of mutual respect and trust, captured by the Latin American term *acompañamiento,* meaning 'accompanying the process' (p. 162). The principles involved include: 'Non-intrusive collaboration, solidarity, mutuality, a focus on process, and the use of language as an expression of culture and power' (Bradbury and Reason, 2003, p. 162). It will be noted that this has correspondence with Gardner's framework for critical reflection and the examples of community-based practice in the UK and Europe above.

Bradbury and Reason (2003) report that action-research was used by staff from the Highlander research centre, Tennessee, USA at Bumpass Cove, a remote mining community in the Appalachian mountains. The mine had closed down in the 1960s, but later a new company announced plans to reopen it and establish a landfill site from household waste, thereby creating new jobs in the local economy. However, the good news about employment for the community proved to be a double-edged sword, as people living near the mine soon began to develop serious illnesses. A protracted campaign by local people, directed at the company and State Health Department officials, identified the source of the problem. It emerged that the company had begun using the mine to dump hazardous chemical waste and this had seeped into the local water supply. In the process of carrying out action-research to expose the nature of the problem and force state health 'experts' to take appropriate action (rescind the company's licence in the public interest), local people became empowered and politicised. This strikes some very resonant chords with the Lancashire pollution example earlier. Here critical practice involved challenging the dominant discourse of environmental health officers (the problem is under control), and persuading them to take appropriate action to protect the community as the first part of a strategy to creating a safer, sustainable and more just community.

A Checklist for Critical Community-Based Practice

How can the vision of critical community-based practice be translated into purposeful action? The following provides a general guide for the practitioner based upon the critical incident technique:

- Identify and describe a critical incident and/or community-based problem from practice (a critical incident can be any practice experience that made the practitioner stop and think).

- Analyse the incident/problem by locating it in its wider theoretical, global policy and local community context. Use a structural analysis to unpack the dominant discourse(s) to achieve depth of understanding, including responses from key stakeholders such as service users, carers, community members, other practitioners, managers and so on.

- Reflect and re-theorise using a range of theory, knowledge and practice wisdom, for example, critical postmodernism to deconstruct the subjective experience of service users and narratives of oppression, structural theories to locate causal mechanisms, practice knowledge and research evidence. Recognise the flow of power between key stakeholders and suggest how this might be changed in favour of subordinate groups to achieve greater social justice.

- Reconstruct and re-create new more emancipatory strategies and community-based initiatives for change (adapted from Stepney, 2006a; see also Fook, 2002 and Morley, 2004).

Practice Focus 3 – From Critical Incident to Critical Practice

Please refer back to the notes you made from the practice focus 2 in Chapter 6 that asked you to identify a critical incident from your own practice. Having described the incident, located it in its theoretical, policy and community context and identified dominant discourses of key stakeholders . . . you are now asked to complete the final two stages from the above checklist:

- reflect and re-theorise to unpack the stories and causal mechanisms that uphold dominant discourses. Identify the flow of power involving key stakeholders and indicate how this could be changed to empower local people/service users/carers;

- develop new strategies and community-based initiatives for change including if possible a research dimension to evaluate effectiveness.

Conclusions

In this final chapter, future possibilities for a critical community-based practice have been explored against a backdrop of economic globalisation and the modernisation and marketisation of the welfare state. Social work has become caught up in this policy shift where a greater emphasis on public accountability, cost containment and risk has created a growing sense of uncertainty about the future. In a climate of 'tough love', often masquerading as consumer 'choice', the profession's long-term commitment to social justice and change has been seriously challenged and reshaped but not eroded. Many service users in the fields of mental health, substance abuse and child protection, as well as new migrants, refugees and asylum-seekers, now receive much harsher and more conditional forms of treatment (Dominelli, 2002). This highlights that social work is now very much associated with risk assessment, resource management and the protection of vulnerable adults and children (Parton *et al.*, 1997). Although practitioners have the necessary knowledge and skills to do preventive work, ironically they are often no longer directly involved in the more enabling projects in the community associated with cultural processes of inclusion (Holman, 1998). Many of these initiatives have migrated to the voluntary sector. Some would argue that mainstream social work has at best lost its way, and at worst had its soul stripped out (Butler and Drakeford, 2001).

According to Hugman (2005), social work is now characterised by two apparently contradictory responses to the current predicament: on the one hand is the 'search for certainty' in evidence-based practice, designed to increase effectiveness and enhance professional standing, whilst on the other is the 'search for uncertainty' in postmodernism and critical practice that emphasises notions of context, contingency and difference. The latter enables social workers to engage with a plurality of meanings as a basis for critical reflection and change. However, this leaves the practitioner with the unenviable task of managing such contradictions, and the future direction of the profession will depend upon how the resulting practice dilemmas are resolved and the quality of the research evidence used to inform practice.

A case has been made throughout the book for developing a more progressive, transformative and critical community-based practice. In this final chapter, we have explored how this might be achieved by considering two versions of critical practice – one combining a structural analysis with elements of critical postmodernism (Fook, 2002), and the other based on critical realism, that seeks to be sensitive to subjective experience and human agency but views this within the context of dominant and powerful social structures (Houston, 2001). Recognising the importance of context, structure and uncertainty is important, but the ability to reconstruct new strategies for change becomes necessary if injustices in the community are to be tackled and not merely understood.

Drawing upon evidence from several community-based projects in a variety of international contexts, five pointers for critical practice emerge:

1. small-scale, 'bottom-up', multi-strategy partnership approaches are more effective than large, top-down prestigious projects;

2. education and training in community development, eco-systems theory and networking are essential and can be integrated with traditional social work methods;

3. research methods training is necessary to facilitate the systematic evaluation of community-based interventions;

4. preventive initiatives can be dovetailed with protection strategies but must be incorporated from the start, and require adequate resources and support;

5. intervention at the structural/policy, community and individual levels are required as three inter-related parts of the same strategy.

We have argued in this book that critical practice can provide a progressive way of working in the community in partnership with community members. It offers practitioners a framework for handling the contradictions that emerge – responding to problems in the community whilst being critical of the structures that contribute to the production of those problems.

Our view is that the government is paying only lip service to issues of autonomy, choice and empowerment, whilst primarily concerning itself with how social work should deal with rationing, risk assessment and court orders. For example, the move to privilege the role of social work service users is a laudable one, but evidence shows that this is often framed in a manner that emphasises the responsibility service users themselves have for their position. The direct payment scheme was introduced to offer choice and control to service users and in many cases represents a laudable increase in power. However, this also heralds a shift of responsibility from service providers to service users. Service users who use direct payments to purchase the services of carers are ultimately responsible as employers for the welfare of their carers and have to deal with any problems that might arise such as finding carers when regular staff are unable to work due to illness or holidays. Service users can also be responsible for carrying out Criminal Record Bureau checks on the carers or other staff they employ which has proved time consuming and complex, leaving service users in a position of vulnerability (Commission for Social Care Inspection, 2004).

The government's approach to social work, which emphasises that people should take responsibility for assessing their own needs and deciding how best these might be met (Department of Health, 2006a), fails to adequately recognise and address the impact of poverty and inequality, which leads to the stigmatising of individuals and communities. Individualism is emphasised at the expense of collectivism, and social justice has been redefined as inclusion and opportunity as opposed to redistribution and transformation. At the same time, increasing bureaucratisation and the control of practitioners through new styles of managerialism and via technological databases, particularly those in local authority employment, has increased stress on front-line workers (Huxley *et al.*, 2005; Jones, 2001) who have less face-to-face contact with service users leaving them to feel their roles are slowly being diluted as voluntary and community sector organisations take over some of their work. All of which is a long way from the more preventive community-based approaches that social work developed and enjoyed in previous decades.

Genuine critical practice will need to be relevant and demanding of itself, evaluation minded, policy informed, sensitive to cultural contexts and diversity, as well as being opposed to injustice in all its forms. The challenge is how to demonstrate that critical community-based practice can be more effective than the current preference for target-driven 'Macdonald-ised welfare' (Harris, 2005). There is an urgent need for the practitioner, subdued by a diet of 'tough love' and 27 'tick box' assessments, to find the inspiration to engage with service users and community members in a process of emancipatory change. We hope that this book will be a helpful resource on the journey and, like the traveller in the Robert Frost poem who took the less travelled road (Frost, 1920), may make a critical and real difference.

Bibliography

Abel-Smith, B. and Townsend, P. (1965) *The Poor and the Poorest*. London: Bell.

Abrams, P. (1978) 'Introduction: social facts and sociological analysis' in P. Abrams (ed.) *Work, Urbanism and Inequality: UK Society Today*. London: Weidenfeld and Nicolson.

Abrams, P. (1980) 'Social change, social networks and neighbourhood care'. *Social Work Service*, **22**, 12–23.

Abrams, P., Abrams, S., Humphrey, R. and Snaith, R. (1989) *Neighbourhood Care and Social Policy*. London: HMSO.

Adams, I. (1993) *Political Ideology Today*. Manchester: Manchester University Press.

Alcock, P. (2004) 'Participation or pathology: contradictory tensions in area-based policy', *Social Policy and Society*, **3**(2), 87–96.

Allatt, P. and Yeandle, S. (1992) *Youth Unemployment and the Family: Voices of Disordered Times*. London: Routledge.

Anning, A. (2001) 'Knowing who I am and what I know: developing new versions of professional knowledge in integrated service settings', *Education On Line*. University of Leeds. www.leeds.ac.uk/educol/documents/00001877.htm.

Apter, T. (1994) *Working Women Don't Have Wives: Professional Success in the 1990s*. New York: St. Martin's Press.

Ashurst, P. and Hall, Z. (1989) *Understanding Women in Distress*. London: Tavistock/Routledge.

Atkin, K. and Twigg, J. (1994) *Carers Perceived*. Buckingham: Open University Press.

Attree, P. (2004) 'It was like my little acorn and it's going to grow into a big tree: a qualitative study of a community support project', *Health and Social Care in the Community*, **12**(2), 155–161.

Austen, J. (1996) *Pride and Prejudice*. Harmondsworth: Penguin (Original work published in 1813).

Bachrach, P. and Baratz, M. (1970) *Power and Poverty*. Buckingham: Open University Press.

Balloch, S. and Taylor, M. (eds) (2001) *Partnership Working: Policy and Practice*. Bristol: Policy Press.

Barclay Committee (1982) *Social Workers: Their Roles and Tasks*. London: National Institute for Social Work/Bedford Square Press.

Barnett, S. A. (1898) 'University settlements in our great towns' in W. Reason (ed.) *University and Social Settlements*. London: Methuen.

Barr, A. (1997) 'Reflections on the enigma of community empowerment', *Scottish Journal of Community Work and Development*, **2**, 47–59.

Barr, H., Hammick, M., Koppel, I. and Reeves, S. (1999) 'Evaluating interprofessional education: two systematic reviews for health and social care', *British Educational Research Journal*, **25**(4), 533–543.

Batten, T. R. (1957) *Communities and Their Development*. London: Oxford University Press.

Batten, T. R. (1962) *Training for Community Development: A Critical Study of Method*. London: Oxford University Press.

Batten, T. R. (1965) *The Human Factor in Community Work*. London: Oxford University Press.

Batten, T. R. (1967) *The Non-Directive Approach to Youth and Community Work*. Oxford: Oxford University Press.

Batten, T. R. with the collaboration with Madge Batten (1967) *The Non-Directive Approach in Group and Community Work*. London: Oxford University Press.

Becker, S. (2004) 'Carers', *Research Matters*, **16**(1), 11–16.

Bell, D. (1993) *Communitarianism and its Critics*. Oxford: Clarendon Press.

Bell, C. and Newby. H. (1971) *Community Studies: An Introduction to the Sociology of the Local Community*. London: Allen & Unwin.

Benington, J. (1975) *Local Government Becomes Big Business*. Coventry: CDP. Occasional Paper No. 11.

Beresford, P. and Croft, S. (1986) *Whose Welfare? Private Care or Public Services*. Brighton: Lewis Cohen Centre for Urban Studies.

Berner, E. and Phillips, B. (2005) 'Left to their own devices? Community self-help between alternative development and neo-liberalism', *Community Development Journal*, 40(1), 17–29.

Beyer, P. F. (1990) 'Privatization and the public influence of religion in global society' in M. Featherstone (ed.) *Global Culture: Nationalism, Globalization and Modernity*. London: Sage.

Bhaskar, R. (1978). *A Realist Theory of Science*. Brighton: Harvester Press.

Billis, D. and Glennerster, H. (1998) 'Human services and the voluntary sector: towards a theory of comparative advantage', *Journal of Social Policy*, 27(1), 79–98.

Blair, T. (2000) 'Transforming the welfare state'. Speech to Institute for Public Policy Research. London. 7 June.

Blair, T. (2004) 'Responsibility, citizenship and the criminal justice system'. Speech to launch new criminal justice policy. London: Kings Cross. 20 July.

Blair, T. (2006) Speech on the Respect Action Plan. 10 January.

Blair, T. and Schröder, G. (1999) 'Der Weg nach vorne fur Europas Sozialdemokraten. Ein Vorschlag von Gerhard Schröder und Tony Blair', quoted in http://www.amos-blaetter.de.

Blakemore, K. (1998) *Social Policy: An Introduction*. Buckingham: Open University Press.

Boddy, M. (1984) 'Local economic and employment strategies' in M. Boddy and C. Fudge (eds) *Local Socialism?* London: Macmillan.

Bornat, J., Pereira, C., Pilgrim, D. and Williams, F. (1993) *Community Care*. Basingstoke: Palgrave Macmillan.

Bourdieu, P. (1992) *An Invitation to Reflexive Sociology*. Chicago: Chicago University Press.

Bradbury, H. and Reason, P. (2003) 'Action research – an opportunity for revitalizing research purpose and practices', *Qualitative Social Work*, 2(2), 155–175.

Bright, M. (2003) 'City of hate'. *The Observer*, 29 June.

Brindle, D. (2007) 'Families told elderly care crisis is looming: relatives to get little help from the state', *The Guardian*, 10 January.

British Council of Churches (1985) *Faith in the City*. London: Church House Publishing.

Bronfenbrenner, U. (1979) *The Ecology of Human Development*. Cambridge, MA: Harvard University Press.

Bryan, B., Dadzie, S. and Scafe, S. (1985) *The Heart of the Race: Black Women's Lives in Britain*. London: Virago.

Bryson, V. (2003) *Feminist Political Theory: An Introduction* (2nd Edition) Basingstoke: Palgrave Macmillan.

Burns, D. (1992) *Poll Tax Rebellion*. Stirling and London: AK Press and Attack International.

Butler, A. (2005) 'A strengths approach to building futures: UK students and refugees together', *Community Development Journal*, 40(2), 147–157.

Butler, I. and Drakeford, M. (2001) 'Which Blair project? Communitarianism, social authoritarianism and social work', *Journal of Social Work*, 1(1), 7–19.

Butler, I. and Drakeford, M. (2005a) 'Trusting in social work', *British Journal of Social Work*, 35(5), 639–653.

Butler, I. and Drakeford, M. (2005b) *Scandal, Social Policy and Social Welfare*. Bristol: Policy Press.

Callwood, I. (2003) 'Collaborative working for primary care practitioners'. Research project for PhD thesis (Unpublished).

Cambridge, P., Hayes, L. and Knapp, M. with Gould, E. and Fenyo, A. (1994) *Care in the Community: Five Years On*. PSSRU: University of Kent.

Cameron, J. (2006) 'Accidental heroes', *Society Guardian, The Guardian*, 6 December.

Carpenter, J., Schneider, J., Brandon, T. and Wooff, D. (2003) 'Working in multidisciplinary community mental health teams: the impact on social workers and health professionals of integrated mental health care', *British Journal of Social Work*, 33, 1081–1103.

Carrington, W. and Detragiache, E. (1999) 'How extensive is the brain drain?', *Finance and Development*, June, 46–49.

Castells, M. (1977) *The Urban Question*. London: Edward Arnold.

Castells, M. (1978) *City, Class and Power*. London: Macmillan.

Castles, M. and Cossacks, G. (1973) *Immigrant Workers and Class Structure in Western Europe*. Oxford: Institute for Race Relations/Oxford University Press.

Centre for Policy on Ageing (1990) *Community Life: A Code of Practice for Community Care*. London: Centre for Policy on Ageing.

Challis, D., Darton, R., Johnson, L., Stone, M. and Traske, K. (1991) 'An evaluation of an alternative to long-stay hospital care for frail elderly patients, part II: costs and effectiveness', *Age and Ageing*, 20, 245–254.

Challis, D., Chesterman, J., Luckett, R., Stewart, K. and Chessum, R. (2002) *Care Management in Social and Primary Health Care: The Gateshead Community Care Scheme*. Aldershot: Ashgate.

Chote, R. and Sibieta, L. (2007) 'Inequalities trends: how the rich and poor have fared under the current labour government' *Britain in 2008*. Swindon: Economic & Social Research Council.

Clarence, E. and Painter, C. (1998) 'Public services under New Labour: collaborative discourses and local networking', *Public Policy and Administration*, 13(3), 8–22.

Clarke, H., Dyer, S. and Hartman, L. (1996) *Going Home: Older People Leaving Hospital*. Bristol: Policy Press.

Clark, H., Dyer, S. and Horwood, J. (1998) 'That bit of help: the high value of low level preventive services for older people'. Joseph Rowntree Foundation. Bristol: Policy Press.

Clarke, J. (2000) 'A world of difference? Globalisation and the study of social policy' in G. Lewis, S. Gewirtz and J. Clarke (eds) *Rethinking Social Policy*. London: Sage.

Clarke, J. (2001) 'Globalisation and welfare states: some unsettling thoughts' in R. Sykes, B. Palier and P. Prior (eds) *Globalisation and European Welfare States*. Basingstoke: Palgrave Macmillan.

Clarke, J. and Cochrane, A. (1998) 'The social construction of social problems' in E. Saraga (ed.), *Embodying the Social: Constructions of Difference*. London: Routledge.

Clarke, J., Gewirtz, S. and McLaughlin, E. (2000a) 'Reinventing the Welfare State' in J. Clarke, S. Gewirtz and E. McLaughlin (eds) *New Managerialism, New Welfare?* London: Sage.

Clarke, J., Gewirtz, S. and McLaughlin, E. (eds) (2000b) *New Managerialism New Welfare?* London: Sage.

Clatworthy, W. (1999) 'Collaborative working', *Journal of Community Nursing*, 13(2), 4–8.

Coates, J. (2003) *Ecology and Social Work: Towards a New Paradigm*. Halifax, NS: Fernwood.

Cohen, R. and Kennedy, P. (2000) *Global Sociology*. Basingstoke: Palgrave Macmillan.

Cohen, R. and Rai, S. (eds) (2000) *Global Social Movements*. London: Athlone Press.

Commission for Social Care Inspection (2004) *Direct Payments: What are the Barriers?* London: Commission for Social Care Inspection.

Community Development Project (1976) *The Costs of Industrial Change*. Nottingham: Russell Press.

Community Development Projects (1977) *Gilding the Ghetto: The State and the Poverty Experiments*. London: CDP Inter-project Editorial Team.

Connolly, N. and Johnson, J. (1996) *Community Care as Policy: Emerging Issues*. Supplement to K259 Workbook 2, part 2, Buckingham: Open University Press.

Cooke, I. and Shaw, M. (eds) (1996) *Radical Community Work: Perspectives from Practice in Scotland*. Edinburgh: Moray House.

Cooper, M. (1983) 'Community social work' in B. Jordan, and N. Parton (eds) *The Political Dimension of Social Work*. Oxford: Blackwell.

Corby, B. (2000) *Child Abuse: Towards a Knowledge Base* (2nd Edition) Buckingham: Open University Press.

Cornwell, J. (1984) *Hard-Earned Lives: Accounts of Health and Illness from East London*. London: Unwin Hyman.

Coulshed, V. and Orme, J. (2006) *Social Work Practice: An Introduction* (4th Edition) especially ch.10, Basingstoke: Palgrave Macmillan.

Coulton, C. (2004) 'The place of community in social work practice research: conceptual and methodological developments'. Paper presented at Aaron Rosen Lecture, Society for Social Work Research, New Orleans, January.

Craig, G. (1979) 'Community work and the state', *Community Development Journal*, **24**(1), 3–18.

Craig, G. and Mayo, M. (eds) (1995) *Community Empowerment*. London: Zed Books.

Craig, G., Derricourt, N. and Loney, M. (eds) (1982) *Community Work and the State: Towards a Radical Approach*. London, Routledge and Kegan Paul.

Craig, G., Mayo, M. and Taylor, M. (2000) 'Globalization from below: implications for the Community Development Journal', *Community Development Journal*, **35**(4), 323–335.

Craig, G., Gaus, A., Wilinson, M., Shrivankova, K. and McQuade, A. (2007) *Contemporary Slavery in the UK: Overview and Key Issues*. York: Joseph Rowntree Foundation.

Cressey, P. (1971) 'Population succession in Chicago, 1898–1930' in J. Short (ed.) *The Social Fabric of the Metropolis*. Chicago: Chicago University Press.

Crow, G. and Allan, G. (1994) *Community Life: An Introduction to Local Social Relations*. Hemel Hempstead: Harvester Wheatsheaf.

Dalley, G. (1988) *Ideologies of Caring*. Basingstoke: Palgrave Macmillan.

Damer, S. (1989) *Glasgow: Going for a Song*. London: Lawrence and Wishart.

Davies, J. K. (2001) 'Partnership working in health promotion: the potential role of social capital in health development' in S. Balloch and M. Taylor (eds) *Partnership Working: Policy and Practice*. Bristol: Policy Press.

Davies, B. and Challis, D. (1986) *Matching Resources to Needs in Community Care: An Evaluated Demonstration of a Long Term Care Model*. Aldershot: Gower.

Davis, R., Cohen, L. and Humes, M. (2000) 'The role of social work in Prevention'. Paper presented at the 128th Annual Congress of American Public Health Association, Boston, MA, USA.

Day, G. and Murdoch, J. (1993) 'Locality and community: coming to terms with place', *Sociological Review*, **41**(1), 82–111.

Denney, D. (1998) *Social Policy and Social Work*. Oxford: Oxford University Press.

Dennis, N., Henriques, F. and Slaughter, C. (1956) *Coal is Our Life*. London: Eyre and Spottiswood.

Department for Education and Skills, DfES (2004) *Every Child Matters: Change for Children*. London: Department for Education and Skills.

Department of Health (1989) *Caring for People*. London: HMSO.

Department of Health (1995) *Child Protection: Messages from Research*. London: HMSO.

Department of Health (1998a) *Modernising the Social Services*. Cm 4169, London: The Stationery Office.

Department of Health (1998b) *Partnerships in Action*. London: The Stationery Office.

Department of Health (1999) *Modernising Mental Health Services*. London: The Stationery Office.

Department of Health (2000) *The NHS Plan*. London: The Stationery Office.

Department of Health (2001) *The National Service Framework for Older People*. London: Stationery Office.

Department of Health (2002) *Fair Access to Care Services: Policy Guidance* [LACS (2002) 13] London: Stationery Office.

Department of Health (2006a) *Our Health, Our Care, Our Say: A New Direction for Community Services*, Cm 6737, London: The Stationery Office.

Department of Health (2006b) *A New Ambition for Old Age: Next Steps in Implementing the National Service Framework for Older People*. London: Stationery Office.

Department of Health and Home Office (2003) *The Victoria Climbie Inquiry: Report of an Inquiry by Lord Laming*. London: Stationery Office.

Department of Work and Pensions (2005) *Households Below Average Income 1994/95–2003/04*. London: Stationery Office.

Department of Work and Pensions (2006) *Security in Retirement: Towards a New Pensions System*. London: Stationery Office.

DoE (Department of Environment) (1977) *Policy for the Inner Cities*. London: HMSO.

Dominelli, L. (2000) 'Empowerment: help or hindrance in professional relationships' in P. Stepney and D. Ford (eds) *Social Work Models, Methods and Theories: A Framework for Practice*. Lyme Regis: Russell House.

Dominelli, L. (2002) *Anti-Oppressive Social Work Theory and Practice*. Basingstoke: Palgrave Macmillan.

Dominelli, L. (2006) *Women and Community Action* (Revised 2nd Edition) Bristol: Policy Press.

Donnison, D. (1982) *The Politics of Poverty*. Oxford: Martin Robertson.

Donzelot, J. (1988) 'The promotion of the social', *Economy and Society*, **17**(3), 395–427.

Dorling, D., Rigby, J., Wheeler, B., Ballas, D., Thomas, B., Fahmy, E., Gordon, D. and Lupton, R. (2007) *Poverty, Wealth and Place in Britain 1968 to 2005*. Bristol: Policy Press.

Dowling, B., Powell, M. and Glendenning, C. (2004) 'Conceptualising successful partnerships', *Health and Social Care in the Community*, 12(4), 309–317.

Driver, S. and Martell, S. (1998) *New Labour Politics after That Hersim*. Cambridge: Polity Press.

Ducklow, F. (2003) 'Self improved citizens: citizenship, social inclusion and the self in the politics of welfare'. Cork: University College.

Engels, F. (1999) (First published 1845) *Condition of the Working Classes in England*. Oxford: Oxford University Press.

Esping-Andersen, G. (1996) *Welfare States in Transition*. London: Sage.

Etzioni, A. (1993) *The Spirit of Community: The Reinvention of American Society*. New York: Touchstone.

Etzioni, A. (1994) *The Spirit of Community: The Reinvention of American Society*. New York: Touchstone.

Etzioni, A. (1995) *The Spirit of Community*. London: Fontana.

European Communities (2007) *Europe in Figures: Eurostat Yearbook 2006–2007*. Luxembourg: Statistical Office of the European Communities. www.europa.eu.int/comm/eurostat.

Everitt, A. and Hardiker, P. (1996) *Evaluating for Good Practice*. Basingstoke: Palgrave Macmillan.

Farrell, G. (2001) 'From tall poppies to squashed weeds: why don't nurses pull together more?', *Journal of Advanced Nursing*, **35**(1), 26–33.

Ferguson, I. and Lavalette, M. (2004) 'Beyond power discourse: alienation and social work', *British Journal of Social Work*, **34**, 297–312.

Finch, J. and Groves, D. (1980) 'Community care and the family: a case for equal opportunities', *Journal of Social Policy*, **9**, 487–511.

Firth, J. (1987) *Public Support for Residential Care: Report of a Joint Central and Local Government Working Party*. London: DHSS.

Fischer, C. S. (1984) *The Urban Experience* (2nd Edition). New York: Harcourt.

Fitzpatrick, T. (2001) *Welfare Theory: An Introduction*. Basingstoke: Palgrave Macmillan.

Fook, J. (2002) *Social Work – Critical Theory and Practice*. London: Sage.

Fook, J. (2003) 'Critical social work: the current iussues', editorial, *Qualitative Social Work*, 2(2), 123–130.

Fook, J., Ryan, M. and Hawkins, L. (2000) *Professional Expertise: Practice, Theory and Education for Working in Uncertainty*. London: Whiting and Birch.

Foot, P. (1969) *The Rise of Enoch Powell: An Examination of Enoch Powell's Attitude to Immigration and Race*. Harmondsworth: Penguin.

Ford, D. and Stepney, P. (2003) 'Hospital discharge and the citizenship rights of older people: will the UK become a test-bed for Eastern Europe?' *European Journal of Social Work*, **6**(3), 257–273.

Forrest, D. (1999) 'Education and empowerment: towards untested feasibility', *Community Development Journal*, **34**(2), 93–107.

Foucault, M. (1977) *Discipline and Punishment*. Harmondsworth: Penguin.

Foucault, M. (1984) *The Foucault Reader*. Paul Rabinov (ed.) Harmondsworth: Penguin.

Francis, D., Henderson, P. and Thomas, D. N. (1984) *A Survey of Community Workers in the United Kingdom*. London: National Institute for Social Work.

Fraser, E. and Lacey, N. (1993) *The Politics of Community: A Feminist Critique of the Liberal-Communitarian Debate*. Hemel Hempstead: Harvester Wheatsheaf.

Freire, P. (1972) *Pedagogy of the Oppressed*. Harmondsworth: Penguin.

Frost, R. (1920) 'The road not taken', *Mountain Interval*. New York: Henry Holt.

Gans, H. J. (1968) *People and Plans: Essays on Urban Problems and Solutions*. New York: Basic Books.

Garbarino, J. and Kostelny, K. (1992) 'Child maltreatment as a community problem', *Child Abuse and Neglect*, **16**, 455–464.

Gardner, F. (2003) 'Critical reflection in community-based evaluation', *Qualitative Social Work*, 2(2), 197–212.

Germain, C. B. and Gitterman, A. (1996) *The Life Model of Social Work Practice: Advances in Theory and Practice* (2nd Edition) New York: Columbia University Press.

Giddens, A. (1981) *A Contemporary Critique of Historical Materialism, Power, Property and the State*. London: Macmillan.

Giddens, A. (1991) *Modernity and Self-identity*. Cambridge: Polity Press.

Giddens, A. (2000) *The Third Way and its Critics*. Cambridge, Polity Press.

Gill, C. (1979) *Plymouth: A New History: 1603 to the Present Day*. Newton Abbot: David and Charles.

Gill, O. (1996) 'Child protection and neighbourhood work: Dilemmas for practice', *Practice*, 8(2), 45–52.

Gilroy, P. (1987) *There Ain't No Black in the Union Jack*. London: Hutchinson.

Glendinning, C., Rummery, K. and Clarke, R. (1998) 'From collaboration to commissioning: developing relationships between primary health and social services', *British Medical Journal*, (11 July), **317**, 122–125.

Godfrey, M. and Moore, J. (1996) *Hospital Discharge: User, Carer and Professional Perspectives*. Leeds: Nuffield Institute for Health.

Goodman, R. M. (2000) 'Bridging the gap in effective program implementation: from concept to application', *Journal of Community Psychology*, **28**(3), 309–321.

Goodman, A., Johnson, P. and Webb, S. (1997) *Inequality in the UK*. Oxford: Oxford University Press.

Gramsci, A. (1971) *Selections from Prison Notebooks*, London: Lawrence and Wishart.

Gramsci, A. (1986) *Selections from Prison Notebooks*. Edited and translated by Q. Hoare and G. Smith. London: Lawrence and Wishart.

Gray, B. (1989) *Collaborating: Finding Common Ground for Multiparty Problems*. San Francisco: Jossey-Bass.

Green, K. (2007) 'Off target', *Progress*, March 16–17.

Grenier, P. and Wright, K. (2001) *Social Capital in Britain: A Critique of Hall's Analysis*. Paper presented at JHU Conference, December.

Griffiths Report (1988) *Community Care: Agenda for Action*. London: Stationery Office.

Grint, K. (2005) *The Sociology of Work* (3rd Edition) Cambridge: Polity Press.

Gunaratnam, Y. (1997) 'Breaking the silence: Asian carers in Britain', in J. Bornat, C. Pereira, D. Pilgrim and F. Williams (eds) *Community Care – A Reader*. Basingstoke: Palgrave Macmillan.

Habermas, J. (1978) *Knowledge and Human Interest*. London: Heinemann.

Hadley, R. and Hatch, S. (1982) *Social Welfare and the Failure of the State*. London: Allen & Unwin.

Hadley, R. and Leidy, B. (1996) 'Community social work in a market environment: a British-American exchange of technologies and experience', *British Journal of Social Work*, **26**(6), 823–842.

Hadley, R. and McGrath, M. (1984) *When Social Services are Local – The Normanton Experience*. London: Allen & Unwin.

Hadley, R., Cooper, M., Dale, P. and Stacey, G. (1987) *A Community Social Workers Handbook.* London: Tavistock.

Hall, S. (1988) *The Hard Road to Renewal: Thatcherism and the Crisis of the Left.* London: Verso.

Hall, S. (1993) 'Basic instinct off target', *The Guardian*, 24 November 1993.

Hall, S. (1998) 'The great moving nowhere show', *Marxism Today.* November/December.

Hall, S. (2003) 'New Labour has picked up where Thatcher left off', *Society, The Guardian*, 6 August.

Hall, S., Critcher, C., Jefferson, T., Clarke, J. and Roberts, B. (1978) *Policing the Crisis: Mugging, the State and Law and Order.* London: Macmillan.

Hamnett, C. (1979) 'Area-based explanations: a critical appraisal' in D. Herbert and D. Smith (eds) *Social Problems and the City: Geographical Perspectives.* Oxford: Oxford University Press.

Haralambos, M. and Holborn, M. (1995) *Sociology: Themes and Perspectives.* London: HarperCollins.

Hardiker, P., Exton, K. and Barker, M. (1991) 'The social policy contexts of prevention in child care', *British Journal of Social Work*, **21**(4), 341–359.

Harman, C. (1997) *How Marxism Works.* London: Bookmarks.

Harrington, M. (1962) *The Other America.* New York: Macmillan.

Harris, J. (1977) *William Beveridge: A Biography.* Oxford: Clarendon.

Harris, J. (1998a) 'Scientific management, bureau-professionalism, new managerialism: the labour process of state social work', *British Journal of Social Work*, **28**, 839–862.

Harris, M. (1998b) 'Doing it their way: organisational challenges for voluntary associations', *Nonprofit and Voluntary Sector Quarterly*, **27**(2), 144–158.

Harris, J. (2005) 'Modernised social services in the UK: franchised social work in the McMunicipality'. Paper presented at conference *The Changing Place of Municipal Social Work in Finland in the 21st Century.* Finland: University of Tampere.

Harris, M., Rochester, C. and Halfpenny, P. (2001) 'Voluntary Organisations and Social Policy: twenty years of change' in M. Harris and C. Rochester (eds) *Voluntary Organisations and Social Policy in Britain.* Basingstoke: Palgrave Macmillan.

HAZnet (2000) Background. www.haznet.org.uk/hazs/background.

Healy, K. (2001) 'Reinventing critical social work: challenges from practice, context and post-modernism', *Critical Social Work*, **2**(1), 201–238.

Healy, K. (2005) *Social Work Theories in Context.* Basingstoke: Palgrave Macmillan.

Heenan, D. (2004) 'Learning lessons from the past or re-visiting old mistakes: social work and community development in Northern Ireland', *British Journal of Social Work*, **34**, 793–809.

Henderson, P. and Thomas, D. (1987) *Skills in Neighbourhood Work.* London: Allen & Unwin.

Henriques, P. (2005) 'General systems theory and eco-systems'. Lecture to BA social work students, University of Wolverhampton, November.

Henwood, M. (1995) *Making a Difference? Implementation of the Community Care Reforms Two Years On.* Leeds: Nuffield Institute for Health, University of Leeds and London: Kings Fund Centre.

Henwood, M. (1996) *Continuing Health Care: Analysis of a sample of Final Documents.* London: NHS Executive.

Higgins, J. (1998) 'HAZs warning', *Health Service Journal*, 16 April, 24–25.

Hillery, C. A. (1955) 'Definitions of community: areas of agreement', *Rural Sociology*, **20**, 86–118.

Hills, J. and Stewart, K. (eds) (2005) *A More Equal Society: New Labour, Poverty, Inequality and Exclusion.* Bristol: Policy Press.

Hills, J., Le Grand, J. and Piachaud, D. (2002) *Understanding Social Exclusion.* Oxford: Oxford University Press.

HMSO (2004) *Social Trends 34.* London: HMSO.

Hobson, D. (2002) *Soap Opera.* Cambridge: Polity Press.

Holman, B. (1976) *Inequality in Child Care.* London: Child Poverty Action Group.

Holman, B. (1981) *Kids at the Door: A Preventive Project on a Council Estate.* Oxford: Blackwell.

Holman, B. (1988) *Putting Families First: Prevention and Child Care*. Basingstoke: Palgrave Macmillan.

Holman, B. (1993) 'Pulling together', *The Guardian*, 20 January.

Holman, B. (1995) *Putting Families First*. Basingstoke: Macmillan.

Holman, B. (1998) *Faith in the Poor*. Oxford: Lion Books.

Holman, B. (1999) *Kids at the Door Revisited*. Lyme Regis: Russell House Publishing.

Holman, B. (2000) *Kids at the Door Revisited*. Lyme Regis: Russell House.

Holman, B. (2001) *Champions for Children*. Bristol: Policy Press.

Holman, B. (2003) 'Social work in the neighbourhood' in V. Cree (ed.) *On Becoming a Social Worker*. London: Routledge.

Holme, A. (1985) *Housing and Families in East London*. London: Routledge and Kegan Paul.

Homans, H. (1987) 'Man-made myth: The reality of being a woman scientist in the NHS' in A. Spencer and D. Podmore (eds) *A Man's World: Essays on Women in Male-Dominated Professions*. London: Tavistock.

Home Office (2002) *Secure Borders, Safe Haven: Integration with Diversity in Modern Britain*. London: Stationery Office.

Horner, N. (2006) *What is Social Work? Context and Perspectives* (2nd Edition) Exeter: Learning Matters.

Houston, S. (2001). 'Beyond social constructionism: critical realism and social work', *British Journal of Social Work*, **31**, 845–861.

Howe, D. (1996). 'Surface and depth in social work practice' in N. Parton (ed.) *Social Theory, Social Change and Social Work*. London: Routledge.

Hoyes, L. and Means, R. (1997) 'The impact of quasi-markets on community care' in J. Bornat *et al.* (eds) *Community Care – A Reader*. (2nd Edition) Basingstoke: Palgrave Macmillan.

Hughes, G. and Mooney, G. (1998) 'Community' in G. Hughes (ed.) *Imagining Welfare Futures*. London, Routledge.

Hugman, R. (2005) 'Looking back: the view from here', *British Journal of Social Work*, **35**, 609–620.

Hutton, W. (1996) *The State We're In: Why Britain is in Crisis and How to Overcome it*. London: Vintage.

Huxley, P., Evans, S., Gately, C., Webber, M., Mears, A., Pajak, S, Kendall, T., Medina, J. and Katona, C. (2005) 'Stress and pressures in mental health social work: the worker speaks', *British Journal of Social Work*, **35**(7), 1063–1079.

Jack, G. (1997) 'An ecological approach to social work', *Child and Family Social Work*, **2**(2), 109–120.

Jack, G. and Jack, D. (2000) ' "Ecological social work": The application of a systems model of development in context' in P. Stepney and D. Ford (eds) *Social Work Models, Methods and Theories: A Framework For Practice*. Lyme Regis: Russell House.

Jack, G. and Stepney, P. (1995) 'The 1989 Children Act: protection or persecution? Family support and child protection in the 1990s', *Critical Social Policy*, **15**(1) 43, 26–39.

Jones, C. (1996) 'Anti-intellectualism and the peculiarities of British social work education' in N. Parton (ed.) *Social Theory, Social Change and Social Work*. London: Routledge.

Jones, C. (2001) 'Voices from the front line: state social workers and New Labour', *British Journal of Social Work*, **31**, 547–562.

Jones, K., Brown, J. and Bradshaw, J. (1978) *Issues in Social Policy*. London: Routledge.

Jordan, B. (1998) *The New Politics of Welfare: Social Justice in a Global Context*. London: Sage.

Jordan, B. (2000) 'Tough love: social work practice in UK society', in P. Stepney and D. Ford (eds) *Social Work Models, Methods and Theories: A Framework for Practice*. Lyme Regis: Russell House Publishing.

Jordan, B. (2001) 'Tough love: social work, social exclusion and the "third way"', *British Journal of Social Work*, **31**(3), 527–546.

Jordan, B. (2002) 'Tough love revisited – the context for practice'. Key note speech given at the Torfaen Conference, *Celebrating Social Work*, Torfaen Social Services in association with the Welsh Office, County Hall, Cymbran, South Wales, 18 November.

Jordan, B. (2004) 'Emancipatory social work? Opportunity or oxymoron', *British Journal of Social Work*, 34(1), 5–19.

Jordan, B. (2006) 'Public services and the service economy: individualism and the choice agenda', *Journal of Social Policy*, 35(1), 143–162.

Jordan, B. (2007) *Social Work and Well-Being*. Lyme Regis: Russell House Publishing.

Jordan, B. with Jordan, C. (2000) *Social Work and the Third Way: Tough Love as Social Policy*. London: Sage.

Jordan, B. and Stepney, P. (1999) 'Collective action and everyday resistance in the community', *Tijdschrift voor Arbeid en Participatie*, 20(3), 215–235.

Karvinen, S., Pösö, T. and Satka, M. (eds) (1999) *Reconstructing Social Work Research*, SoPhi. Finland: University of Jyväskylä.

Kazi, M. (2003) *Realist Evaluation in Practice*. London: Sage.

Kendall, J. and Knapp, M. (2001) 'Providers of care for older people: the experience of community care' in Harris, M. and Rochester, C. (eds) *Voluntary Organisations and Social Policy in Britain*. Basingstoke: Palgrave Macmillan.

Kendall, J. (2003) *The Voluntary Sector*. London: Routledge.

Knapp, M., Robertson, E. and Thomason, C. (1990) 'Public money, voluntary action: whose welfare?' in H. Anheier, and W. Seibel (eds) *The Third Sector: Comparative Studies of Nonprofit Organisations*. Berlin: de Gruyter.

Kuhn, T. (1970) *The Structure of Scientific Revolutions*. Chicago: University of Chicago Press.

Laming, Lord (2003) *Report of the Enquiry into the Death of Victoria Climbié*. London: The Stationery Office.

Langan, M. (2000) 'Social services: managing the third way' in J. Clarke, S. Gewirtz, and E. McLaughlin (eds) *New Managerialism New Welfare?* London: Sage.

Ledwith, M. (2005) *Community Development: A Critical Approach*. Bristol: BASW/Policy Press.

Lee, J. (2001) *The Empowerment Approach to Social Work Practice: Building the Beloved Community* (2nd Edition) New York: Columbia University Press.

Lees, R. and Mayo, M. (1984) *Community Action for Change*. London: Routledge and Kegan Paul.

Leiba, T. (1996) 'Inter-professional and multi-agency training and working', *British Journal of Community Health Nursing*, 1(1), 8–12.

Lenard, P. (2004) *Communitarianism and Communitarian Critiques of Liberalism*. University of Bristol.

Leonard, P. (1997) *Postmodern Welfare*. London, Sage.

Lewis, O. (1968) *La Vida*. London: Panther Books.

Lewis, J. and Glennerster, H. (1996) *Implementing the New Community Care*. Buckingham: Open University Press.

Lipset, S. (1960) *Political Man: The Social Basis of Politics*. London: Heinemann.

Lister, R. (2001) 'New labour: a study in ambiguity from a position of ambivalence', *Critical Social Policy*, 21(4), 425–447.

London to Edinburgh Weekend Return Group (1980) *In and Against the State*. London: Pluto Press.

Loney, M. (1983) *Community Against Government: The British Community Development Project 1968–1978 – A Study of Government Incompetence*. London: Heinemann.

Lorenz, W. (1997) 'Social work in a changing Europe'. Keynote paper presented at the International Conference, *Culture and Identity: Social Work in a Changing Europe*. Dublin, August.

Lorenz, W. (2001) 'Social work responses to New Labour in continental European countries', *British Journal of Social Work*, 31, 595–609.

Lukes, S. (1974) *Power: A Radical View*. London: Macmillan.

Lund, B. (1999) '"Ask not what your community can do for you": Obligations, New Labour and welfare reform', *Critical Social Policy*, **19**(4), 447–462.

Lupton, R. (2003) *Poverty Street: The Dynamics of Neighbourhood Decline and Renewal*. Bristol: Policy Press.

Lymbery, M. (1998a) 'Care management and professional autonomy', *British Journal of Social Work*, **28**, 863–878.

Lymbery, M. (1998b) 'Social Work in general practice: dilemmas and solutions', *Journal of Inter-professional Care*, **12**(2), 199–208.

MacDonald, G. and Sheldon, B. (1992) 'Contemporary studies of the effectiveness of social work', *British Journal of Social Work*, **22**(6), 615–643.

Macfarlane, A. (1993) 'The right to make choices' J. Bornat, C. Pereira, D. Pilgrim and F. Williams (eds) *Community Care: A Reader*. Basingstoke: Palgrave Macmillan.

MacIntyre, A. (1981) *After Virtue: A Study of Moral Theory*. London: Duckworth.

Macpherson, S. W. (1999) *The Stephen Lawrence Inquiry*. London: HMSO.

Maguire, D. J., Brayshay, W. M. and Chalkely, B. S. (1987) *Plymouth in Maps: A Social and Economic Atlas*. Plymouth: Department of Geographical Sciences, Plymouth Polytechnic.

Malin, N., Wilmot, S. and Manthorpe, J. (2002) *Key Concepts and Debates in Health and Social Policy*. Buckingham: Open University Press.

Mann, K. (2006) 'Three steps to heaven? Tensions in the management of welfare: retirement pensions and active consumers', *Journal of Social Policy*, **35**(1), 77–96.

Markova, E. and Black, R. (2007) *East European Immigration and Cohesion*. York: Joseph Rowntree Foundation.

Marris, P. (1987) *Meaning and Action: Planning and Conceptions of Change*. London: Routledge and Kegan Paul.

Marris, P. and Rein, M. (1967) *Dilemmas of Social Reform*. London: Routledge.

Marsh, P. and Doel, M. (2005) *The Task-Centred Practice Book*. London: Routledge.

Marwick, A. (2000) *A History of the Modern British Isles 1914–1999*. Oxford: Blackwell.

Mason, D. (2000) *Race and Ethnicity in Modern Britain*. Oxford: Oxford University Press.

Massey, D. (1991) 'A global sense of place'. Unit 23, Social Sciences Foundation course D103. Milton Keynes, The Open University.

Matthies, A.-L., Järvelä, M. and Ward, D. (eds) (2000a) *From Social Exclusion to Participation: Explorations Across Three European Cities*. Working paper number 106, Finland: University of Jyväskylä.

Matthies, A.-L., Turunen, P., Albers, S., Boeck, T. and Närhi, K. (2000b) 'An eco-social approach to tackling social exclusion in European cities: a new comparative research project in progress', *European Journal of Social Work*, **3**(1), 43–52.

Mayo, M. (1975) 'The history and early development of CDP' in R. Lees and G. Smith (eds) *Action Research in Community Development*. London: Routledge.

Mayo, M. (1980) 'Beyond CDP: reaction and community action' in R. Bailey and M. Brake (eds) *Radical Social Work and Practice*. London: Edward Arnold.

Mayo, M. (1994) *Communities and Caring: The Mixed Economy of Welfare*. London: Macmillan.

Mayo, M. (1998) 'Community work' in R. Adams, L. Dominelli and M. Payne (eds) *Social Work: Themes, Issues and Critical Debates*. 1st Edition, Basingstoke: Palgrave Macmillan.

Mayo, M. (2002) 'Community work' in R. Adams, L. Dominelli, and M. Payne (eds) *Social Work: Themes, Issues and Critical Debates*. 2nd Edition, Basingstoke: Palgrave Macmillan.

Mayo, M. (2008) 'Introduction: community development, contestations, continuities and change' G. Craig, K. Popple and M. Shaw (eds) *Community Development in Theory and Practice: An international reader*. Nottingham: SpokesmanBooks.

Means, R. and Smith, R. (1998) *Community Care: Policy and Practice* (2nd Edition) Basingstoke: Palgrave Macmillan.

Mellor, R. (1977) *Urban Sociology in an Urbanized Society*. London: Routledge and Kegan Paul.

Metropolitan Police Authority (2004) *Report of the MPA Scrutiny on MPS Stop and Search Practice*, May. London: MPA.

Meyer, C. H. (ed.) (1983) *Clinical Social Work in the Eco-Systems Perspective*. New York: Columbia University Press.

Midwinter, E. (1994) *The Development of Social Welfare in Britain*. Buckingham: Open University Press.

Mishra, R. (1999) *Globalisation and the Welfare State*. Cheltenham: Edward Elgar.

Mizrahi, T. (2001) 'The status of community organizing in 2001: community practice context, complexities, contradictions and contributions', *Research on Social Work Practice*, **11**(2), 176–189.

Morley, C. (2004) 'Critical reflection in social work: a response to globalisation?', *International Journal of Social Welfare*, **13**, 297–303.

Mullaly, B. (2007) *The New Structural Social Work*. Ontario, Canada: Oxford University Press.

Murray, C. (1996) 'The underclass' in J. Muncie and E. McLaughlin (eds) *Criminological Perspectives*. London: Sage.

Nichols, M. (2004) 'An ounce of prevention is worth a pound of cure – social worker funding deserves as much attention as the police budget'. *Las Vegas Review Journal*, April 11.

Nisbett, R. and Ross, L. (1980) *Human Inference: Strategies and Shortcomings of Social Judgement*. Englewood Cliffs, NJ: Prentice Hall.

Noble, C. (2004) 'Postmodern thinking: where is it taking social work?', *Journal of Social Work*, **4**(3), 289–304.

Oakley, A. and Rajan, L. (1991) 'Social class and social support: the same or different?', *Sociology*, **25**(1), 31–59.

Office of National Statistics (2002) *Focus on Ethnicity and Identity*. London: Office of National Statistics. www.statistics.gov.uk/downloads/theme_compendia/foe2004/Ethnicity.pdf.

Ohmae, K. (1990) *The Borderless World*. London: Collins.

Ohmer, M. and Korr, W. (2006) 'The effectiveness of community practice interventions: a review of the literature', *Research on Social Work Practice*, **16**(2), 132–145.

Oliver, M. and Campbell, J. (1996) *Disability Politics: Understanding Our Past, Changing Our Future*. Basingstoke: Routledge.

ONS (Office of National Statistics) (2003) *Carers: 5.2 Million Carers in England and Wales*, London: ONS.

OPCS (Office of Population Sensus Surveys) (2002) *General Household Survey: Carers in 2000*. London: Government Statistical Service.

Orwell, G. (1982) *The Lion and the Unicorn: Socialism and the English Genius (with an introduction by Bernard Crick)* Harmondsworth: Penguin.

Pain, R., Barke, M., Fuller, D., Gough, J., MacFarlane, R. and Mowl, G. (2001) *Introducing Social Geographies*. London: Arnold.

Park, R. E. (1952) *Human Communities: The City and Human Ecology*. New York: Free Press.

Parry, N. and Parry, J. (1979) 'Social work, professionalism and the state' in N. Parry, M. Rustin and C. Satyamurti (eds) *Social Work, Welfare and the State*. London: Edward Arnold.

Parton, N. (ed.) (1996) *Social Theory, Social Change and Social Work*. London: Routledge.

Parton, N., Thorpe, D. and Wattam, C. (1997) *Child Protection, Risk and the Social Order*. London, Basingstoke: Palgrave Macmillan.

Patterson, S. (1965) *Dark Strangers: A Study of West Indians in London*. Harmondsworth: Penguin.

Paxton, W. and Dixon, M. (2004) *The State of the Nation: An Audit of Injustice in the UK*. London: Institute of Public Policy Research.

Payne, M. (1995) *Social Work and Community Care*. London: Macmillan.

Payne, M. (2005a) *Modern Social Work Theory* (3rd Edition). Basingstoke: Palgrave Macmillan.

Payne, M. (2005b) *The Origins of Social Work: Continuity and Change*. Basingstoke: Palgrave Macmillan.

Pearson, G. (1975) *The Deviant Imagination*. Basingstoke: Palgrave Macmillan.

Pease, B. (2007) 'Critical social work theory meets evidence-based practice in Australia: towards critical knowledge informed practice in social work' in K. Yokota. (ed.) *Empowering People Through Emancipatory Social Work*. Kyoto, Japan: Sekai Shisou-sya, pp. 103–138.

Pierson, J. (2002) *Tackling Social Exclusion*. London: Routledge.

Pincus, A. and Minahan, A. (1973) *Social Work Practice: Model and Method*. Itasca, IL: Peacock.

Pinker, R. (1982) 'An alternative view', *Social Work Today – The Barclay Report*, **13**(33), 23.

Pinkney, S. (2000) 'Children as welfare subjects in restructured social policy' in G. Lewis, S. Gewirtz and J. Clarke (eds) *Rethinking Social Policy*. London: Sage.

Piven, F. and Cloward, R. (1972) *Regulating the Poor*. London: Tavistock.

Plantenga, J. and Hansen, J. (1999) 'Assessing equal opportunities in the European Union', *International Labour Review*, **138**(4), 351–379.

Pollitt, C. (1996) 'Business and professional approaches to quality improvement…'. Paper presented to International Conference at Centre for Social Welfare and Research, Helsinki.

Pollitt, C. (2003) 'Joined-up government: a survey', *Political Studies Review*, **1**(1), 34–50.

Pollitt, C. and Harrison, S. (1992) *Handbook of Public Services Management*. Oxford: Blackwell.

Popper, K. (1959) *The Logic of Scientific Discovery*. New York: Basic Books.

Popple, K. (1995) *Analysing Community Work: Its Theory and Practice*. Buckingham: Open University Press.

Popple, K. (2000) 'Critical commentary: community work', *British Journal of Social Work*, **30**, 109–114.

Popple, K. (2002) 'Community Work' in R. Adams, L. Domeinelli and M. Payne (eds) *Critical Practice in Social Work*. Basingstoke: Palgrave Macmillan.

Popple, K. (2006a) 'Critical commentary: community development in the 21st century: a case of conditional development', *British Journal of Social Work*, **36**, 333–340.

Popple, K. (2006b) 'Plymouth, paternalism and the Astors: the origins of Virginia House Settlement' in R. Gilchrist, T. Jeffs and J. Spence *Drawing on the Past: Studies in the History of Community and Youth Work*. Leicester: Youth and Police/National Youth Agency.

Popple, K. (2006c) 'The first forty years: the history of the *Community Development Journal*', *Community Development Journal* (Advanced Access published 5 September 2006).

Popple, K. (2006d) 'Community development in the 21st century: a case of conditional development', *British Journal of Social Work*, **39**, 333–340.

Popple, K. (2007) 'Community development strategies in the UK' in L. Dominelli (ed.) *Revitalising Communities in a Globalising World*. Aldershot: Ashgate.

Postle, K. (2002) 'Working "Between the idea and the reality": Ambiguities and tensions in care managers work', *British Journal of Social Work*, **32**(3), 335–351.

Powell, E. (1968) 'Text of Speech Delivered in Birmingham, 20 April 1968', *Race*, X(1), 80–104.

Powell, M. (2000) 'New Labour and the third way in the British welfare state: a new and distinctive approach?', *Critical Social Policy*, **20**(1), 39–60.

Powell, M. and Moon, G. (2001) 'Health Action Zones: the "third way" of a new area-based policy?', *Health and Social Care in the Community*, **9**(1), 43–50.

Powell, M., Boyne, R. and Ashworth, R. (2001) 'Towards a geography of people poverty and place poverty', *Policy and Politics*, **29**(3), 243–258.

Prochaska, F. (1980) *Women and Philanthropy in 19th Century England*. Oxford: Oxford University Press.

Putnam, R. (2000) *Bowling Alone: The Collapse and Revival of American Community*. New York: Simon and Schuster.

Quinney, A. (2006) *Collaborative Social Work Practice*. Exeter: Learning Matters.

Rake, K. (ed.) (2000) *Women's Incomes over the Lifetime*. London: Stationery Office.

Ray, L. (2006) 'Community studies' entry in Turner, B. S. (ed.) *The Cambridge Dictionary of Sociology*. Cambridge: Cambridge University Press.

Rees, S. (1991) *Achieving Power: Policy and Practice in Social Welfare*. London: Allen & Unwin.

Rex, J. and Moore, R. (1967) *Race, Community and Conflict: A Study of Sparkbrook*. London: Oxford University Press.

Riger, S. (1993) 'What's wrong with empowerment?', *American Journal of Psychology*, **21**(3), 279–292.

Riley, D. (1983) *War in the Nursery: Theories of the Child and Mother*. London: Virago.

Rimmer, J. (1980) *Troubles Shared: The Story of a Settlement 1899–1979.* Birmingham: Phlogiston.

Robinson, L. (1995) *Psychology for Social Workers: Black Perspectives.* London: Routledge.

Robson, T. (2000) *The State and Community Action.* London: Pluto.

Roof, M. (1972) *A Hundred Years of Family Welfare.* London: Michael Joseph.

Rose, H. and Ashcroft, R. (1979) *Area-Based Approaches to Inner-City Deprivation: A Review of the Literature.* Bradford: University of Bradford.

Rose, H. and Hanmer, J. (1975) 'Community participation and social change' in D. Jones and M. Mayo (eds) *Community Work Two.* London: Routledge.

Rousseau, C. and Drapeau, A. (2003) 'Are refugee children an at-risk group? A longitudinal study of Cambodian adolescents', *Journal of Refugee Studies,* 16(1), 67–81.

Rummery, K. and Glendinning, C. (1997) Working Together: Primary Care Involvement in Commissioning Social Care Services, Debates in Primary Care. Manchester: University of Manchester.

Salt, J. (2001) 'International labour migration'. Paper presented to Home Office conference *Bridging the Information Gaps.* London, 21 March.

Sanders, C. (1992) 'Bengal to Brick Lane revisited'. *The Higher,* 7 February, 15.

Sanders, J. and Munford, R. (2005) 'Activity and reflection: research and change with diverse groups of young people', *Qualitative Social Work,* 4(2), 197–209.

Saunders, P. (1979) *Urban Politics: A Sociological Interpretation.* Harmondsworth: Penguin.

Sawdon, D. (1986) *Making Connections in Practice Teaching.* Heinneman: NISW.

Sawicki, J. (1991) *Disciplining Foucault: Feminism, Power and the Body.* New York: Routledge.

Scholte, J. A. (2000) *Globalization: A Critical Introduction.* London: Macmillan.

Scott, D. and Russell, L. (2001) 'Contracting: the experience of service delivery agencies' in M. Harris and C. Rochester (eds) *Voluntary Organisations and Social Policy in Britain.* Basingstoke: Palgrave Macmillan.

Scull, A. (1984) *Decarceration.* Cambridge: Polity Press.

Seebohm Report (1968) *Report of the Committee on Local Authority and Allied Personal Social Services.* Cmnd 3703. London: HMSO.

Seed, P. (1973) *The Expansion of Social Work in Great Britain.* London: Routledge.

Seed, P. (1990) *Introducing Network Analysis in Social Work.* London: Jessica Kingsley.

SEU (Social Exclusion Unit) (1998) *Bringing Britain Together: A National Strategy for Neighbourhood Renewal.* London: Cabinet Office.

SEU (2001) *A New Commitment to Neighbourhood Renewal: National Strategy Action Plan.* London: Cabinet Office.

Sheldon, B. (2000) 'Cognitive behavioural methods in social care' in P. Stepney and D. Ford (eds) *Social Work Models, Methods and Theories: A Framework for Practice.* Lyme Regis: Russell House.

Sheldon, B. and MacDonald, G. (1999) *Research and Practice in Social Care: Mind the Gap.* Centre for Evidence Social Services: University of Exeter.

Shenton, N. and Barr, A. (1974) *The Allocation of Council Housing and the Racial Conundrum.* Oldham: CDP and Oldham Metropolitan Borough.

Sheppard, M. (1998) 'Practice validity, reflexivity and knowledge for social work', *British Journal of Social Work,* 28, 763–781.

Sibbald, B. (2000) 'Inter-disciplinary working in British primary care teams: a threat to the cost-effectiveness of care?', *Critical Public Health,* 10(4), 439–451.

Skeggs, B. (1997) *Formations of Class and Gender: Becoming Respectable.* London: Sage.

Smale, G., Tuson, G., Cooper, M., Wardle, M. and Crosbie, D. (1988) *Community Social Work: A Paradigm for Change.* London: NISW.

Smale, G., Tuson, G. and Statham, D. (2000) *Social Work and Social Problems.* Basingstoke: Palgrave Macmillan.

Smith, G. (1996) *Community-arianism.* http://homepages.uel.ac.uk/G.Smith/community-arianism/chap9.html.

Social Services Inspectorate and NHS Executive (1995) *Community Care Monitoring Report 1994: Findings from Local Authority Self Monitoring and Survey*. London: HMSO.

Solomos, J. (2003) *Race and Racism in Britain* (3rd Edition). Basingstoke: Palgrave Macmillan.

Southwell, P. (1994) 'The integrated family centre', *Practice*, 7(1), 45–54.

Stacey, M. (1969) 'The myth of community studies', *British Journal of Sociology*, 20(2), 134–147.

Stedman-Jones, G. (1984) *Outcast London*. Harmondsworth: Penguin.

Stepney, P. (2000) 'An overview of the wider policy context' in P. Stepney and D. Ford (eds), *Social Work Models, Methods and Theories*. Lyme Regis: Russell House.

Stepney, P. (2006a) 'Mission impossible? Critical practice in social work', *British Journal of Social Work*, 36(8), 1289–1307.

Stepney, P. (2006b) 'The paradox of reshaping social work as "tough love" in the Nordic welfare states', *Nordisk Sosialt Arbeid*, 26(4), 293–305.

Stepney, P. and Davis, P. (2004) 'Social inclusion, mental health and the green agenda', *American Journal of Social Work in Health Care*, 39(3/4), 387–409.

Stepney, P. and Evans, D. (2000) 'Community social work: towards an integrative model of practice' in P. Stepney and D. Ford (eds) *Social Work Models, Methods and Theories: A Framework for Practice*. Lyme Regis: Russell House.

Stepney, P. and Ford, D. (eds) (2000) *Social Work Models, Methods and Theories: A Framework for Practice*. Lyme Regis: Russell House Publishing.

Stepney, P., Lynch, R. and Jordan, B. (1999) 'Poverty, exclusion and New Labour', *Critical Social Policy*, 19(1), 109–127.

Strange, S. (1995) 'The limits of politics', *Government and Opposition*, 30(3), 292–312.

Tam, H. (1998) *Communitarianism: A New Agenda for Politics and Citizenship*. Basingstoke: Palgrave Macmillan.

Taylor, M. (2001) 'Partnership: insiders and outsiders' in M. Harris and C. Rochester (eds) *Voluntary Organisations and Social Policy in Britain*. Basingstoke: Palgrave Macmillan.

Thane, P. (1996) *The Foundations of the Welfare State*. London: Longman.

Thatcher, M. (1993) *The Downing Street Years*. London: HarperCollins.

The Guardian (2006) 'The reporter', *Money Guardian*, 28 October.

The Times (2006) '1,300 planes needed to fly Britons abroad'. 23 November.

Thompson, N. (2001) *Anti-discriminatory Practice*. Basingstoke: Palgrave Macmillan.

Thompson, N. (2005) *Understanding Social Work: Preparing for Practice* (2nd Edition). Basingstoke: Palgrave Macmillan.

Thompson, N. and Thompson, S. (2005) *Community Care*. Lyme Regis: Russell House Publishing.

Tonnies, F. (1955) *Community and Association*. London: Routledge and Kegan Paul.

Toynbee, P. (2007) 'Finally ministers are off the leash and free to say the rich are too bloody rich', *The Guardian*, 18 May.

Tuckman, B. W. (1965) 'Developmental Sequence in Small Groups', *Psychological Bulletin*, 63(6), 384–399.

Tunstill, J., Allnock, D., Akhurst, S. and Garbers, C. (2005) 'Sure Start local programmes: implications of case study data from the national evaluation of sure start', *Children and Society*, 19(2), 158–171.

Turunen, P. (1999) *TSER Project: Making New Local Policies Against Social Exclusion – Executive Summary*. Magdeburg Bd: Schriften der Fachhochschule.

Twigg, J. (1998) 'Informal care of older people' in M. Bernard and J. Phillips (eds) *The Social Policy of Old Age*. London: Centre for Policy on Ageing (CPA).

Ungerson, C. (1987) *Policy is Personal*. London: Tavistock.

United Nations Development Programme (2005) *Human Development Report*. New York: United Nations.

Utting, D., Bright, J. and Henricson, C. (1993) *Crime and the Family*. London: Family Policy Studies Centre.

Van de Veen, R. (2003) 'Community development as citizen education', *International Journal of Lifelong Education*, 22(6), 580–596.

Vaux, G. (2004) 'Social security', *Research Matters*, **16**(1), 63–68.

Vertovec, S. (2007) 'New ethnic communities: from multiculturalism to super-diversity'. *Britain Today: The State of the Nation in 2007*. Swindon: Economic and Social Research Council.

Vickery, A. (1983) *Organising a Patch System*. London: NISW.

Waddington, P. (1983) 'Looking ahead – community work into the 1980s' in D. N. Thomas (ed.) *Community Work in the Eighties*. London: National Institute for Social Work.

Wagner, G. (1988) *Residential Care: A Positive Choice*. London: HMSO.

Walker, A. (1997) 'Community care policy: From consensus to conflict' in J. Bornat, C. Pereira, D. Pilgrim and F. Williams (eds) *Community Care – A Reader* (2nd Edition) Basingstoke: Palgrave Macmillan.

Walsall Council, (2007) News and Views, Social Care and Inclusion Internal Bulletin, January 2007.

Walton, R. G. (1975) *Women in Social Work*. London: Routledge.

Walton, R. (2005) 'Social work as a social institution', *British Journal of Social Work*, **35**(5), 587–607.

Webb, S. (2001) 'Some considerations on the validity of evidence-based practice in social work', *British Journal of Social Work*, **31**(1), 57–79.

Webb, S. (2006) Beyond Critical Social Work in Advanced Liberal Societies. Unpublished.

Wheen, F. (2000) *Karl Marx*. London: Fourth Estate.

Whitehead, A. (1976) 'Sexual antagonism in Hertfordshire' in D. L. Barker and S. Allen (eds) *Dependence and Exploitation in Work and Marriage*. London: Longman.

Williams, R. (1976) *Keywords*. London: Fontana/Croom Helm.

Williams, R. (1983) *Keywords*. London: Fontana Press.

Williams, F. (1996) 'Postmodernism, feminism and the question of difference' in N. Parton (ed.) *Social Theory, Social Change and Social Work*. London: Routledge.

Williams, F. (1997) 'Women and community' in J. Bornat, C. Pereira, D. Pilgrim and F. Williams (eds) *Community Care: A Reader*. Basingstoke: Palgrave Macmillan.

Williams, C. (2003) Book review of Sullivan, R. (2000) *Liberalism and Crime: The British Experience*, Lanham: Rowman and Littlefield, published by H-Albion.

Willmott, P. (1986) *Social Networks, Informal Care and Public Policy*. London: Policy Studies Institute.

Wilson, E. (1980) *Only Halfway to Paradise: Women in Post-War Britain 1945–1968*. London: Tavistock.

Wilson, E. (1982) 'Women and community care' in A. Walker (ed.) *Community Care*. Oxford: Basil Blackwell.

Wirth, L. (1938) 'Urbanism as a way of life?', *American Journal of Sociology*, **44**(1), 1–24.

Wistow, G. (1995) 'Community care at the crossroads', *Health and Social Care*, **3**(4), 227–240.

Wistow, G. (2000) 'Working in the NHS' in *Research Matters*, published by Community Care, April 2000.

Wolfenden Committee (1978) *The Future of Voluntary Organisations*. London: Croom Helm.

Women's National Council (2000) *Treating Women Well: Women and the NHS*. www.thewnc.org.uk/pubs/treatingwomenwell.pdf [Accessed 2 June 2007].

Woods, R. (2007) 'Super-rich treble wealth in last 10 years', *Sunday Times*, 29 April.

Writson, W. (1988/1989) 'Technology and Society', *Foreign Affairs*, **67**, 63–75.

Yoo, S., Weed, N., Lempa, M., Mbondo, M., Shada, R. and Goodman, R. (2004) 'Collaborative community empowerment: an illustration of a six-step process', *Health Promotion Practice*, **5**(3), 256–265.

York, A. (1984) 'Towards a conceptual model of community social work', *British Journal of Social Work*, **14**(1), 241–255.

Young, A. F. (1956) *British Social Work in the Nineteenth Century*. London: Routledge and Kegan Paul.

Young, J. (1998) 'Breaking windows: situating the new criminology' in P. Walton and J. Young (eds) *The New Criminology Revisited*. London: Macmillan.

Young, J. (1999) *The Exclusive Society: Social Exclusion, Crime and Difference in Late Modernity.* London: Sage.

Young, M. and Willmott, P. (1957) *Family and Kinship in East London.* London: Routledge and Kegan Paul.

Younghusband, E. L. (1959) *Report of the Working Party on Social Workers in the Local Authority Health and Welfare Services.* London: HMSO.

Index